MANAGING WORKFORCE REDUCTION

By the same author

New Firm Formation and Regional Development
US Corporate Personnel Reduction Policies

MANAGING WORKFORCE REDUCTION

An International Survey

Edited by Michael Cross

PRAEGER

PRAEGER SPECIAL STUDIES • PRAEGER SCIENTIFIC

New York • Philadelphia • Eastbourne, UK
Toronto • Hong Kong • Tokyo • Sydney

Published in 1985 by Praeger Publishers
CBS Educational and Professional Publishing,
a Division of CBS Inc.
521 Fifth Avenue, New York, NY 10175 USA

Library of Congress Catalog Card Number: 84-18088
456789 052 9876545321

Library of Congress Cataloging in Publication Data
Main entry under title:

Managing workforce reduction.

    Includes index.
    1. Employees, Dismissal of − Management − Addresses,
essays, lectures. 2. Employees, Dismissal of − Law and
legislation − Addresses, essays, lectures. I. Cross,
Michael.
HF5549.5.D55 M36 1985   658.3'134   84-18088
ISBN 0-03-002654-7 (alk. paper)

Published and Distributed by the
Praeger Publishers Division
(ISBN Prefix 0-275)
of Greenwood Press, Inc.,
Westport, Connecticut

Printed and bound in Great Britain

CONTENTS

TABLES AND FIGURES

Tables

Figure

1 INTRODUCTION

Michael Cross

In the period since the oil crises of the early- and mid-1970s employment in much of the Western industrialised world has rapidly declined. This decline, which almost amounts to a collapse in some industries and locations, has led to many thousands of people being thrown out of work. This book is an international study of how the common problem of reducing workforces in individual plants and, in some cases, in whole industries has been tackled.[1] The balance of state to company (employer) and to individual (employee) initiatives is noteworthy. In the USA and Australia, for example, the state (at both levels) has played a relatively minor role (though there are signs of it increasing) when compared to the United Kingdom or West Germany. The middle position is taken by Japan, where the state acts more as a facilitator by allowing cartels to be formed in troubled industries to allow adjustments to take place and so lessen the impact on the individual.

What is also evident is the treatment of layoffs or redundancies as almost independent and isolated events in some countries, and not as an integral part of other developments in the labour market. Layoffs are one means of adjusting the existing supply and the new demand for labour. It is difficult not to also consider those measures which reduce working time (and hence the supply of labour), e.g. short time working, advance training and re-training, raising of the school leaving age, early retirement and reduced pensionable age, increased holidays, reduced working week and part-time working.[2] Each of these seven measures reduces the supply of labour without directly adding to those already without work. True, there is a strong element of redefining unemployment, but it does represent a recognition, however tacit, that there is an alternative to layoffs and redundancies.

The most striking example of adopting alternative methods of layoffs and redundancies is to be found in Japan. An annual survey is conducted by the Economic Planning Agency which deals with a range of subjects of common concern to Japanese businesses including: (1) economic growth and the business environment; (2) trends in plant and equipment investment; (3) employment trends; and (4)

1

Table 1.1: Employment Adjustment Measures in Japan, 1978–86

Employment adjustment measures	Taken in the past five years or so (%)	Planned for the next three years or so (%)
Reducing new hirings (regular employment)	63	62
Intra-company reassignment	41	57
Loan and transfer to other companies	38	35
Holding down wage increases (excluding regular raises)	15	21
Voluntary retirement	14	10
Slowing down promotions and reducing regular wage increases	7	3
Other measures	1	2
No measures taken	25	19

Source: Economic Planning Agency, Japan, Annual Survey, 1983.

foreign import restrictions and foreign direct investment. A total of 1,038 companies listed in the first or second sections of the stock exchange, excluding banks and insurance companies, responded to the questionnaire in January 1983. As regards employment adjustment the survey found that conspicuous moves are underway to use intra-company reassignments. In all, 75 per cent of companies stated they have adjusted their workforces during the past five years or so, and 81 per cent said they are considering doing so in the next three years or so. Table 1.1 indicates the range and frequency with which different measures have been used.[3]

Contrast the practice in Japan to that in the United Kingdom. The most recent comprehensive survey of redundancy provisions[4] found assistance being made available to redundant workers as shown below:

(1) 91 per cent of those made redundant received none of the following types of training — re-training in new skills, enhancement of existing skills, job sampling (experimenting with alternative jobs) or job search (counselling, occupational guidance, instruction on how to write job applications);
(2) only 2 per cent of those made redundant benefited from any re-training, enhancement training or job sampling;
(3) about 10 per cent of all those people made redundant were given some job search training (usually half a day in duration); and

(4) about 90 per cent of companies did not report redundancies to other local firms.

Hence the community aid programmes which have been developed in the steel closure towns of Consett and Shotton in the United Kingdom are isolated instances, and only deal with small numbers of people relative to the million or so made redundant each year in the UK at the present time.[5] The Japanese system is one of employee retention and employment protection in the main, whereas the UK system, whilst recognising the protection aspect, tends to focus upon the finding of alternative employment. The Swedish system sits between the two. In Sweden the state seeks to subsidise labour for the employer of ex-redundant workers and pay for their re-training. There is also state provision which encourages the retention of redundant employees for re-training. The aim of the Swedish system is to provide a breathing space while the security of the declared redundant jobs is temporarily re-established, and to aid job mobility positively. Lump sum payments — which form the basis of the UK system — are regarded as being a measure of last resort.[6]

While there are undoubtedly differences in the approach, extent and resources devoted to managing workforce adjustments, there are also a number of common threads and developments. First, because of the frequency and magnitude of redundancy the level and range of assistance would appear to be increasing. Secondly, the success of national industrial restructuring programmes will lead to the displacement of many thousands of workers (e.g. 300,000 in France over the next five years),[7] and in order that these programmes may proceed the co-operation of the workforces concerned is necessary. Hence measures which ensure the rapid restructuring of an industry with minimum social disruption are being adopted. Thirdly, the advent of an era based on 'new technologies' may lead to a need for its rapid uptake and use to ensure the continuance of an internationally competitive position. In turn this may lead to the displacement of workers, the need for re-training, and possibly migration. Again, with these thoughts gaining increasing ground, both macro- and micro-labour market adjustment policies are being developed. Fourthly, and in part as a result of the above three developments, international pressures are being brought to bear upon the behaviour of major multinational corporations. These pressures, particularly noticeable within the EEC, are encouraging employers to consult with workers before changes are introduced to the workplace.[8]

The five country reports which form the basis of this book have been chosen to cover and highlight the full range of measures used to aid and allow worker adjustment. As editor, my approach has been to identify a number of key topics and to ask each author to discuss them where possible with regard to a particular country.[9] Coverage of topics varies from one chapter to another, and this indicates the lack of importance and/or lack of information on the topic for that country, and the interests of the authors themselves.

In considering the wealth of material presented, the reader is asked to keep two questions in mind. First, what is the degree of state involvement in the labour market of the particular country? And secondly, is the labour market employer- or employee-oriented? It is the answers to these two questions which explain many of the differences between countries in the ways workforce reductions are handled.

Notes

1. European Industrial Relations Review, 'International-Collective Dismissals in 10 Countries', No. 76, 19-24, May 1980. R. Blanpain, 'Job Security and Industrial Relations', *Bulletin of Comparative Industrial Relations*, No. 11, Kluwer Publishers, Netherlands, 1980. E. Yemin (ed.), *Workforce Reductions in Undertakings*, International Labour Office, Geneva, 1982.

2. Federal Employment Institute, *Employment Policy in Germany — Challenges and Concepts for the 1980s*, Federal Employment Institute, Nurnberg, 1980.

3. I. Yamashita, 'Industry in Japan — Changes in Structure and Strategy', *The Robbins Lecture*, University of Stirling, Scotland, 1983.

4. Institute of Manpower Studies, 'Redundancy Provisions Survey', Part 1: Commentary, *IMS Manpower Commentary*, No. 13, 1981.

5. R. Hudson and D. Sadler, 'Anatomy of a Disaster: The Closure of Consett Steelworks', *Northern Economic Review*, No. 6, 2-17, Spring 1983. K. Jones, *The Human Face of Change. Social Responsibility and Rationalization at British Steel*, Institute of Personnel Management, London, 1974. E. Robson, 'Face to Face with Change in the British Steel Industry — A Recipe with Potential'. Paper presented to the symposium organised by the International Committee on Occupational Mental Health, Heidelberg, May 1981.

6. Economists Advisory Group, 'Swedish and Swiss Manpower Policy — Its Relevance for the EEC', Main Report. Programme of Research and Actions on the Development of the Labour Market, Study No. 77/6.

7. D. Green, *Managing Industrial Change? French Policies to Promote Industrial Adjustment*, HMSO, London, 1981. Also see on the loss of jobs in the car industry: D. Housego, 'Why Peugeot's jobs mean so much to so many. The Poissy plant is a test case', *Financial Times*, 12 December 1983; P. Betts, 'The future of Peugeot. Behind the battle of Poissy', *Financial Times* 9 January 1984; D. Housego, 'Unions will take harder line over future job losses', *Financial Times*, 13 January 1984; D. Housego, 'Mitterrand and the Unions. Why warning lights are

flashing', *Financial Times* 1 February 1984.

8. R. Blanpain, *The Badger Case and the OECD Guidelines for Multinational Enterprises*, Kluwer Publishers, Netherlands, 1977. Commission of the European Communities, 'Information, Consultation and Negotiation Procedures for the Introduction of New Technology', Information Note, Doc. No. V/373/82-EN, EEC, Brussels, March 1982. Commission of the European Communities, 'Worker Participation in Decision Making — Fifth Draft Directive on Public Companies', Background Report, ISEC/B29/83, EEC, Brussels, December 1983. P. Davies and M. Freedland, *Transfer of Employment. The Transfer of Undertakings (Protection of Employment) Regulations 1981 with Annotations*, Sweet and Maxwell, London, 1982.

9. A copy of the authors' brief is available on request from the editor.

2 THE UNITED STATES OF AMERICA AND CANADA

Morris L. Sweet

Introduction

The subject of redundancies in the United States and Canada is examined from three standpoints: existing and proposed redundancy legislation, foreign influences on domestic redundancy policy and adjusting to layoffs and re-employment measures. The emphasis is on significant programmes in these areas.

As the world economy becomes increasingly integrated, national redundancy policy is viewed from an international perspective. On this basis the US is unique among industrialised countries in not having enacted legislation affecting the ability of management to make decisions freely and without mandated financial obligations for the closing of facilities and/or large scale reductions in the workforce. There is no national legislation calling for advance notice or severance pay. Canada has taken modest steps toward initiating national redundancy legislation.

The questions that ensue are whether this freedom, i.e. the ability of management to make closing and reduction decisions without public restraints, will continue. What is the current economic environment and how is it affecting the direction of redundancy policies and programmes? The first step is to review the domestic redundancy picture within a world context.

According to the American Productivity Council, labour in the US has priced itself into the world labour market by settling not only for moderate wage increases but for not insisting on as much job security as European workers.

> American corporations ... continue to have, by European standards, an extraordinary freedom to lay off workers when orders shrink. So they fret less about the risk of a labor surplus (a flexible cost) than a capital surplus (a fixed cost).[1]

The ability to streamline a company has been considered a

6

major factor in investments in the US by European chemical companies.[2] The difference in national attitudes toward layoffs is further illustrated by the General Motors response in 1980 to declining auto sales in the US and West Germany. Workers in West Germany were able to negotiate a more favourable separation programme supported by pressure from the government, works councils, worker representatives on the supervisory board and the German press.[3]

Redundancy in the US

In 1982, 1,287,411 workers in the US were placed on either temporary or permanent layoff, including 215,525 workers who lost their jobs when plants or facilities were permanently or indefinitely closed (Table 2.1). The largest number of workers laid off, 86.7 per cent, and permanent closings, 68.5 per cent, were in manufacturing. By industry the largest number of layoffs, 32.3 per cent, took place in the transportation equipment industry, largely because of the depressed auto industry. In turn the downturn in the auto industry spread to the primary metals industry with 10.2 per cent of all layoffs.

In terms of unemployment by occupation, production workers in February 1983 constituted some 47 per cent of the total. These workers also had the highest unemployment rates. The service and technical, sales and administrative occupational categories also had high unemployment rates which indicates that extensive unemployment is not confined to any one occupational group (Table 2.2).

Dislocated and Disadvantaged Workers

In the US the dislocated worker has not been the primary focus of Federal programmes dealing with employment and training for the unemployed. The greater emphasis has been on the disadvantaged who differ as a group from the redundant. The disadvantaged are more likely to consist of low income individuals with little or no work experience, an unstable work record or low skill levels. 'Canada's manpower system is generally similar to that of the US, except that it is not nearly so strictly targeted on the disadvantaged.'[4]

On the other hand the redundant, displaced or dislocated workers have been unable to cope with changes in demand for their occupational skills, have been working in a declining industry or reside in depressed regions. Their problems are compounded with the restructuring of industry and modernisation of plant and equipment which are designed for production with a decreased number of workers.

Blue collar workers are the most severely affected group; the

Table 2.1: Employees Laid Off[a] and Permanent Closings[b] by Industry, 1982

Industry	Employees laid off		Permanent closing	
	Number	%	Number	%
Manufacturing				
Apparel, other finished textiles	56,338		47	
Chemical, allied products	9,990		23	
Electrical machinery, equipment	163,089		24	
Fabricated metals	40,100		36	
Food & beverages	35,118		42	
Furniture	4,105		13	
Leather & leather products	1,340		4	
Lumber & wood products	7,203		10	
Machinery (except electrical)	147,686		30	
Miscellaneous manufacturing	15,149		7	
Paper & allied products	10,636		11	
Petroleum & allied products	7,952		15	
Primary metals	131,876		40	
Printing & publishing	6,861		15	
Instruments, related products	12,805		2	
Rubber products	17,425		17	
Stone, clay & glass	10,763		18	
Textile mill products	20,446		34	
Tobacco	1,262		5	
Transportation equipment	416,189		31	
Total-manufacturing	1,116,333	86.7	424	68.5
Non manufacturing				
Communications services	719		2	
Construction & housing	5,234		16	
Mining	76,324		48	
Retail stores	23,533		98	
Services	16,894		20	
Transportation services	47,567		9	
General miscellaneous	807		2	
Total non-manufacturing	171,078	13.3	195	31.5
Total all industries	1,287,411	100.0	619	100.0

a. Temporary and permanent layoffs resulting from production cutbacks and permanent layoffs from plant closings.

b. Permanent or indefinite closings, covers 215,525 employees.

Source: The Bureau of National Affairs, *Layoffs, Plant Closings and Concession Bargaining: BNA's Summary Report for 1982*, Washington, DC, February 1983, p. 15.

Table 2.2: Unemployed Persons (16 years and over) by Occupation, Industry and Duration of Unemployment, February 1982 and February 1983 and Unemployment Rate, February 1983 (thousands of persons)

	Feb. 1982 Number	Feb. 1982 %	Feb. 1983 Number	Feb. 1983 %	Unemployment rate Feb. 1982	Unemployment rate Feb. 1983	Feb. 1983 Duration in weeks Mean	Feb. 1983 Duration in weeks Median
Occupation								
Managerial & professional	690	6.7	840	6.8	2.9	3.5	19.0	12.1
Technical, sales, administrative	1,891	18.2	2,390	19.5	5.9	7.3	18.2	10.1
Service	1,493	14.4	1,718	13.9	10.2	11.3	18.0	9.9
Precision, production, craft, repair	1,493	14.7	1,972	16.1	11.6	14.4	19.6	11.4
Operators, fabricators, labourers	1,530	32.7	3,791	30.9	17.0	19.9	21.7	13.3
Farming, forestry, fishing	363	3.5	491	4.0	10.6	14.1	14.6	9.3
No previous work experience	1,017	9.8	1,084	8.8				
Total	10,378	100.0	12,286	100.0	9.6	11.3	19.4	11.0
Industry								
Agriculture	257	2.5	366	3.0	18.1	21.7	13.2	9.1
Mining	118	1.2	236	1.9	10.0	21.5	NA	NA
Construction	1,310	12.6	1,399	11.3	25.8	27.3	18.3	10.4
Manufacturing	2,586	24.9	3,151	25.4	11.4	14.3	24.2	16.5
Durable	1,644	15.8	2,030	16.4	12.0	15.8	26.4	20.0
Non-durable	942	9.1	1,121	9.1	10.4	12.3	20.2	10.8
Transportation, public utilities	388	3.7	526	4.2	6.8	9.2	19.5	10.9
Wholesale & retail	2,010	19.4	2,453	19.8	10.1	12.0	16.9	9.1
Finance insurance, real estate	252	2.4	293	2.4	4.2	4.9	17.8b	10.6b
Service	1,442	13.9	1,677	13.5	7.4	8.2	b	b
Government, self employed, unpaid family workers	999	9.6	1,198	9.7	3.9	4.6	NA	NA
No previous work experience	1,017	9.8	1,084	8.8				
Total	10,378	100.0	12,382a	100.0	9.6	11.3	19.4	11.0

a. Totals do not agree in source tables.
b. Finance, insurance, real estate combined with service.

Source: *Employment and Earnings* (US Department of Labor), vol. 30, no. 3 (March 1983), Tables A-11, A-12, A-15, A-17, pp. 41, 42, 46.

unemployment rate for blue collar workers in November 1982 was 16.5 per cent, compared to 5.6 per cent for white collar workers (Table 2.3). The older workers are even more severely affected (Table 2.4). Blue collar workers may have substantial job experience but not a great deal of formal education and thus experience difficulty in adapting to changed employment conditions. The level of past earnings is often based on firm-specific skills and seniority which are not readily transferable to other types of jobs or industries. Often they have been sheltered for many years from the vicissitudes of the labour market. These workers also find mobility difficult to accept in view of attachments to their communities.

In terms of allocation of government resources, the question has been raised:

Should workers dislocated by economic change become a new high-priority target group for Federal employment and training programs? Are their needs sufficiently urgent, and the potential

Table 2.3: Selected Unemployment Rates by Demographic and Occupational Groups (seasonally adjusted, in per cent)

Group	July 1981[a]	November 1982
All workers	7.2	10.8
Adult men	5.8	10.1
Adult women	6.7	9.1
Teenagers	18.7	24.2
White	6.3	9.7
Black	13.8	20.2
White collar workers	4.0	5.6
Professional & technical	2.8	3.8
Managers & administrators	2.6	3.9
Sales workers	4.9	6.3
Clerical workers	5.7	7.9
Blue collar workers	9.5	16.5
Craft & kindred workers	6.9	12.2
Operatives except transport	11.1	21.2
Transport equipment operatives	7.3	14.1
Non-farm labourers	14.4	19.4
Service workers	8.0	11.2
Farm workers	4.8	7.7

a. Month corresponding to the most recent low period of unemployment.

Source: US Congress, Congressional Budget Office, *Strategies for Assisting the Unemployed* (Washington, 8 December 1982), p. 5 from US Department of Labor, Bureau of Labor Statistics Data.

returns to that investment sufficiently high, to justify serving their needs at the expense of disadvantaged workers who are currently the main focus of such activity?

The conclusion is that the disadvantaged should have priority.[5]

A different conclusion has been reached by a trade union representative from the United Auto Workers (UAW). Their members have suffered disproportionately in terms of unemployment.

While the UAW in no way wishes to see reductions in public employment and training services for those who are already disadvantaged, it is a cruel irony and grossly unfair that workers displaced from auto and other basic industries presently are denied otherwise-available assistance because they are 'guilty' of having a prior history of lifelong gainful and remunerative employment. To force such workers to endure months of unemployment without assistance because of the bureaucratic notion

Table 2.4: Estimated Number of Dislocated Workers in January 1983 under Alternative Eligibility Standards and Economic Assumptions (in thousands)

Eligibility criteria	Number of workers[a]
Single criteria	
Declining industry	1,240–1,590
Declining occupation	1,700–2,200
Ten years or more of job tenure	840–1,200
More than 45 years of age	1,120–1,370
More than 26 weeks of unemployment	840–1,200
Multiple criteria	
Declining industry and:	
10 years' job tenure	270–330
45 or more years of age	270–340
26 weeks of unemployment	185–240
Declining occupation and:	
10 years' job tenure	300–390
45 or more years of age	390–520
26 weeks of unemployment	310–490
Mass layoff and plant closing	1,090–1,400

a. The range reflects a variety of assumptions related to general economic conditions and to patterns of growth among different sectors of the economy.

Source: US Congress, Congressional Budget Office, *Strategies for Assisting the Unemployed* (Washington, 8 December 1982), p. 60.

that such assistance should be restricted to the 'disadvantaged' does a disservice, not only to the unemployed worker, but also to the American public. Appropriate intervention is more likely to be successful if it is *timely*, not months or years after the displaced worker becomes unemployed. Demeaning and irrelevant 'means tests' deter thousands from seeking vitally needed assistance.[6]

As dislocated workers remain unemployed for long periods, the financial needs of both disadvantaged and dislocated become similar. In February 1983, the duration of unemployment averaged a sizeable 19.4 weeks, an increase of 36 per cent over the figure for February 1982 (Table 2.5). But in respect to re-employment there are differences and a single uniform employment and training programme would not be appropriate.

Layoffs and Dismissals in Canada

Comparison with the US

The Canadian government has gone beyond the US in imposing limitations on employers, thus moving away from the approach to redundancy management in the US and closer to, but not yet reaching the stage in Western Europe. It should be kept in mind that 'the restrictions imposed on the right of Canadian employers to lay off

Table 2.5: Unemployed Persons (16 years and over) by Reasons and Duration of Unemployment, February 1982 and February 1983 (thousands of persons)

Reasons	February 1982		February 1983	
	Number	%	Number	%
Job losers	6,132	59.1	7,939	64.1
Job leavers	931	8.9	842	6.8
Re-entrants	2,300	22.2	2,521	20.4
New entrants	1,015	9.8	1,079	8.7
Total	10,378	100.0	12,382	100.0
Duration in weeks				
Average (mean)	14.3		19.4	
Median	8.5		11.0	

Source: *Employment and Earnings* (US Department of Labor), vol. 30, no. 3 (March 1983), Tables A-14 and A-14, p.42.

employees are neither very severe nor very extensive'.[7]

In contrast to other major industrial nations, there is greater freedom in the US to dismiss employees for economic reasons. Some exceptions exist where there is a collective bargaining agreement, an individual employment contract or anti-discrimination statutes. Under common law and in the absence of special conditions an employee can be dismissed at any time under the doctrine of 'employment at will' without reason or notice. However, the law on non-economic discharges is evolving and becoming increasingly involved; the legal decisions on discharge have tended to limit the unbridled freedom of management in this respect. With respect to layoffs for economic reasons management is free to use normal business judgement in determining whom and when to lay off employees.[8]

There are similarities and differences in the social and economic environments of the two countries. The dual Federal and provincial jurisdiction in Canada parallels the Federal–state relationship in the US. In addition, the multiple Canadian political system includes the territories of Yukon and Northwest.

As indicated in Table 2.6, though the size of each country is fairly close, the Canadian population, labour force and unemployment are about a tenth of those of the US. The unemployment rate and unemployment benefits are comparable. The industrial structure is about the same in terms of the percentage of workers in manufacturing. But the Canadian economy is more heavily based on natural resources.

The large degree of foreign control of Canadian industry, particularly by US interests is a sensitive and controversial issue:

> ... there is an overriding concern about the high levels of foreign control in Canada. A situation has developed whereby key decisions affecting not only individual firms but the economy as a whole, are made in boardrooms outside Canada, in a manner that can be insensitive to and inconsistent with our Canadian priorities.[9]

Examples of the differences between the two countries can be found in the attitudes of many US companies with operations in Canada that they can literally dismiss personnel at will in their Canadian subsidiaries as they have been able to do in their home country. The US-controlled management of a Canadian subsidiary

Table 2.6: United States–Canada: Comparison for Selected Items

Item	United States		Canada	
	Year	Value	Year	Value
General				
Population (millions)	1980	222.0	1980	23.0
Square miles (millions)	1981	3.6	1981	3.9
Median family income ($)	1978	20,428	1978	17,500[a]
Per capita income ($)	1979	10,745	1979	8,954[a]
Growth of real output	1977	4.4	1977	2.8
Labour				
Labour force (millions)	1980	104.8	1980	11.5
Labour force/Population	1980	47.0	1980	50.1
Employment (millions)	1980	97.5	1980	10.7
Unemployment (millions)	1980	7.4	1980	0.9
Unemployment rate	1980	7.1	1980	7.5
Average duration of unemployment (weeks)	1980	11.9	1980	14.8
% of Employees in manufacturing	1980	21.8	1980	19.8
% of Employees unionised	1979	23.6	1977	31.0
Unemployment insurance recipients (thousands)	1980	3,095	1979	2,322
Unemployment insurance average weekly benefits ($)	1980	96.41	1979	92.76[a]

Job search data (millions of persons)	US — 1980		Canada — 1980	
	Persons	% of unemployed	Persons	% of unemployed
Persons unemployed	7.45	100	.87	100
Persons looking	5.85	79	.79	91
Persons not looking	1.60	21	.08	9
Contacted employers directly	4.28	57	.56	65
Used employment service	1.62	22	.40	46
Used advertisements	1.81	24	.31	35
Used other	1.50	20	.21	24

a. Canadian dollar amounts were adjusted using Canadian–US exchange rates.

Source: National Alliance of Business, Worker Adjustment to Plant Shutdowns and Mass Layoffs: An Analysis of Program Experience and Policy Options (Washington, March 1983) pp. 4-13.

may have little grasp of the variation between US and Canadian law, particularly on wrongful dismissal;[10] for example, it could be 'somewhat of a shock to the American parent company to discover the extent of its liability as a result of discharging one of its Canadian management personnel'.[11]

Collective Bargaining

As in the US, the core of Canadian employment law has tradi-
tionally been the common law right of management to run the
business as it deems most suitable and to dispense with the services
of any employee no longer wanted or needed. Two key developments have served as catalysts in changing this approach: the
growth of collective bargaining, and the gradual enactment of
legislation abridging the uncurtailed freedom of management to
terminate workers' employment.

Some 30 per cent of the 11 million labour force are union
members. In a 1978 analysis of some 1,000 major collective agreements covering some 2 million employees, almost three-fourths
permitted the employer to decide unilaterally to lay off workers
subject to seniority restrictions. About half the contracts contained
provisions for a simple notice of layoff and a fourth called for
notice of a week or less. Advance notice or consultation preceding
the introduction of new methods or techniques was in almost 30
per cent of the agreements.[12]

An important limit on management's right to lay off workers is
the collective bargaining restrictions on contracting out to persons
not covered by the agreement. Arbitrators have generally maintained that unless specifically prohibited by the agreement
employers are free to do so even if there are layoffs. Unions are
most concerned about this practice and it is restricted in almost 40
per cent of the agreements analysed.[13]

Severance pay is cited in some 40 per cent of the agreements
and supplementary unemployment benefits in almost ten per cent.
Provisions for training and re-training in the event of technological
change are contained in over 20 per cent of the agreements.

There is a further question as to what protection and benefits an
employee is entitled to after a shut-down or closing. Few agreements limit the right of management to close all or part of an
operation but the agreement itself is not necessarily cancelled by
such an action. Until the expiration date either party can have the
terms enforced.

The courts have held that unless and until either party performs
in such a way as to give notice that it will no longer be committed
to the terms of the expired agreement those terms will have been
considered to be incorporated into the individual employment
contract and thus continue to be valid.

Collective bargaining, other than giving senior employees preference, has not had any great impact on reductions in the number of employees, even union members. Management's right to dismiss for cause has been restricted but collective bargaining has accomplished little in giving protection from economically caused reductions. A partial explanation for the limited protection is the traditional attitude of management and labour in North America toward each other, i.e. adversaries with gains for each side at the expense of the other. The adversary positions are closely bound to the narrow focus of collective bargaining practices in Canada and the US.

Legislative Actions

In view of the limited role of common law and collective bargaining in restricting management's right to cut the workforce, legislative actions have been taken within the past decade at both the Federal and provincial levels. In 1971, the Federal government approved legislative requirements covering advance notice of individual and collective dismissals. The requirements are incorporated in the Labour Code which prescribes the rules for industrial relations and labour standards for industries under Federal jurisdiction. The Code is administered by Labour Canada; key sections are Part III — labour standards, Part IV — employee safety, and Part V — industrial relations. The Federal agency responsible for labour market policies and programmes is the Canada Employment and Immigration Commission (CE&IC). It is the major agency at the Federal level responsible for the development, supervision and administration of national programmes designed to solve manpower problems.

The separate jurisdictions, Federal and provincial, are a feature of the Canadian political system that is closer to the US than to the Western European systems. The divided jurisdiction over employment and industrial relations causes a lack of clarity over which government jurisdiction has responsibility for layoffs. The applicable requirements for severance pay and advance notice depend on which jurisdiction the industry or firm falls into.

Federal work, undertaking or business means any within the legislative authority of the Parliament of Canada 'including without restricting the generality of the foregoing':

a work, undertaking or business operated or carried on for or in

connection with navigation and shipping, whether inla
maritime, including the operation of ships and transportat
ship anywhere in Canada;
a railway, canal, telegraph or other work or undertaking connecting any province with any other or others of the provinces,
or extending beyond the limits of a province;
a line of steam or other ships connecting a province with any
other or others of the provinces, or extending beyond the limits
of a province;
a ferry between any province and any other province or
between any province and any other country than Canada;
aerodromes, aircraft or a line of air transportation;
a radio broadcasting station;
a bank;
a work or undertaking that, although wholly situated within a
province, is before or after its execution declared by the Parliament of Canada to be for the general advantage of Canada or
for the advantage of two or more of the provinces; and
a work, undertaking or business outside the exclusive legislative
authority of provincial legislatures.[14]

Essential to an undertaking of the Canadian system are the differences among individual and group layoffs or just and unjust dismissals. The objective is to enhance individual job security by
offering unjustly dismissed, non-unionised employees the remedy
of possible reinstatement available to union members under collective bargaining.

When a cut in the workforce is caused by a shortage of orders or
other economic adversities, employees may still feel they have
been unjustly dismissed. But the dismissal is not deemed to be
unjust though the employer may have to provide an adjudicator
with the reasons for the action. The employer's decision will be
upheld if due only to such reasons as declining production or phas-
ing out of a function or operation.

The legislation does not seek to define just or unjust dismissal.
The Minister of Labour refers the matter to an independent adjudicator if previous attempts to resolve the disagreement have been
unsuccessful. The provinces of Nova Scotia, Ontario and Quebec
have similar legislation.

Advance Notice and Severance Pay

Advance notice is mandated by both Federal and provincial governments prior to the termination of large numbers of employees (Table 2.7). Severance pay as a statutory right is required only by the Federal government and the province of Ontario.

For the termination of the employment of 50 or more workers in a four-week period within a particular industrial establishment or location, an employer must provide the Minister of Labour, Employment and Immigration a certified trade unions' advance notice before the effective date: 50–100 employees, 8 weeks; 101–300 employees, 12 weeks; over 300 employees, 16 weeks.

In the case of an individual separation, an employee who has finished three consecutive months of continuous work, except for just cause dismissals, is entitled to notice in writing at least two weeks before the termination date. In lieu of such notice, two weeks' wages at regular work rates must be paid.

At the provincial level, there are also advance notice requirements. Five provinces — Manitoba, Newfoundland, Nova Scotia, Ontario and Quebec — call for employers to give advance notice of a forthcoming termination of a group of employees. The minimum period for pre-notification is two months, with the maximum four months (Table 2.7).

Along the lines of the Federal regulations for notice to individual workers, nine provinces — Alberta, British Columbia, Manitoba, Newfoundland, Nova Scotia, Ontario, Prince Edward Island, Quebec and Saskatchewan — also call on employers to notify an individual worker who is to be separated.

Employers subject to the Federal regulations must give severance pay to an employee who completes five consecutive years of continuous work unless the termination is for just cause. The amount is calculated as the lesser of two days wages for each year of employment or 40 days wages. Neither the statutory minimum nor the nominal rates generally agreed upon are deemed to be sufficient to replace the lost income.

In 1981, Ontario enacted legislation mandating severance pay. The employer must give each terminated employee who has been with the firm for a minimum of five years, pay equal to the amount received at the regular rate for a normal work-week multiplied by the number of years of employment with the firm. Twenty-six years is the maximum number of years.

Table 2.7: Canadian Pre-notification Requirements for Group Terminations

Jurisdiction	Minimum layoff period	Workers laid off	Length of pre-notification
Federal	4 weeks	50–100	8 weeks
		101–300	12 weeks
		over 300	16 weeks
Manitoba	same as Federal		
Newfoundland	4 weeks	50–199	8 weeks
		200–499	12 weeks
		over 499	16 weeks
Nova Scotia	4 weeks	10–99	8 weeks
		100–299	12 weeks
		over 299	16 weeks
Ontario	4 weeks	50–199	8 weeks
		200–499	12 weeks
		over 499	16 weeks
Quebec	2 months	10–99	2 months
		100–299	3 months
		over 299	4 months

Changes Causing Redundancy

In view of the redundancies caused by technological change, there is one provision of the Federal Labour Code which has particular relevance. It provides that where a collective agreement exists a trade union may apply to the Labour Relations Board for an order mandating the employer to furnish 90 days advance notice of technological change and bargain for revision of the agreement. Technological change is defined as:

> ... the introduction by an employer into his work, undertaking or business of equipment or material of a different nature or kind than that previously utilized by him in the operation of the work, undertaking or business; and
> a change in the manner in which the employer carries on the work, undertaking or business that is directly related to the introduction of that equipment or material.[15]

The notice must include a description of the nature of the technological change, the date it is to take effect, the number and type of employees affected and the impact on terms, conditions and employment security of concerned workers.

Labour unions allege that the definition of technological change is too restrictive and there are constant disputes with management over what changes fit into the category of 'technological'. Instead the regulation should apply to all changes.

In 1979, the Federal (Carrothers) Commission of Inquiry into Redundancies proposed that all employers in both Federal and provincial jurisdictions should provide notice of 'an intent to introduce a change likely to cause redundancy'.[16] The Commission found that the resolution of redundancy problems does not lend itself ideally to the traditional adversary system found in collective bargaining; instead, there should be a 'more cooperative and constructive relationship of "partners", rather than of adversaries'.[17]

The Commission surveyed employers and found they caution against too long advance notice contending that the efficiency and well-being of a firm could suffer; also that managements' decisions should be executed as soon and as decisively as possible. But they do agree that there is a basis for varying lengths of advance notice. Labour union representatives usually prefer an advance notice with sufficient time to devise comprehensive adjustment plans as well as time for workers to qualify for new positions.

The Carrothers Commission concluded that severance pay should not be relied upon as a general adjustment measure.[18] A finding was that labour unions do not wish to assume part of the operational responsibilities of the enterprise; 'The decision to introduce a change is acknowledged as purely a management decision.' However, unions would like joint consultations with management with respect to the conditions of human resource management.[19] But the Commission acknowledged the limitations in looking to a company for resolution of the problems of surplus workers. The objective of redundancy management, if employment retention is impossible, should be re-employment elsewhere.

Plant Closing Legislation — US

The subject of plant closing legislation has been one of continuing controversy. One viewpoint is that it is restrictive legislation, counterproductive to the economy and detrimental to the welfare of workers generally.[20] Another opinion is that not enough corporations are assuming their social obligations and that the Federal and state governments cannot ignore the costs of maintaining a mobile economy. Despite the heated controversy, there have been very few legislative victories.[21]

Federal Legislation

The first major effort in the US to enact plant closing legislation was the National Employment Priorities Act of 1974, HR 13541, introduced by Representative William D. Ford of Michigan. A co-sponsor was then Senator Walter F. Mondale, later Vice President and a leading Democratic contender for the 1984 presidential nomination. The bill made little progress in Congress, but sub-sequently plant closing bills have been regularly introduced in Congress and various state legislatures.

Almost a decade later, in May 1983, Representative Ford introduced a revised plant closing bill, the National Employment Priorities Act (NEPA), HR 2847, which applies to firms with over 50 employees. NEPA provides Federal financial assistance to workers, communities and businesses preferably to take effect before the closings or failures occur. Advance notice is called for when the job loss in an establishment in any 18-month period equals or exceeds the lesser of 100 employees or 15 per cent of the employees. The notice given must be not less than six months where fewer than 100 employees are involved and one year where there are more than 100.

The firms must make severance payments, continue health and welfare benefits and provide opportunities for transfer to other company facilities. Employees receive severance payment of 85 per cent of their average wage for a period of 52 weeks with a maximum payment of $25,000. Older workers receive extended benefit payments reimbursed by the Federal government. There is a provision to penalise a firm that transfers operations outside the US when an economically viable domestic alternative exists.

According to Representative Ford, the bill does not restrict the operations of a small business since it is applicable only to firms with 50 or more employees.[22] The question might be posed whether the exclusion means that employees of small businesses are being treated unfairly. NEPA does not give the government the power to prevent a closing or relocation but only to delay the shutdown for six months to a year, depending on the number of employees. As with other similar pieces of legislation, the likeli-hood of the passage of NEPA is dim, particularly so in view of the opposition of the Reagan administration to this type of programme.

State Legislation

Following the failure of NEPA at the Federal level, the legislative effort moved to the states. The Ohio Community Readjustment Act, first introduced in the State of Ohio in 1977, has been a model for bills introduced in other states. The bill covers closing, relocation, or reduction in operations. Any commercial, industrial or agricultural corporation with 100 or more employees operating in the state for a minimum of five years is subject to the legislation. The basic provisions call for a two-year advance notice filing of an economic impact statement, severance payments to employees, payments to communities and continuation of health insurance coverage and rights of transfer to other units in the company.

An individual state enacting plant-closing legislation would be placed at a disadvantage in retaining or attracting industry as opposed to states without the legislation. Thus, the most effective and practical approach would be through Federal legislation.

The only plant-closing legislation passed at the state level have been two 'less stringent and loosely enforced' bills in Maine and Wisconsin. The penalties for non-compliance are not particularly severe.[23] Following the closing of the Alpha Carbide facilities, the Maine legislation (Revised Statutes, Section 625-B) was enacted in 1976 to protect employees. The legislation mandates both severance pay and advance notice.

A covered employer is liable for severance pay if an industrial or commercial operation is relocated within or outside the state a 100 or more miles from the original location. A covered employer is defined as one that employs at any one time in the preceding 12-month period 100 or more persons. The severance pay to a terminated worker consists of a lump sum equal to the worker's average weekly wage times the number of years employed.

There is no liability for severance pay if: (1) relocation is due to a physical calamity; (2) there is a contract covering severance pay for the employees; (3) the employee accepts employment at the new location; or (4) the employee has been employed by the employer for less than three years.

Any employer proposing to relocate a covered establishment outside the state must notify employees and the municipality concerned not less than 60 days prior to relocation. Violation of the 60-days notice provision subjects the employer to a maximum fine of $500 unless there is a physical calamity or unforeseen circumstances.

In the 18 months preceding April 1983, 1,374 persons were paid a total of $2,219,614 in severance pay, an average per employee of $1,615 — not a particularly munificent sum. All except one of the industries involved willingly made the mandated severance payment without any legal action being necessary.[24]

The Wisconsin legislation, Section 109.75, enacted in 1975, was directed at mergers, liquidations, dispositions, relocations and closings. It requires corporations with 100 or more employees to give 60 days advance notice to affected employees, communities and the State Department of Labor, Industry and Human Relations. There is no provision for severance pay. Violation of the law is a misdemeanour subject to a fine of $150 for each employee losing a job. One reason the Wisconsin law has not been enforced is because the legislation does not define 'cessation of business'.[25]

Municipal Legislation

Even though one criticism of the proposed state plant-closing bills is that passage would keep business out of any state that passed such a bill, in 1982 the city of Philadelphia put into effect a bill that mandates employers to provide employees, unions and the municipality with 60 days' notice before closing or leaving the city. If proper notice is not given, the city can either ask the court to stop the closing or require the company to give employees up to 60 days' pay. The City Council which enacted the bill over the Mayor's veto contended that employees would have more time to search for new jobs and possibly give the city an opportunity to prevent the departure. The Mayor vetoed the bill on the grounds that the sanctions were illegal and would send a negative message to companies that might otherwise move to Philadelphia.[26]

In 1983, Bill No. 2643 was introduced by the Pittsburgh City Council calling for at least one year's advance notice of plant closings, reductions or relocations. Parties affected by the failure of employers to comply can bring civil action. The court can enjoin employers from carrying out the action until proper notice has been given or otherwise there is compliance with the Ordinance. An employer is subject who has at least 50 employees for more than six months. The reduction in operations comes under the bill when there is a permanent closing of a portion of the operations so as to reduce the number of employees at any establishment by 15 per cent or more over any one year period or 25 employees, which ever is more. The bill also creates a unit to help affected employees or the community to acquire ownership.

Components of Plant-Closing Bills

Though advance notice and severance pay are incorporated in collective bargaining agreements, little progress has been made on the legislative front. They are key elements in proposed plant-closing bills.

The advocates of pre-notification contend that it could provide time to prevent or delay closing decisions or strategies can be devised to find other jobs for workers. Localities would be given time to seek replacement industries, prepare for the loss of tax revenues and increases in social expenditures and seek Federal and state intervention and aid

Opponents state that as soon as notice is given labour–management conflict will emerge and employee productivity and morale will decline. Key employees, including managerial, will leave. Customers will be lost to competitors, particularly in the area in which the facility is located. The company's credit rating could drop. Once the announcement is made of the closing, potential buyers assume a harder bargaining stance.

How necessary is formal advance notice? It may merely be a confirmation of what employees already sense. Deferred maintenance, declining sales and production, news reports of takeovers, mergers or weak financial condition are signals. But these signals are tentative and may not necessarily be synonymous with shutdowns. Firms can close a facility gradually without shutting down completely and having to comply with mandated pre-notification. Any growth or expansion in production can be shifted to other company facilities or areas at the expense of the older facility.

A potential source of controversy is the length of the pre-notification period. An excessively long period may be impractical. A marginal company may be in a precarious position for years and suddenly find the end comes quickly at the instigation of outside forces or, vice versa, recover.

How does business view advance notice for plant closing? A revealing survey in May 1980 of *Fortune 500* companies elicited 105 responses.[27] Twenty-seven per cent of the respondents considered three to six months to be ideal; 21 per cent indicated two to three months. Fifty-three per cent thought a realistic period in which to notify a community would be between two and six months.

In regard to a one- to two-year advance notice requirement, a provision included in much of the proposed plant-closing legislation, 74 per cent of the executives felt their companies 'could not reasonably meet this requirement'. Fourteen per cent were unsure; and only 12 per cent felt their companies could comply.

When asked to give the most important reason for not giving advance notice, 51 per cent cited 'potential loss of worker productivity'; 25 per cent said 'potential loss of business'; 6 per cent said employee morale; and 3 per cent said 'stock market considerations'.

Forty-eight per cent of the respondents mentioned that their firms had recently closed plants. Of this group 6 per cent gave no notice; 4 per cent, one week; 14 per cent, one month; 54 per cent, 2 to 6 months; 14 per cent, 6 months to a year; and 6 per cent, a year or more. Eighty-two per cent of this group felt the notice given was sufficient. The survey results indicate that management is not unalterably and unilaterally opposed to having to give advance notice. The controversy may be more over the length of time than actually having to give notice.

Severance pay can ease resistance to closings, make employees more amenable to re-training or relocation and allow management more flexibility to close plants. In a period when multinationals can shift production among countries, severance pay can be one of a number of factors determining locational decisions. The US has been attractive to multinationals for its lack of requirements such as severance pay. A high level of severance pay could encourage the increased substitution of capital for labour. The role of severance pay in causing such substitution is no longer as important an element as automation or robotisation.

Advance notice and severance pay, *per se*, have a limited effect in preventing or delaying job loss in the face of economic realities. But they do serve to mitigate the hardships of job loss and provide for an interim readjustment period.

Preventing Relocation

In view of the lack of success in having plant-closing legislation enacted at either the Federal or state levels, communities and labour are attempting through other methods to deter companies from relocating. Among states and municipalities there is strong competition to attract and retain industry through the use of generous incentives. It may be that the acceptance of subsidies will eventually limit the ease with which companies can close and relocate subsidiaries. A number of municipalities, notably Yonkers, New York, are questioning the right of companies to relocate after accepting assistance.

In November 1982, Otis Elevator, a subsidiary of the conglomerate, United Technologies, announced it would close their Yonkers plant which then employed some 375 hourly, salaried and managerial employees engaged in the manufacture of geared and gearless elevator machines. According to the company management, the closing decision results from significant technological changes which have affected the ability to manufacture at the Yonkers plant, e.g. changes from electro-mechanical to electronic controls and new types of elevator drives. Since the Yonkers facility is a heavy industrial facility, the company asserts it is not suited for the production of the newer products. Recessionary conditions and product changes have reduced the plant workforce from a peak of 1,500.

The elevator was invented in Yonkers where the company had its roots as an independent entity. Though there have been hints for some 20 years that Otis would leave Yonkers, the Mayor reacted sharply to the announcement. In the early 1970s, the municipality put together some $14 million in public funds, supplying about a sixth, to help Otis expand in Yonkers. At that time Otis employed some 1,300 workers.

The importance of the dispute rests on whether a community can hold a company wishing to depart responsible for the public assistance it received. The Yonkers Mayor wants to take legal action to have Otis compensate the city for the subsidy. If the city is successful in obtaining reparations, it could be a serious obstacle to relocation by major employers. If legal action is taken and is successful, Professor Charles Haar of the Harvard Law School, an urban law specialist, predicts cases like the one in Yonkers and a similar one in Detroit will set legal precedents. Courts will be encouraged to create a new 'common law notion of fairness when a city commits resources to help an employer. The law is evolving and I think you may see some obligations placed on a major employer to the community and its employees'.[28]

Labour is pursuing another tactic to block plant closings, relying on a National Labor Relations Board interpretation of Federal labour law. Either party to a contract would be barred from modifying it before expiration. A company is prevented from moving while the collective bargaining contract is still in effect. Court decisions have reaffirmed the Board's rulings that, during the term of a labour contract, work cannot be moved from a union to a non-union facility to reduce labour costs. Such moves for economic reasons are prohibited without the union's consent.[29]

Foreign Influences on Domestic Policy

Despite the lack of national redundancy legislation in the US, the future course of such legislation could be influenced by the existence of various arrangements outside the US.[30] Government, business and labour are directly and indirectly affected by a number of international, regional and national guidelines, codes and laws, notably those under the aegis of the Organisation for Economic Co-operation and Development, the International Labour Organisation, the European Economic Community and national co-determination legislation. The impact of these codes, guidelines and laws derives from the overlapping foreign and domestic operations of multinationals and as models for initiating and structuring domestic programmes. They prevent government, business and labour from avoiding the subject of redundancy legislation.

The subject of redundancies cannot be examined simply from a national perspective; world investment and trade transcend national boundaries as exemplified by the growth of multinationals. About half of the industrial output of the non-communist world is produced by firms that have a multinational structure. Practically all the 400 or 500 largest world enterprises have substantial business interests in the form of operating units located outside their home country.[31]

In the mid-1970s, US multinationals were reported to employ seven million workers at home against 750,000 US residents who worked for foreign-owned enterprises. An estimated one third or more of manufacturing employment is in the home country of US multinationals; Canada follows closely. The larger US multinationals employ more nationals at home than foreign workers in their subsidiaries abroad, 6.7 million versus 3.3

million.[32] The proportion, however, has been shifting toward an increasing share of employment outside the US.

The importance of US multinationals has involved the US government at the international level in what it has been able to ignore domestically. The involvement has been with codes of conduct in the form of declarations, resolutions, conventions, recommendations and guidelines dealing with redundancy.

These are not necessarily legally binding until ratified as a treaty when they are incorporated into the legislation of the signatory parties and the provisions become binding. A non-binding code can have force by virtue of voluntary acceptance and observance or moral persuasion. The mere adoption by a host country of an agreement that has been negotiated over a number of years has political impact. Thus, US multinationals may be called upon to comply with codes by host countries and find it difficult to resist complying in the home country. 'Standards that are developed on international codes have a way of finding themselves expressed in national legislation at some time in the future.'[33]

OECD Guidelines

The first major multilateral understanding or code of conduct for acceptable activities and treatments of multinationals and foreign investment including closures was formulated in 1976 and reconfirmed in 1979 by the Organisation for Economic Development and Co-operation (OECD). The OECD emerged from the institutions established in 1948 to implement the European Recovery Plan (Marshall Plan). It was formally organised in 1960, the membership consisting of 24 market economy countries, including the US.

The OECD members including the US adopted the Declaration of International Investment and Multinational Enterprises, outlining new rules or guidelines for multinationals operating in their respective jurisdictions. It was drafted in close consultation with the Business and Industry Advisory Committee (BIAC) and the Trade Union Advisory Committee (TUAC). The significance or importance of the Declaration has not been so much in its enforcement but as a model or prototype for use by the United Commission on Transnational Corporations, the International Labour Organisation Convention and the European Community Vredeling proposal.

The guidelines call for an enterprise to give reasonable notice of changes and co-operate with employees and governments to lessen to the greatest possible extent the adverse effects of the changes. Compliance should be within the framework of national law, regulations, labour relations and employment practices of the countries in which they operate. With respect to large scale layoffs or dismissals the guidelines call for enterprises:

> in considering changes in their operations which would have major effects upon the livelihood of their employees, in particular in the case of the closure of an entity involving collective layoffs or dismissals, provide reasonable notice of such changes to representatives of their employees, and where appropriate to the relevant governmental authorities, and co-operate with the employee representatives and appropriate governmental authorities so as to mitigate to the maximum extent practical the adverse effects.[34]

The guidelines are voluntary but governments have suggested to the multinationals that they comply. Some multinationals include statements in their annual reports that they comply; however, unions have complained that governments and multinationals are not overly concerned about adherence to the guidelines.

The attitude of the US government in respect to the guidelines is illustrated by its actions in the Badger case. Badger, a subsidiary in Belgium of the US multinational, Raytheon, was to be closed by the US management in 1977. The subsidiary was declared bankrupt, not leaving enough assets to cover the workers' claims for severance pay as mandated by Belgian law.

The unions and the Belgian government claimed the US multinational violated the spirit of the guidelines and made the case the first OECD review of experience under the guidelines. The case moved to the Committee for Investment and Multinational Enterprises (CIME). The key issue was whether the parent company was liable for financial obligations of a subsidiary operating as a limited liability company. The CIME was averse to accepting the case, holding that its role was limited to general principles, not the merits of a particular case.

The US government representative contended that any discussion of a specific dispute would be inappropriate and harmful by transforming the OECD into a semi-judicial body rather than a consultative mechanism. In other words, the merits of a particular case were better handled under the laws and practices of the country concerned. The company argued that the guidelines were misinterpreted to impose burdens on the multinationals beyond those applied to national companies. The majority of the OECD members agreed with the US. However, Raytheon did cover Badger's obligations.

The OECD decision could be interpreted that multinational subsidiaries operating in the US have no mandated obligation to follow the OECD guidelines in the host country. But labour has pushed for stronger codes.

ILO Convention and Recommendations

The International Labour Organisation (ILO) General Conference in June 1982 adopted a Convention, No. 158, and Recommendations, No. 166, on 'Termination of Employment at the Initiative of the Employer'. Their objective is to give workers protection against unfair dismissals and terminations for economic reasons.

The Convention covers unfair dismissals and procedures for workers to appeal if dismissal is considered unjustified. The worker has the right to a reasonable period of notice and severance allowances or social security benefits according to national law and practice. Reasons are cited that are not considered valid as a basis for termination.

There are supplementary provisions concerning terminations of employment for economic, technological, structural or similar reasons. Employers should inform workers' representatives of contemplated terminations and provide an opportunity for consultation on measures to avert or minimise the terminations and mitigate the adverse effect. The employer should inform the competent authority of such terminations.

The supplementary provisions in the Recommendations in respect to termination for economic reasons are especially detailed. They provide governments with major guidelines and numerous examples of possible measures to prevent or limit economic terminations and their negative effects.

The Convention recommends that national legislatures adopt its provisions by giving them effect through law or regulations. The Convention and Recommendations are not legally binding in the US until ratified. The US government adviser prior to adoption stated that the stability and quality of employment through sound dismissal policies and protection of individuals and groups

... was best accomplished through less government intervention in the free marketplace, in attacking the root cause of unemployment and economic problems, rather than just coping with short-term factors or symptoms ... the key was to be found in reliance on private arrangements to solve private controversies and the creation of an environment of private co-operation rather than adversarial confrontation.[35]

The US government considered the proposed text as not truly comprehensive because it almost completely ignores guidelines for voluntary efforts by the parties to correct underlying problems which give rise to many terminations.[36] US business is not concerned about Congress adopting the ILO Convention but is worried about the effect on the subsidiaries operating abroad if adopted by foreign national legislatures. There is also concern that domestically an ILO convention would add momentum to pending state legislation covering large-scale layoffs and the unions would gain credibility by using the provisions for collective bargaining. But labour does not anticipate Congressional approval. Since 1934, US management has been successful in convincing the government to oppose all ILO conventions.[37]

While the immediate impact in the US may be limited, there may be effects eventually on an international level. In the long run the ILO Convention and Recommendations may supersede the OECD guidelines as the source of pressure on multinational operations; the ILO as contrasted to the OECD has almost universal applicability. Another source of pressure would be adoption by the United Nations of a code of conduct for multinationals. The ILO Convention on Termination of Employment will be incorporated into the Code of Conduct which is the responsibility of the UN Commission on Transnational Corporations. The Commission hopes to have the Code approved in 1983.

Vredeling Directive

The proposed Vredeling Directive provides another indication of US business and government reaction to requirements that multinationals operating in the European Economic Community (EEC) keep workers informed of major corporate changes likely to effect them, especially closures, redundancies and transfers of production. The proposal has made considerable progress towards

EEC ratification; final approval by the Council of Ministers, subject to agreement on a number of points, is a distinct possibility.

According to EEC officials, the OECD guidelines are inadequate because they are too vague, are voluntary and there is only partial compliance by US firms. As contrasted to the OECD guidelines and the ILO Convention and Recommendations on Termination of Employment, the Directive would be legally binding on meeting the overall goals. The individual countries would have considerable latitude in putting it into effect.

The mandatory nature of the Directive has stirred up strong opposition from US business and government and has engendered more controversy than any EEC proposal of the past quarter century. The National Foreign Trade Council (NFTC), a nonprofit organisation, has been firmly against the proposal. The unanimity of the opposition by US multinationals is reflected by the membership of the NFTC — over 600 US corporations engaged in foreign trade and investment. The membership includes most of the multinationals accounting for some $77 billion of direct investment in Europe. The uproar over Vredeling and similar proposals has prompted several US congressmen to introduce legislation that would forbid US companies to comply with EEC rules or regulations that contravene domestic law.[38]

The concerns of US business over the proposal are about the impact inside and outside the EEC. It would interfere with established labour practices and impair the competitiveness of their European-based subsidiaries. Though the Community officials dismiss the fears as unfounded, US parent companies are concerned that they will be subject to extra-territorial legislation, i.e. the EEC will legislate for their behaviour outside the Community.[39]

Disclosure requirements would be on a worldwide basis and US multinationals could end up being polarised on both sides of the Atlantic.[40] There is also the fear that confidential information or company secrets would go to competitors or adversely affect stock prices.

The different foreign and domestic viewpoints stem from the mandatory and permanent nature of the Vredeling Directive. In the US, as part of give-back bargaining, more companies are opening their books to unions. But it is questionable whether the current information-sharing will endure. Management may find that a cost calculus indicates it is temporarily advantageous to cede a modicum of power or control in return for substantial financial concessions.

As with other such proposals, enactment of the Directive could be a take-off point for demands that the involvement of workers not be limited to the European subsidiaries of US multinationals but rather that there should be equal treatment on both sides of the Atlantic. It could represent another means for US labour to demand similar treatment, if not politically then through collective bargaining.

Co-determination

Another example of the influence of external factors on investment and divestment decisions, including openings and closings, is co-determination (CD).[41] Though non-existent in the US in any mandatory form, European legislation has led to demands that it be started in the US, not necessarily by legislation but at the corporate level. More immediately there is the connection from multinationals with facilities in the US and in countries with CD, notably West Germany and the Netherlands.

The differences between CD and collective bargaining with respect to large-scale layoffs or dismissals should be clarified. Under CD, employee representatives serve on the supervisory board which is the equivalent to the board of directors in the US. National legislation in Europe mandates that employee representatives be elected to the board. Thus under CD employee members of the board are informed and involved before major decisions to reduce the workforce are made. Under collective bargaining, labour is formally involved, if at all, at a later stage, most likely after the decision-making process is well under way and efforts may be limited to overturning or delaying implementation. Collective bargaining does not encompass the range of substantive decisions considered under CD, such as investment, disinvestment, location, closings, takeovers, mergers and product lines.

Labour unions in the United States, with few exceptions, have shown little interest in CD as indicated in the widely quoted May 1976 statement by Thomas R. Donahue, now Secretary-Treasurer of the American Federation of Labor–Congress of Industrial Organizations (AFL–CIO):

We do not seek to be a partner in management, to be, most

likely, the junior partner in success, and the senior partner in failure.

We do not want to blur in any way the distinctions between the respective roles of management and labor in the plant.

We guard our independence fiercely — independent of government, independent of any political party and independent of management.

We've watched codetermination and its offshoot experiments with interest, and will continue to do so, but it is our judgment that it offers little to American unions in the performance of their job unionism role (given our exclusive representative status and our wide-open conflict bargaining) and it could only hurt US unions as they pursue their social unionism functions — seeing through legislation, political action, community involvement and a host of other approaches, improve our members' lot by improving society generally.[42]

According to Lane Kirkland, President of the AFL–CIO, control over pensions, welfare and other funds is a far more effective tool for labour unions than participation on boards of directors. There is much greater potential in obtaining an effective voice in the flow of investment capital based on accumulated pension and welfare funds. Also that directors are not significant policy makers; rather most companies are management-controlled. The theoretical legal liability of directors has grown without a commensurate increase in real power.[43] The question with respect to control over pension and welfare is what happens in the event of large-scale displacement of workers. As contributions fall and payments increase, the capital of the funds diminishes with a commensurate loss in the importance of the funds.

The few examples of worker representation on US boards of directors have occurred in financially impacted companies. 'Only three groups can make financial concessions to keep an ailing company alive — banks, governments and employees. In America, employees of troubled companies are increasingly making wage-cut sacrifices.'[44] Board membership has been gained in return for worker co-operation in rescue plans, usually in the form of financial concessions.

What was considered a breakthrough in avoiding layoffs took place in 1979 with the nomination of Douglas Fraser, President of the United Automobile Workers (UAW), to the Chrysler board of directors. The offer to Fraser came as a tradeoff for union support in lobbying for Federal loan guarantees and concessions enabling the company to reduce cost-of-living raises and benefits. Initially, other UAW officers were cool to union representation on the corporate board but changed their minds after a surprising decision by Chrysler to close the Hamtramck, Michigan assembly plant which employed 5,000 members. Mr Fraser conceded he could not have reversed the decision but he might have had the plant phased out over a longer period or done more to see that workers found new jobs, thereby moderating the effects of the closing.

In early 1983, the UAW wanted Fraser to keep his seat on the Chrysler board but the continuation of worker representation was doubtful. Chrysler contended that Fraser was invited as an individual and wanted him to remain on the board but the union was not automatically entitled to have a member. The Chrysler approach illustrates the difference between the mandated representation based on legislation and the purely voluntary selection of board members.

The other major corporation with union representation on the board is Pan American World Airways. In May 1982, Robert L. Gould, a Pan Am pilot and representative of the Air Line Pilots Association, was elected to the airline's board of directors. In March 1983, five labour unions requested an additional seat on the seventeen-member company board.

As already indicated, many US trade union leaders have little desire for CD to be formalised; but they will have to become increasingly involved, not by choice, as CD becomes more widespread outside the US. This will be particularly true if CD is instituted in the European Economic Community. Unions in the US will find themselves dealing increasingly with multinationals who also have facilities in countries with CD. Some 40 of the 600-odd companies subject to CD in West Germany are major US firms, such as Ford, General Motors, IBM, Proctor and Gamble, and DuPont. On the other hand, major German companies have facilities in the US.

Multinational or transnational unions have experienced some growth. For example, West German subsidiaries of US multinationals such as Ford and DuPont have had international trade unionists on their supervisory boards. In January 1973, Herman Rabhan, an American, General Secretary of the International

Metalworkers Federation, was elected as the workers' representative on the Ford Werke supervisory board. A vocal critic of
multinationals, Charles Levenson, a Canadian and General
Secretary of the International Federation of Chemical, Energy and
General Workers Union was elected to the DuPont supervisory
board.

Their election reflects demands by European trade unions for
an employees' voice on multinationals. They want not only to be
involved in global investment but also in disinvestment because of
the employment implications. In contrast, North American unions
have indicated that they were not pleased to share responsibility
with management on investment decisions. 'In this particular
context, they saw difficulties in reconciling European ideas of
"participation" with the North American approach to collective
bargaining with an employer.'[45]

As opposed to US trade union leaders, many European trade
union officials recognised earlier that headquarters decisions
concerning investment and production rationalisation have greater
consequences for workers than the traditional issues of wages,
fringe benefits and working conditions.

> The really substantive decisions, they say, are made in the
> very remote and inaccessible headquarters of the multinational
> firms and they want worker representatives to have a say in
> those decisions, as well as in those which are generally left to
> subsidiary managers.[46]

But the US trade union leaders, though not yet willing to
demand CD, are finding that the shrinkage of industry is bringing
the matter of job loss to the forefront and the traditional issues
have become relatively less significant.

The employment ramifications of CD that transcend national
boundaries are illustrated by the Volkswagen (VW) decision to set
up facilities in the US despite opposition from particular groups on
the company's subsidiary board. The investment of $250 million in
the US was unanimously approved in April 1976 only after certain
conditions were agreed upon:

> Supervisory board approval would be necessary for any
> specified increase in the amount of US-produced components
> in any US-assembled cars and for any changes in German

employment due to the foreign project.

A pledge of DM 40 million to retool the Emden plant producing VWs for export to the US; operations could thus be continued in the plant after loss of the US sales.

Labour given guarantee that employment levels would be maintained for ten years.

Incorporation of the VW subsidiary in the US was devised so that the supervisory board in Germany oversees operations of the US company and expansion of its operations must be approved by the supervisory board. This method gave the union strong leverage to bargain with management about location and relocation plans.

Paradoxically some seven years later, VW sales both in Germany and the US have been at an unsatisfactory level due to Japanese competition. Employment has suffered and expansion plans have been suspended.

Another example of the complexities of transnational arrangements is the relationship between Renault, the French state-owned manufacturer and the American Motors Corporation (AMC). Renault purchased 46.4 per cent of American's stock, thus giving it effective control. As a state-owned company, Renault is mandated to have a tripartite supervisory board with a third of the members each from trade unions, management and the government, all with equal voting rights. What is the role of the AMC workers and trade unions in such an arrangement when decisions affecting employment are being considered?

Another unresolved and related factor is the placement of a union representative on the AMC board of directors. The company has accepted in principle the seating of a UAW representative on the board of directors but the actual seating has been held up on antitrust grounds, i.e. the connection between the UAW, AMC and Chrysler.

How does CD work in regard to cutbacks? Worker directors as a group are generally active proponents of investment or expansion that purportedly strengthens the company and increases employment security. They are under great pressure to oppose any action that could adversely affect workers.

How influential on management is the existence of CD in a decision to curtail operations; given a choice, would the country without CD be selected for the cutback in view of the greater ease with which it could be accomplished? However, other considerations are the mandated costs of large-scale layoffs and it is possible that the initial choice for operations would be negatively influenced by the existence of CD.

To what extent, if at all, national codetermination laws can motivate foreign companies to relocate or to limit future investment depends on a number of factors. Despite restricted corporate freedom of decision, the relevant country may still offer cost and other advantages, unless equally profitable access to its markets exists indirectly from other locations not governed by codetermination laws. In general, codetermination regulations should not initiate an exodus of foreign corporation production facilities, but they could motivate foreign companies to look for equivalent alternatives without codetermination for future investment, especially if they exist within a common market.[47]

An American labour specialist finds it

... eminently reasonable that corporations seeking to establish production facilities abroad should be required to discuss their plans with the organizations representing their employees prior to taking final decisions ... and would like to see the employee representatives armed with the same power they have under German codetermination. The unions might object to any and all investments that meant loss of jobs, but they would be on much weaker ground where the investment was essential to maintain the firm's viability, as it might be where semiskilled labor-intensive production was involved.[48]

If CD should be adopted in the US, it would probably start without government sanction and in financially troubled companies. Much is being made in the US of industry–labour co-operation or partnership as a key component of industrial policy, leading to a modified form of CD. Employees would be increasingly involved in reduction decisions. But with less than a fourth of the labour force unionised and the weakness of unions in the face of the restructuring of industry, management is not under extreme pressure to accept labour as an equal partner and to readily accept CD. Thus, the progress of CD in the US is likely to be gradual.

Despite the reluctance of US labour readers to embrace CD,

there are predictions that more labour representatives will be found on company boards and the unilateral ability of management to make personnel cutbacks will be curtailed. To preserve companies, management will seek increased co-operation from labour to rationalise production or make concessions.

Professor George C. Lodge of the Harvard University Graduate School of Business Administration, guesses

> ... that more companies will want worker representation on the board because it is more profitable. The workers will obviously be more sympathetic to the competitive situation if they are represented on the board and that any contributions they make will go into preserving their jobs and into other businesses.[49]

Another academic, Professor George Strauss of the University of California, Berkeley Institute of Industrial Relations, finds 'The unions in this country haven't had the ideology to go in this direction [CD], but now I think they see this as the only way to save their jobs'.[50] From a corporate perspective, the Vice President for industrial relations for Asarco projects worker-directors to be a thing of the future and can see some situations where they would be a good thing for companies in trouble.[51]

Adjusting to Layoffs and Re-employment Measures

Though the US has no comprehensive redundancy programme along the lines of those in Western Europe, there has been a policy of reliance on unemployment insurance (UI) and a large number of *ad hoc* programmes dealing with a relative small number of workers in special situations. In 1983 a new national policy of job training for dislocated workers is scheduled to begin.

Unemployment Insurance

The oldest, largest and most encompassing government systems in Canada and the US for compensating unemployed workers are the unemployment insurance systems. They are the major income support for workers following loss of their jobs.

The principle of UI was first discussed in the US as a possibility in Massachusetts in 1916 but the first state bill was enacted by Wisconsin in 1932. At the Federal level the government role in dealing with unemployment originated in the Great Depression of the 1930s when the rate of unemployment reached 25 per cent. The Federal government was not too willing to become involved, perhaps paralleling the current reluctance to consider seriously plant-closing legislation.

The Federal/state UI system was created as Titles III and IX of the Social Security Act of 1935. Temporary financial aid became a matter of right rather than one of benevolence. The basic model was borrowed from Europe, especially France and Great Britain but with a difference. 'The European approach emphasized the *worker* and his needs, while the American emerging variant stressed the responsibility of the *employer* to reduce unemployment.'[52]

The thrust of UI was on workers whose unemployment was expected to be transitional and of relatively short duration. They would be re-employed 'without a major change in themselves or in their environment. All that these workers require is a temporary and usually partial, replacement of lost income. Programs to aid these unemployed may be called *alleviative* programs ...' Unemployment compensation relied on the alleviative approach, whereas the new programmes of regional development and job training of the 1960s were defined as *'curative'*.[53] In the 1980s the shift is to job training and de-emphasis on regional development.

The Federal UI programme adopted a then seldom-used form of fiscal incentive to assure state action. A uniform payroll tax of three per cent was levied on employers of eight or more workers but had provisions for a credit of 90 per cent to employers contributing 2.7 per cent to a state unemployment compensation system. The uniform tax encourages states to provide unemployment benefits without foregoing their competitive advantage but allowed states to be flexible in fixing the amount and duration of benefits.

Over the years the coverage has been extended to some 97 per cent of wage and salaried workers and the amount and duration of benefits has grown. The Federal levy on employers' payrolls has increased to 3.4 per cent. Employers still get a credit of 2.7 per cent for payments into the appropriate state UI system from which unemployed workers are actually paid benefits. The remaining 0.7 per cent balance goes to the Federal government to administer Federal and state systems, to finance extended benefits and the Federal UI loan fund. The states can vary the 2.7 per cent requirement according to layoff experience by which employers are rated.

UI nominally pays benefits to qualified unemployed workers for 26 weeks which has been periodically but not permanently extended. Eligibility is contingent upon previous work experience and demonstrating that the recipient was actively seeking employment. Most states restrict eligibility to workers involuntarily separated from their jobs.

Despite the 97 per cent coverage, because of work experience requirements, only an estimated 50 per cent of unemployed workers with recent job experience actually receive benefits. Workers with recent job experience are defined as those who held covered jobs and whose unemployment was due to job termination. Taking into account new entrants to the labour force and those who leave jobs voluntarily, categories that are for the most part ineligible, some 30 per cent of all the unemployed received UI benefits. The calculation of benefit amounts varies by state usually by a fixed proportion of earnings. Several states add allowances for dependants. Weekly maximums in January 1980 ranged from $90 to $202. As of December 1982, the weekly average benefit approximated $115. Iowa offers up to 13 additional weeks of benefits in cases of job terminations resulting from firms going out of business.[54]

As of October 1982, some 4 million unemployed were recipients of regular UI benefits; another 475,000 were receiving extended benefits; and Federal Supplemental Compensation was paid to another 800,000. Regular UI is financed entirely by states and available for up to 26 weeks. Extended benefits are financed equally by Federal and state governments, payable up to 13 additional weeks when unemployment in a state exceeds certain thresholds. Federal Supplemental Compensation was authorised to continue from October 1982 to March 1983 and financed by general Federal revenues with benefits payable for up to ten weeks.[55]

A criticism of the Federal/state arrangement has been the differences in benefits and costs among the 50 states. For example, the maximum benefit available in 1979 to unemployed workers in Massachusetts was more than twice the level prevailing in Georgia and Alabama. The maximum tax on employers was as much as 50 per cent higher in some Northern and Mid-western states.[56]

As a result of this and other criticisms, demands have been made that the UI system be federalised and made uniform throughout the country. Among the bases for seeking federalisation is that unemployment is not a local but a national phenomenon. Uniform benefit standards and a single system of experience tax rated schedules would assure an adequate and fair level of benefits to all workers, negating the efforts of various states to attract industry from other states by keeping down UI costs. The costs of unemployment would be assumed by all regions and groups. Eligibility standards would be equalised among states in which they are either too lenient or too stringent. An argument against federalisation is that UI rates. in states with lower benefit levels will increase significantly to meet Federal standards and that individual states would have no incentive to keep UI costs low as a means of attracting or retaining industry.

The likelihood that Congress would accept federalisation is doubtful given the constellation of state interests represented in the national legislature. 'This shows the continuing utility of the pragmatic political balance struck more than four decades ago.'[57]

If federalisation is not the most urgent problem facing the UI system, then the most pressing issue is one of continued solvency. The difficulties with UI solvency vary by state. For example, they started in Illinois in 1974 when the state started to borrow from the Federal government to cover shortages in the unemployment compensation fund. At that time state governments showed little concern for the debt. The Federal government then made interest-free loans but in April 1982 began charging ten per cent interest. The problems stemming from the greater demands on the fund from the larger number of unemployed were thus compounded. In June 1983, the Illinois UI system owed the Federal government close to $2.4 billion with the prospect of having to borrow $3 billion more to keep the system afloat through 1985.

Illinois in 1983 is only one of 27 states in debt to the Federal government for their unemployment compensation systems. But only three, Michigan, Pennsylvania and Ohio, are as heavily in debt as Illinois. Of the $12.8 billion that states have borrowed to pay jobless benefits, $9.5 billion comes from these four states with high unemployment rates and who are expected to have continued high unemployment and depressed business conditions: the Illinois debt is $2.4 billion, Michigan, $2.5 billion, Pennsylvania, $2.6 billion; and Ohio, $2.0 billion.

Illinois, Michigan and Ohio have either frozen or reduced worker benefits. Illinois and Michigan have also raised employer

UI rates, further lowering the ability of these states to retain and/or attract business.

In 1982, Michigan raised the UI tax paid by employers by some 20 per cent and increased the wage base on which the tax is computed from $6,000 to $9,500 by 1986. The workers' weekly maximum benefits were frozen at $197 for a four-year period. Jobless workers receiving less than the maximum lose an average of some seven per cent in weekly benefits.[58]

The rate and benefit changes intended to make the fund solvent by 1988 were based on assumptions that Michigan's unemployment rate would decline steadily to 11.7 per cent in 1983, 10.7 per cent in 1984, 9.7 per cent in 1985 and 9.4 per cent in 1986. However, the state's unemployment rate has been in the neighbourhood of 17.0 per cent.

US Employment Service

A companion system to UI, the US Employment Service (ES) created by the Wagner Peyser Act of 1933, represented the first differentiation between employment services and charity. The separation first emerged in the creation of a public employment office or employment exchange by the State of Ohio in 1890. Other states and municipalities followed. The need to allocate manpower resources during World War I resulted in the formation of the US Employment Service in the Department of Labor. After World War I, the Employment Service and state agencies were quiescent until the 1930s depression.

The US Employment Service serves as a national clearing house to match the skills of job seekers with the needs of prospective employers. Though funded by Federal grants to the states, the responsibility for administering and operating ES rests with the states.

ES has had limited effectiveness in aiding experienced workers. Reduced resources have not been sufficient to meet expanded responsibilities. Also there is the problem of inability to get private sector firms to use ES and thus build up employment listings. A reason for the reluctance is that ES has a reputation for dealing with economically disadvantaged job seekers with low skill levels. UI recipients register with the ES but the chances of obtaining employment in this way are poor.

Though UI and ES were conceived in the midst of the 1930s depression, they have not proved adequate to deal with the large-

Table 2.8: Special Protection Programmes, Federal Legislation

---

Interstate Commerce Act of 1887, and Amendments of Rail Passenger Service Act
   (Amtrak) of 1976
Railroad Unemployment Insurance Act of 1939
Federal Communications Act Amendments of 1934
Urban Mass Transportation Act of 1964
Public Works and Economic Development Act of 1965
High Speed Ground Transportation Act of 1965
Demonstration Cities Act of 1966
Rail Passenger Service Act of 1970
Regional Railroad Reorganization Act (Conrail) of 1973
Federal Aid Highway Act of 1973
Trade Act of 1974
Disaster Relief Act of 1974
Juvenile Justice and Delinquency Prevention Act of 1974
Developmental Disabilities Services and Facilities Construction Act of 1975
Special Health Revenue Sharing Act of 1975
Comprehensive Employment and Training Act of 1978
Airline Deregulation Act of 1978
Amendments to Redwoods National Park Act of 1978
Milwaukee Railroad Restructuring Act of 1979
Health Planning and Resources Development Amendments of 1979
Rock Island Railroad Transition and Employee Assistance Act of 1980
Rail Act of 1980

Source: Pat Choate, *Retooling the American Work Force: Toward a National Strategy*
(Northeast–Midwest Institute, Washington, July 1982), p.41.

scale redundancies of the 1980s. The rapid rate of technological change and the restructuring of total industries when unemployment can no longer be considered primarily transitional necessitates adapting these systems to a changed economic environment.

Special Protection Programmes

Largely during the 1960s and 1970s, the US Federal government created some 22 special protection programmes (SPPs) to help workers who become unemployed because of Federal actions (Table 2.8). The rationale is that there is a special obligation to workers and firms harmed by actions that distribute benefits to a much larger number of beneficiaries. Most SPPs were set up on an *ad hoc* basis to assist workers in specific industries or areas and to restore affected workers to their prior status. The private sector cannot be expected to assume the costs of these programmes.

The criticism is that windfalls are given to selected workers and adaptation to change is not facilitated. Because of its *ad hoc* nature and the relatively small numbers who meet the specialised qualifications, equally distressed displaced workers do not obtain equivalent assistance. The SPPs operate independently without any coordinated policy or administration; each has a unique set of benefits and eligibility standards.

The overriding questions with respect to SPPs are whether the existing programmes should be phased out, no new programmes initiated and the displaced workers incorporated into the unemployment insurance system. One response is that no further SPPs be initiated and active SPPs be folded into a reformed unemployment insurance system. Employers would be required to give six months or a year's advance notice for sizeable layoffs. From a time perspective reforming or revising the unemployment insurance system and instituting pre-notification will not be easily accomplished.

The best reform option is to phase out SPPs and channel all unemployment assistance through an improved UI system. Benefits that assure unemployed workers 60 percent of their previous wages promise the optimal tradeoff between adequacy and work incentives. The special circumstances that surround layoffs traceable to government actions should lengthen the period of eligibility for benefits and trigger special retraining and relocation assistance. Advance notice of dismissals should be mandatory to permit as many adjustments as possible before workers are unemployed.[59]

Two SPPs are examined. The Redwood Employee Protection Program (REPP) is the most controversial. The largest is the Trade Adjustment Assistance (TAA).

Redwood Employee Protection Program.[60] The Redwood Employee Protection Program was established in 1978 to compensate some 1,500 loggers affected by the addition of 48,000 acres to the Redwood National Park in Northern California. The programme came about after loggers and lumber companies protested that newly-protected acreage would curtail business operations and displace workers in a high wage but isolated industry. These workers would be unlikely to find similar work at high wages (up to $35 an hour for piece rate tree fellers). A coalition of environmentalists, workers and lumber companies united to have adversely affected workers protected by a range of monetary and non-monetary benefits.

The exceptionally generous monetary benefits are in the form of weekly or lump sum severance payments and include fringe benefits such as health and pension coverage.

Workers with five or more years of service are eligible for weekly benefits equal to highest wage earned between 1 January 1977 and 31 March 1978. The weekly cash benefit is reduced dollar for dollar if unemployment insurance or social security is received or if the worker has timber-related earnings. To encourage loggers to obtain other employment, the weekly benefit is reduced by 50 cents for each dollar earned outside the lumber industry. Weekly benefits have averaged $300 with some payments reaching $1,000.

Severance pay in lieu of weekly payments is calculated on the basis of one week's pay for every month of paid employment up to a maximum of 72 weeks for six or more years of service. Workers have frequently received lump sum severance pay in the $30,000 to $50,000 range. Eligibility for benefits has been quite liberal. REPP benefits are scheduled to end in 1984, except for workers aged 50 or over who can continue to receive benefits until the age of 65.

Obviously, SPPs such as REPP give workers benefits that are extremely liberal, especially when compared to what other workers get in similar situations. In defence of the workers, the lumber companies were scheduled to receive one billion dollars for the land; whereas original land settlement costs were estimated at $359 million.

Trade Adjustment Assistance. The closest approximation to plant closing legislation in the US is the Trade Adjustment Assistance Act, the major SPP in terms of number of workers and amount of expenditures. The Act is designed to assist workers, firms and communities harmed by increases in imports. The US was one of the first countries to offer adjustment assistance to compensate for lowered trade barriers. The rationale for this legislation, as well as other SPPs, was that particular groups were assuming a dispro-portionate share of the burden stemming from Federal policy while other groups were obtaining the gains. Adjustment assistance is deemed preferable to maintaining high tariff levels; it is con-sidered a short-run social investment or cost to facilitate the trans-ition of the damaged parties from the no longer viable industry. On the other hand, tariffs and quotas impose costs on most of the public for many years.

The Trade Expansion Act (TEA) of 1962, PL 87-794, initiated the programme as a response to import-related problems, not necessarily industry-wide but involving particular sets of workers, firms and communities. The US Labor Department would certify workers in a company or subdivision for group eligibility and US Commerce Department would certify firms and communities. Compensation for workers would be added to benefits of existing programmes.

(a) Provisions. Few workers were able to meet TEA's stringent eligibility standards and the Trade Act of 1974, PL 93-618, relaxed the standards and broadened the applicability of TAA. Benefits in the form of a weekly cash allowance, trade readjustment allowances (TRA), were added to unemployment insurance, as well as employment and relocation services. The more liberal benefits reflected the belief that trade-impacted workers differed from most unemployed workers in that they would have to seek or accept jobs in a less favourable job environment.

In December 1980, a worker with no dependants collecting the maximum unemployment insurance received only $142 for a limit of 26 weeks whereas a worker under TAA could receive $269 for up to 78 weeks.[61] As a result, the 1974 Act was amended in 1981, Title XXV, PL 97-35, reversing the liberalisation of TAA by reducing benefits. The 1981 amendment brought TAA more in line with UI; an earlier provision whereby an additional 26 weeks of TRA could be paid to workers of 60 years of age or older was removed.

A new provision allows the government to require workers after eight weeks of TRA to extend their active job search beyond the immediate area or agree to accept training. Workers' benefits after the 1981 amendment consisted of cash payments (TRA), employment services, job search and relocation allowances:

> TRA is generally set at the level of unemployment insurance benefits, payable when workers exhaust their UI entitlement.
>
> UI and TRA combined can't exceed 52 times the TRA weekly benefit amount, except that 26 additional weeks are payable to workers in approved training programs.
>
> Special help provided in finding a new job.

Training in a new skill covered when suitable employment is not otherwise available. If the training facility is beyond the normal commuting distance, transportation and subsistence expenses may be reimbursed.

Job search allowance payable to cover expenses of looking for work outside of the commuting area. Workers may be paid 90 percent of necessary transportation and subsistence costs not to exceed $600.

Relocation allowances available to help workers move their families and household goods to a new job area. Workers may be paid for 90 percent of their moving expense plus a lump sum payment, not to exceed $600 to get settled.[62]

(b) Use of Assistance. For the most part the emphasis of TAA has been one of income maintenance rather than readjustment. Most workers have awaited recall rather than accept other jobs. Firms with job openings offering lower wages and/or benefits have been hesitant to employ laid off workers, fearing they will leave to return to former jobs if recalled. However, with less likelihood of returning to former jobs in depressed industries, there may be greater willingness to accept new jobs.

Prior to the 1981 amendment little use was made of employment and training services. From financial year 1976 to 1980, about a quarter of applicants applied for employment services.[63]

Table 2.9: Trade Adjustment Assistance: Certifications by Major Industry, Cumulative, April 1975 to April 1983

Industries	Certifications	
	Number of workers	%
Coal	5,436	0.4
Textiles	25,913	1.9
Apparel	156,247	11.3
Footwear	79,477	5.8
Steel	186,455	13.5
Electronics	59,587	4.3
Automobiles	724,143	52.6
Fabricated metal products	30,434	2.2
Other industries	109,702	8.0
Total	1,377,394	100.0

Source: US Department of Labor, Employment and Training Administration, Office of Trade Adjustment Assistance, Washington, DC.

Table 2.10: Metropolitan New York Trade Adjustment Assistance Center, Trade Adjustment Assistance Provided, October 1975 to December 1982

Fiscal year[a]	No. of firms		Loans		No. of jobs		Init. & Impl. Tech. Assist.		Non-TAAC Fin. Assist.	
	Total	Certified	No. of firms	$ (000)	Preserved	Additional	No. of firms	Amount $[c]	No. of firms	$ (000)
1976	9	8	6	5,080	570	1,089	6	35,160	1	300
1977	53	52	5	3,950	329	582	26	85,072	0	0
1978	85	36	31	26,014	3,049	2,993	32	121,440	0	0
1979	173	40	19	16,429	1,436	1,723	34	111,274	3	490
1980	255	55	15	12,678	2,083	923	53	218,924	5	2,800
1981	170	18	3	4,660	1,147	634	32	158,430	7	3,325
1982	148	16	1	1,000	150	129	33	335,023	11	3,140
1983[b]	67	14	1	300	51	31	13	67,180	—	—
Total	960	239	81	70,111	8,815	8,104	229	1,132,503	27	10,055

a. Fiscal year, October 1 to September 30.

b. October to December 1982.

c. Figure includes certification, initial and implementation costs.

Source: Metropolitan New York Trade Adjustment Assistance Center, New York, NY.

From January 1975 to November 1981, nationally only 3.2 per cent of the certified workers entered training and only 37.2 per cent completed the training.[64]

Another source of controversy has been the high cost of TRA. From only $70 million in financial year 1976, the cumulative costs of TRA by March 1983 reached $3,987,805,540. The major cause of the increase was declaring the auto industry eligible. The importance of the auto industry is reflected in that 52.6 per cent of the certified workers were in this industry (Table 2.9); also the state receiving the largest amount of TRA, 30.4 per cent, was Michigan, home of the auto industry.[65]

Technical and financial assistance is available to affected companies. In regard to technical assistance, the Federal government pays up to 75 per cent of the costs for preparing the certification petition, the economic adjustment proposal and the proposal implementation. Financial assistance may be in the form of a direct loan or loan guaranteed by the Federal government. The maximum direct loan to an eligible firm is $1 million and for a guaranteed loan, $3 million, with 90 per cent guaranteed by the Federal government. Loans and guarantees are not available if they can be obtained from private sources at no higher than government rates. In the New York metropolitan area, much greater use has been made of financial than technical assistance (Table 2.10)

Evaluation

The US General Accounting Office found that firms in the TAA programme are generally in such poor financial condition that when they receive benefits the loans prove to be inadequate in terms of making any significant difference to the firm's financial condition. Most firms have been unable to use the proceeds to improve their competitive position. Instead, the loan proceeds are too frequently used to pay debts or for working capital and thus, are insufficient to modernise plant or equipment, improve production or make product changes. 'Relatively few import-impacted firms that received financial assistance under the Trade Act have made the adjustments needed to successfully compete with other firms.'[66]

Industries may receive technical assistance for industry wide programmes for development of new products or new export markets. The maximum per industry is $2 million per annum.

There is another component of adjustment assistance aimed at creating new job opportunities for trade-impacted communities. It would facilitate the survival and growth of existing industry and/or attract new industry. The eligibility basis is that trade-impacted communities must show that increased imports of articles similar to or directly competitive to production in the community present a threat to sales and employees.

In line with criticism of SPPs, the US Department of Commerce has preferred not to give trade-impacted Communities special treatment but rather to encourage them to use existing programmes. The trade-impacted communities have had to compete against communities with similar economic problems though attributable to other factors. The allocation problem is compounded by the cuts in programme funding since 1981. Imports are only one cause of economic dislocation and there is the question as to whether limited funds should go to import-impacted areas or to areas of greatest need regardless of cause. Like assistance to firms, can sufficient help be given to communities to attain economic viability? Will the aid be used for promotion, recruiting and subsidies to attract industries from other depressed areas or for infrastructure and improved services for long-term economic improvements.

Another criticism has been that firms and workers providing component parts and services related to the manufacture of imported products have been ineligible for certification. For example, a firm producing yarn for sweaters was deemed ineligible though the firm producing sweaters was declared eligible. The yarn firm had petitioned for assistance but was refused since it did not produce the end product — the sweaters.[67] Proposals are before Congress to include independent firms producing component parts for import-affected firms as well and to add eligibility on the basis of transfers of production overseas, regardless of whether there is an import impact on the domestic side.

A basic problem of TAA is that by the time disaster occurs and remedial action is taken too much time has elapsed for corrective action to be taken. In a good number of cases imports pose a danger because management failed to make earlier decisions, such as product and production adaptation.

A harsh judgement was pronounced on adjustment assistance by a Congressional committee in that 'the adjustment assistance provisions of the Trade Expansion Act have generally been conceded to be a failure'. The Committee found this to be a judgement shared by unions, companies and administrators of the programme. Reasons for failure could be summarised by 'labor's oft-repeated comment that adjustment assistance is essentially burial assistance'.[68]

The major theme of a World Bank study is that economic welfare both at home and abroad can be improved by means of worker adjustment assistance programmes. Trade liberalisation offers long-run benefits for consumers and workers in general at the short-run cost of high unemployment for displaced workers and capital.

> These [adjustment assistance] benefits will obviously be greater if reemployment occurs in expanding industrial sectors rather than in declining sectors which are reliant upon various protective measures for their continued survival, and an economically efficient reemployment program ought to vary its incentives accordingly.[69]

The problems with suggestions such as the foregoing for shifting labour and capital into expanding sectors is that it is unlikely to occur in a depressed economy and particularly for certain segments of the labour force, e.g. the ageing re-employment for this group may never occur. The Canadian government has taken steps to remedy this type of situation — the Labour Adjustment Benefits Act.

The outlook for the programme in terms of existence is likely to be somewhat of a standoff. President Reagan has called on Congress to phase out TAA and merge it into more general assistance programmes. The programme is scheduled to end in the latter part of 1983 but Congress is likely to extend TAA. The House of Representatives has proposed a two-year extension and the Senate, six years.

Labour Adjustment Benefits Act — Canada

The special problems of the older displaced worker in finding new employment have been recognised by a distinctive Canadian programme that is a variation of the US Trade Adjustment Assistance programme. First called the Adjustment Assistance Benefits Programme (AAB), it was changed and renamed the Labour

Adjustment Benefits Act (LAB) in 1982.

Protection is offered in the form of income maintenance to certain older workers permanently laid off in industries designated by the Federal government. The workers must have exhausted their unemployment insurance entitlement and have no prospects of further employment. The benefits are considered a last resort since the targeted individuals, because of age and industry-specific skills, have special difficulty adapting to layoff and re-employment through placement programmes.

Genesis of the Programme

The programme had its beginnings in 1970 when the Government's Textiles and Clothing Policy recognised that competition from imports would result in rationalisation and modernisation of these industries and the displacement of large numbers of workers. AAB was initiated to lessen the burden for older employees as the level of protection was lowered and structural readjustment took place in these industries. In 1978, workers in the footwear and tanning industries were included.

A subsequent review of Federal adjustment programmes in connection with Multilateral Trade Negotiations identified gaps in the existing programme for displaced workers. Older workers lacked the educational, skill and mobility traits for existing employment programmes.

The LAB is concerned with laid-off employees in industries and regions designated under the Industry and Labour Adjustment Program ILAP for labour adjustment assistance. An industry may be designated if it is undergoing major economic adjustment of a non-cyclical nature because of import competition or industrial restructuring, including technological change and where such adjustment results in a significant loss of employment. The general industries designated as eligible at the beginning of 1983 were clothing, textiles, footwear and tanning. An industry may also be designated regionally where an industry in a region is undergoing significant economic adjustment with a related loss of employment. Eleven regional designations were in effect from August 1982 to August 1983.

Benefits. The first step for laid-off workers is to be certified; this is granted to an employee from a designated industry. The number of employees in the establishment must have been reduced over a twelve-month period due to layoffs by 10 percent or 50 employees whichever is the lesser. The layoff must be due to economic adjustment which is the basis for the designation of the industry.

For individual eligibility, applicants must be at least 54 years of age but not more than 65; be Canadian citizens or permanent residents of Canada; have been employed in a designated industry for at least 10 of the 15 years preceding the layoff; been paid for at least a thousand hours in each of these years; have claimed and exhausted all unemployment benefits; have no prospect of employment; or have accepted employment with earnings less than their previous weekly earnings in the industry. In cases of financial hardships, benefits may be payable to individuals 50 to 54 years of age, who have worked in a designated industry for at least 30 years and who have been paid for at least a thousand hours of employment in each of those years.

The LAB benefits payable are about 60 per cent of average weekly insurable earnings based on the last 20 weeks of employment prior to layoff. The benefits are fully indexed for inflation and continue until the age of 65.

Operations. In the period 1 May 1983 to 31 December 1982, programme expenditures totalled $5,439,049; the bulk was paid to workers from the clothing and textile industries; $4,973,506 or 93.7 per cent of the total expenditure for 309 allowed claims and $332,134 or 6.3 per cent for 31 claims in footwear and tanning. For the same period there were 184 applications by firms approved as general designations and 49 as regional designations. On the other hand, of the 18,877 employees certified, 10,173 or 53.9 per cent came under the regional designation versus 8,704 or 46.1 per cent under the general designation. With respect to the age of the 18,877 certified laid-off employees, 2,816 or 14.0 per cent were aged 50 and over. Of the 2,816, 899 or 31.0 per cent were aged 50 to 54 and 1,917 or 68.1 per cent were 54 and over.[70]

The significance of the programme is in the recognition of the difficulties of older workers in obtaining jobs and thus it is a realistic approach in an era of shrinking employment opportunities. Eligibility at age 50 might be questioned. The ever present factor in any special protection programme is the matter of equity for those excluded by virtue of being in a non-eligible establishment, industry or region.

Manpower Consultative Service — Canada

The Canadian Manpower Consultative Service (MCS) has received much attention as a prototype for adoption in the US, particularly for job training programmes. MCS, which is part of the Employment and Immigration Commission, was established in 1963 to encourage joint action by employers and employees as a response to technological change. When plant closings in 1974 became a major economic problem in the industrial areas of Ontario and Quebec, MCS operations were expanded. The added responsibilities were to avoid and mitigate the severe effects of large-scale layoffs and closings by increasing the profitability of troubled firms and re-train or find new jobs for employees.

Operations. The approach is to assist management and labour in firms undergoing critical decline or growth through the formation of tripartite committees to resolve these problems. Placement, training and mobility are typical activities when employment is being curtailed. The committee is free to select the approach they consider most suitable. The first stop in the typical MCS case starts after firms give the provincial authorities the mandatory advance notice of a shutdown or large-scale layoff; MCS is informed and an officer is assigned. Employers and unions may directly request MCS intervention. MCS will not become involved when: there is a refusal by the parties to co-operate; there is a labour dispute; or collective bargaining is under way.

The assigned officer requests management and labour to form a Manpower Adjustment Committee with two representatives from management, two from labour and an impartial chairman (usually a retired business person) suggested by the MCS officer. The MCS officer acts in an advisory capacity and sees that the committee gets off the ground, assists the committee in obtaining resources from Federal and provincial manpower services. To keep bureaucracy to a minimum the MCS staff is intentionally chosen from outside government.

The financial arrangements vary by case. In the typical layoff situation MCS matches the contribution of the provincial government, employer and union. Thus, the Federal contribution is 50 per cent while the union contribution is generally nominal. In bankruptcies, MCS can cover the entire cost.

Results. The majority of cases are from small population centres of

50,000 or fewer people and from the manufacturing sector (67 per cent) with the emphasis on declining industries such as textiles, autos and machine parts. In 59 per cent of the cases between 1975 and 1977, there were fewer than 100 people laid off. Large foreign-owned firms are least apt to accept MCS intervention. MCS officials believe that the least able workers with the greatest difficulty finding work are most likely to seek MCS assistance. About 65 per cent of those seeking help are placed. Since 70 per cent of workers request help, about 46 per cent are actually placed (0.70 × 0.65 − 0.46).[71] The 65 per cent rate looks good but there is no indication of how well these workers would have done without MCS. After the MCS agreement ends and MCS withdraws, unemployed workers no longer receive assistance.

The placement has been accomplished with moderate costs. The average costs in 1975–7 for 13,706 employees (10,763 without mobility assistance and 2,943 with mobility assistance) were as follows:

Cost per employee

Without mobility assistance	With mobility assistance
$US 68.74	$US 86.21
$C 93.10	$C 116.77

The cost per employee in 1980 was almost double the 1975–7 average. The 1980–1 financial year budget was some $C 2.5 million.[72]

On the credit side, MCS can respond rapidly and speed up the personnel process. Bureaucracy is kept to a minimum in terms of paperwork, rules and oversight. The approach is flexible in that no fixed or set method has to be used. However, the Canadian government and taxpayers are starting to demand increased documentation on how the money is spent, bringing MCS closer to traditional programmes.

On the debit side, already unemployed workers or those from firms not utilising MCS lose out in favour of those in the MCS placement service. MCS has not worked particularly well in depressed areas such as Windsor, Ontario (sister city of Detroit), or in other cities where jobs are scarce. There are doubts as to its effectiveness in solving large-scale displacement or counteracting high unemployment.

Job Training Partnership Act — US

By 1982, there was belated recognition by the US Federal government of the need for special assistance to dislocated workers. But instead of following the example of Western European governments requiring employers to make efforts to prevent closings, give advance notice and severance payments to displaced employees, the principal course chosen was training. The Canadian Manpower Consultative Service was an important model. None of income maintenance, job creation or efforts to prevent the displacement was given high priority. The new legislation, the Job Training Partnership Act (JTPA) of 13 October 1982, PL 97-300, follows a series of manpower programmes with limited applicability and success for displaced workers.

The first such programme was the Area Redevelopment Act (ARA) of 1961 which was largely oriented to relieving unemployment and underemployment in rural areas through technical assistance and loans for development activities. A small share of the expenditures was allocated to re-training and trainee stipends. The ARA evolved into the Economic Development Administration (EDA) which has not been particularly concerned with training but rather with improving the economic base of localities; the emphasis shifted from rural to urban areas.

Other programmes more directed to manpower followed ARA. 'From that modest beginning in 1961, statutes succeeded statutes and amendment succeeded amendment.'[73] In programmatic sequence, they were the constantly-amended Development and Training Act of 1962 and the much-amended Economic Opportunity Act of 1964, superseded by the Comprehensive Employment and Training Act of 1973 (CETA).

Between 1973 and 1982, CETA was amended eight times and proliferated into twelve separate programmatic titles, parts and sub-parts. The instability of CETA was compounded by the funding vagaries. There were 26 separate approaches for the programme including regular, supplemental, and emergency appropriations plus a surfeit of continuing resolutions.[74] The constant revisions reflect the changes in goals and objectives and constant power struggles which often overshadow the substance of pro- grammes. Based on the history of these programmes, the outlook for JTPA could be turbulent.

In devising the legislation, the President and Congress felt there was a need to include provisions for the dislocated worker. There had to be a private sector perspective which was limited under CETA, an emphasis on federalism with the states and not the Federal government having greater direct participation in the pro- gramme. Also the emphasis had to be on job training and not income maintenance or public service employment.

States

State governments under JTPA are the primary agents in dealing with dislocated workers with major responsibility for the oper- ations and oversight.

> The state's role is *not* that of the design and implementation of the details of the training programs; but its coordination, supervision, review, monitoring and assignment of performance goals and sanctions for non-performance. The basic role of the state in this Act has not been achieved by the transfer of functions from the local government; rather it has been accom- plished by the transfer of functions in the Federal government.[75]

Each state must develop its own procedures. To receive its share of formula funds, a state must submit a plan to the US Secretary of Labor detailing how funds will be spent and how the various involved agencies will be co-ordinated. States must have an overall programme strategy for dislocated workers. No expendi- tures are allowed for unplanned and *ad hoc* responses to individual cases of dislocation.

Funding

From the amount appropriated in any fiscal year for Title III, up to 25 per cent can be allocated for help to persons affected by mass layoffs, natural disasters, Federal government actions such as relocation of Federal facilities, or persons who reside in areas of high unemployment or in designated enterprise zones.

The remainder or balance is divided among the states as follows:

One-third on the basis of the relative number of unemployed individuals in each state as compared to the total number of unemployed in the country.

One-third on the basis of the relative excess number of unemployed in each state compared to the excess number of unemployed in the country. Excess number means unemployed in excess of 4.5 per cent of the civilian labour force in the state.

One-third on the basis of the relative number of individuals who have been unemployed for 15 weeks or more compared to the total number of such individuals in the country.

The states must develop their own procedures to identify substantial groups of eligible individuals. The states must seek help from private industry councils (PICs) in identifying these groups and assessing what, if any, job opportunities exist for which individuals could be re-trained. The state must determine whether training opportunities exist and, if so, notify eligible individuals.

The definition of a dislocated worker is fairly flexible. A notice of termination of layoff is sufficient for workers to qualify for help. Under UI regulations a recipient must search for and be available for a job which could nullify the ability of a worker to enter a training programme and still subsist. Title III waives the UI regulation for recipients in a training programme.

There is flexibility in the types of activities that can be funded. They can start prior to a layoff and continue until relocation. The activities include but are not limited to the following:

job search assistance including job clubs;
job development;
training in job skills for which demand exceeds supply;
support services including community assistance;
financial and personal counselling;
pre-layoff assistance;
relocation assistance;
programmes conducted in co-operation with employers or labour organisations to provide early intervention in the event of closures of plants or facilities.

Relocation assistance is available if the state decides that individuals cannot find employment within their community area and there is a job or an offer of a job 'in a relocation area in a state'.

The intra-state requirement points to a potential deficiency in the programme that could limit its effectiveness.

To qualify for financial assistance, a state must match the amount available from the Federal government. The equal matching requirement at first glance appears to be a substantial obstacle to participation; however, there are various methods of lowering the state's matching portion. Included in the state's matching contribution are the direct cost of employment or training services provided under state and local programmes, private non-profit organisations or private for-profit employers.

When the average rate of unemployment in a state exceeds the national average, the matching contribution can be reduced by ten per cent for each one per cent of excess. Any state expenditure to give UI benefits to an eligible individual enrolled in a training programme can be credited up to 50 per cent of the mandated non-Federal matching.

Before a programme can be approved by a state, it must consider the recommendations of PICs and elected officials. Consultation with labour organisations is mandated if an assistance programme will furnish services to a substantial number of labour organisation members. There is the question of who will represent workers where there is no union representation.

To target the bulk of funding on training, no more than 30 per cent of Title III funds can be used for administration, supportive services, wages, allowances or stipends. When specified conditions are met, the 30 per cent can be exceeded.

Costs of Services

The number of people assisted under Title III will depend on the level of appropriations and the mix of services provided. The Congressional Budget Office estimates the cost of job assistance to be about $90 by traditional methods and $500 per worker for job clubs. Relocation assistance is estimated to cost an average of $1,200 per family; and with re-training added, $2,500 per person. Assuming that all workers receive job search assistance, five per cent receive relocation help and 50 per cent receive training, costs of assistance under Title III would entail an average of some $2,000 per eligible worker, including administrative costs. If half of this amount were paid from non-Federal matching funds, 100,000 workers could be helped with $100 million in Federal funds.[76]

To get the programme moving immediately in financial year 1983, the initial Federal appropriation is expected to be $110 million and the President's request for Title III funds in financial year 1984 is $240 million.[77]

Since the states have been assigned the responsibility for implementing and administering JTPA, they must enact legislation to accomplish this. Maryland is the first state to pass legislation to implement and supplement JTPA. On 10 May 1983, the Governor signed House Bill 1226, codifying the framework within which JTPA will be implemented; this establishes a structure for state funding of employment and training programmes, attempts to merge or co-ordinate employment, training and economic development and seeks to establish uniform labour market and information management systems. The management system will generate uniform financial reports, as well as information on local programme performance, participant characteristics and facility usage. The legislation does not go far enough beyond administration in specifying a state role.

Evaluation

To date the primary emphasis on discussing JTPA has been on administration and management. Even though it may take some time before the programme becomes fully operational, it would be well to raise questions on its likely effectiveness. This is particularly important when redundancy programmes may be quickly transferred to or adapted in different countries.

A redundancy policy which consists largely of reliance on government-financed training relieves employers of obligations for severance payments, advance notice and payments to affected communities. These are components of the proposed plant-closing bills.

What is the likelihood of workers who have completed the training courses being absorbed by private employers in a period when the economy is weak or when the Federal government is doing little about economic development or job creation? Few jobs will be available in a depressed area or region. Can the programme operate on a limited geographical basis, i.e. in a locality where plants are closing?

There are no provisions for income maintenance; workers are left to cope themselves while undergoing training. The UI benefits are inadequate in terms of length of time and amount to support adequately an individual or family.

The plethora or multiplicity of training projects will be difficult to assess. There is a need for an overall strategy or guidelines to assess the type of training needed in respect to occupations or industries. Is there an adequate training infrastructure to handle the large number of eligible workers? A caveat is that a few individual successes with limited applicability will be over-publicised.

There are questions about giving the business sector major responsibility in the programme. Does the private sector have the experience or the capacity to start training programmes rapidly? There is a potential contradiction if businesses are sharply reducing the number of workers in their companies while being given a major role in seeing that workers are re-employed.

Despite these comments, there is obviously a need for training. But it is incomplete as a substitute for a comprehensive redundancy policy. Training can only be considered as one component.

Conclusions

The existence of large numbers of displaced or redundant workers will persist and is unlikely to disappear even in a robust economy. Changing employment and skill demands, robotisation, international economic competition, inter-regional competition for industry within the country and decline of old line industries are among the continuing and varied causes of displacement.

The US lacks a comprehensive strategy to deal with this problem whereas Canadian public policy has been more concerned with preventing and easing displacement and attempting to create new jobs. Though not mentioned in this review, Canada has maintained a regional policy to retain and establish jobs in the depressed areas. In contrast the US under the Reagan administration has shown little interest in regional problems.

A start has been made in the US to assist displaced workers directly through re-training. The questions posed about the programme must be tentative since they are raised shortly after passage of the legislation and before it has become operational. But the outlook for continued and large-scale displacement indicates that training will not be sufficient; it can only be successful if it is a part of a broader strategy together with the allocation of adequate public and private resources. The comprehensive strategy must be based on the experience of other countries in their efforts to prevent closings, inform and compensate workers for closings, provide transitional support, offer training opportunities and create jobs.

Notes

1. 'American jobs: Why so many more?' *The Economist,* vol. 271, no. 7076 (14 April 1979), p. 80.

2. Geoffrey Owen, 'European chemical industry's national crutches', *World Business Weekly,* vol. 2, no. 21 (28 May 1979), p. 63.

3. Robert Coulson, *The Termination Handbook* (The Free Press, New York, 1981), p. 139.

4. National Alliance of Business, *Worker Adjustment to Plant Shutdowns and Mass Layoffs; An analysis of Program Experience and Policy Options* (Washington, March 1983), p. ES4.

5. Marc Bandick, Jr. and Judith Radlinski Devine, 'Workers Dislocated by Economic Change: Do They Need Federal Employment and Training Assistance?' in National Commission for Employment Policy, *Seventh Annual Report: The Federal Interest in Employment and Training* (Washington, October 1981), p. 217

6. Sheldon Friedman, statement in US Congress, House of Representatives, Committee on Education and Labor, Subcommittee on Employment Opportunities and Senate, Committee on Labor and Human Resources, Subcommittee on Employment and Productivity, *Employment and Training Policy: Joint Hearings* 97th Congress, 2nd Session, 1982, Part 2, p. 44.

7. Bernard Adell, 'Canada' in Edward Yemin (ed.) *Workforce Reductions in Undertakings* (International Labour Office, Geneva, 1982), p. 46.

8. David W. Ewing, 'Your right to fire', *Harvard Business Review,* vol. 61, no. 2 (March/April 1983), p. 33.

9. Herb Gray, 'Reviewing Canada's Foreign Investment Review Act', *Area Development,* vol. 17, no. 6 (June 1982), p. 50.

10 Brian A. Grossman, *The Executive Firing Line: Wrongful Dismissal* (Carswell/Methuen, Toronto, 1982), p. 182.

11. David Harris, *Wrongful dismissal,* 2nd edn. (Richard DeBoo Ltd, Ontario, 1980), p. 3.

12. Adell, 'Canada', pp. 38-9.

13. Ibid., p. 40.

14. Labour code, Part III.

15. Ibid., Part V, Section 149.

16. Canada, Minister of Labour, *Report of the Commission of Inquiry on Redundancies and Lay-offs* (Labour Canada, Ottawa, March 1979), p. 233.

17. Ibid., p. 232.

18. Ibid., p. 262.

19. Ibid., p. 193.

20. Richard B. McKenzie (ed.), *Plant Closings: Public or Private Choices?* (Cato Institute, Washington, 1982).

21. The Business Week Team, *The Reindustrialization of America* (McGraw Hill Book Co., New York, 1982), p. 99.

22. US, *Congressional Record* vol. 129, no. 57 (2 May 1983), p. H2727.

23. 'An American Exit Tax', *The Wall Street Journal* (7 December 1978), p.|20.

24. Letter, William R. Malloy, Commissioner, State of Maine, Department of Labor, Bureau of Labor Standards, 11 April 1983.

25. Joseph A. Cipparone, 'Advance Notice of Plant Closings: Toward National Legislation', *Journal of Law Reform*, vol. 14, no. 2 (Winter 1981), fn. 37, p. 289.

26. 'Keeping jobs in Philly', *Business Week*, no. 2746 (5 July 1982), p. 32.

27. 'How Much Advance Notice Before Closing a Plant?' *Corporate Issues Monitor: A Quarterly Survey of Communications Executives*, Peter Small and Associates (15 July 1980).

28. Lawrence J. Tell, 'Plant shutdowns: The cities fight', *The New York Times* (15 May 1983), p. 8F.

29. 'Labor's bid to keep plants from moving', *Business Week*, no. 2774 (24 January 1983), p. 25; and 'Moving on: Unions win the right to restrict some company relocations', *The Wall Street Journal* (22 March 1983), p. 1.

30. Morris L. Sweet, 'Dismissals of Employees — Labor Laws in Other Countries Could Become Models for US', *Area Development*, vol. 17, no. 11 (November 1982), p. 28.

31. Raymond Vernon and Louis T. Wells, Jr., *Manager in the International Economy* 4th edn. (Prentice Hall, Englewood Cliffs, New Jersey, 1981), p.4.

32. 'MNs and employment', *ILO Information*, vol. 9, no. 3 (August 1981), p. 2.

33. Herbert R. Northrup and Richard L. Rowan, *Multinational Collective Bargaining Attempts: The Records, the Cases and the Prospects*, Multinational Industrial Relations Series No. 6 (University of Pennsylvania, Philadelphia, 1979), p. 563.

34. Organisation for Economic Co-operation and Development, *International Investment and Multinational Enterprises*, revised ed. (Paris, 1979), p. 20.

35. International Labour Office, *Termination of Employment at the Initiative of the Employer*, Report V (1) (Geneva, 1981), p. 64.

36. International Labour Office, *Termination of Employment at the Initiative of the Employer*, Report V (2) (Geneva, 1982), p. 9.

37. 'No International Labor Laws?', *The Journal of Commerce* (19 May 1982), p. 4A.

38. John Dennis, 'European Economic Community Efforts to Regulate Multinational Corporations and the Business Response', unpublished paper (February 1982), p. 5.

39. 'Only the tiddlers will escape', *The Economist*, vol. 284, no. 7246 (17 July 1982), p. 49.

40. Dennis, 'European Economic Community', pp. 5 and 17.

41. Morris L. Sweet, *Industrial Location Policy for Economic Revitalization: National and International Perspectives* (Praeger Publishers, New York, 1981), Chapter 7, p. 105.

42. International Conference on Trends in Industrial Relations. 'Remarks' (mimeographed), p. 5 in Milton Derber, 'Collective Bargaining: The American Approach to Industrial Democracy', *The Annals*, vol. 431 (May 1977), p. 92.

43. 'Labor chief seeks investment power', *The New York Times* (16 November 1981), p. 1.

44. 'Banking on recovery: a survey of international banking', *The Economist*, vol. 286, no. 7282 (26 March 1983), p. 10.

45. Alun Morgan and Roger Blanpain, *The Industrial Relations Employment Impacts of Multinational Enterprises* (Organisation for Economic Co-operation and Development, Paris, 1977), p. 17.

46. Tom Devos, 'American Multinationals in Europe and Worker Participation: Rejection, Conversion or Adaptation', paper presented at the annual meeting of the American Political Science Association, September 1976, p. 15.

47. Rainer Hellman, *Transnational Control of Multinational Corporations* (Praeger Publishers, New York, 1977), pp. 99-100.

48. Walter Galenson, School of Industrial and Labor Relations, Cornell University, 'Comments' in National Commission for Manpower Policy, *Trade and Employment: A Conference Report*, Special Report No. 30 (Washington, November 1978), p. 249.

49. 'UAW urges Fraser to keep Chrysler seat', *The New York Times* (23 February 1983), p. 9.

50. 'Tasting a new kind of power. Now workers get a look at the books. Later a real role on decisions', *Business Week* no. 2724 (1 February 1982), p. 16.

51. Tom Devos, *US Multinationals and Worker Participation in Management* (Quorum Books, Westport, Connecticut, 1981), p. 213.

52. US Advisory Commission on Intergovernmental Relations, *The Federal Role in the Federal System: The Dynamics of Growth* (Washington, February 1982), p. 19.

53. Ibid., p. 40.

54. US Congress, Congressional Budget Office, *Dislocated Workers: Issues and Federal Options* (Washington: July 1982), pp. 25, 26.

55. US Congress, Congressional Budget Office, Resources and Community Development Division, *Strategies for Assisting the Unemployed* (Washington, 8 December 1982), p. 43.

56. Barry Bluestone and Bennett Harrison, *The Deindustrialization of America* (Basic Books, New York, 1982), p. 187.

57. Advisory Commission, *The Federal Role*, p. 26.

58. David Hess, 'States Struggle with Jobless Fund Shortfalls', *The Journal of Commerce* (2 June 1983), p. 7A.

59. Philip L. Martin, *Labor Displacement and Public Policy* (Lexington Books, Lexington, Massachusetts, 1983), p. 105.

60. Ibid., pp. 72-3 and US General Accounting Office, *Congress Should Scale Down Redwood Employee Program Benefits*, HRD 80-63 (Washington, 8 July 1980).

61. Massachusetts, Division of Employment Security, Job Market Research, *Trade Adjustment Act: Impact on the Massachusetts Economy*, 2nd edn. (Boston, 1982), p. 3A.

62. 'Trade Adjustment Assistance Program Fact Sheet', *Program Highlights*, US Department of Labor, ETA 82-5.

63. Congressional Budget Office, *Dislocated Workers*, p. 27.

64. Massachusetts, Division of Employment Security, p. 29.

65. Martin, *Labor Displacement*, p. 68, and US, Department of Labor, Employment and Training Administration, Office of Trade Adjustment Assistance, Management Information Report, 'Worker Adjustment Assistance under the Trade Act of 1974' (30 April 1983), p. 4.

66. US General Accounting Office, *Management of Trade Adjustment Program Shows Progress*, CED 82-58 (Washington, 2 April 1982), p. i.

67. Sweet, *Industrial Location Policy*, p. 131.

68. US Congress, Joint Economic Committee, *Anticipating Disruptive Imports*, 95th Congress, 2nd Session, 1978, p. 2.

69. World Bank, *Worker Adjustment to Liberalized Trade: Costs and Assistance Policies*, Staff Working Paper No. 426 (Washington, October 1980), p. 4.

70. Labour Canada, *Report on the Administration of the Labour Adjustment Benefits Act to 31 December 1982* (Ottawa, 1983).

71. National Alliance of Business, *Worker Adjustment* p. 4-7.

72. National Alliance of Business, *Worker Adjustment*, pp. 4-1, 4-3.

73. Robert Guttman, 'Job Training Partnership Act: New Help for the Unemployed', *Monthly Labor Review*, vol. 106, no. 3 (March 1983), p. 3.

74. Ibid.

75. Ibid., p. 5.

76. Congressional Budget Office, *Strategies*, p. 63.

77. 'Dislocated Worker Training Programs under JTPA', *Business Currents Technical Report*, National Alliance of Business, no. 8 (29 March 1983).

THE UNITED KINGDOM

W.W. Daniel

Introduction

The management of redundancy in Britain is of special interest for two reasons. First, there has been a very high rate of redundancy in recent years particularly in manufacturing industry. That rate contributed to a net reduction of the manufacturing workforce of one-quarter between June 1979 and June 1983. Secondly, that massive reduction has been achieved with remarkably little organised resistance or overt conflict. The distinctive system for managing redundancy that predominates in Britain has made a major contribution to the acceptability of job losses.

Unfortunately, it is not possible to provide a simple picture of the extent of redundancy in Britain over recent years owing to the lack of satisfactory official statistics. There are three distinct sets of public figures but all are by-products of the statutory arrangements

Table 3.1: Paid Redundancies in Great Britain, 1977–82

	All industries and services	Manufacturing industries	Service industries
(a) Number of paid redundancies (thousands)			
1977	267	123	72
1978	255	139	70
1979	255	153	63
1980	491	338	98
1981	810	531	180
1982	635	363	182
(b) Rates per thousand			
1977	12	17	6
1978	12	20	5
1979	11	22	5
1980	22	50	7
1981	38	89	14
1982	31	64	14

Source: Department of Employment, *Gazette*, June 1983.

regarding redundancy and none of them provides an accurate measure of the extent of redundancy. Table 3.1 is based on the number of people who received statutory redundancy payments over the years 1977 to 1982. The inadequacy of those figures is that they exclude people who were made redundant but did not qualify for redundancy payments. I report later in the chapter how surveys of the unemployed suggest that only about one-half of all people who lose their jobs for reasons of redundancy receive statutory payments. Accordingly, the figures in Table 3.1 are a very substantial understatement of the extent of redundancy. Nevertheless, they provide clear indications of variations in the incidence of redundancy between different sectors and years. They show that the rate of redundancy in Britain has been concentrated in manufacturing industry and that it peaked in 1981. In that year four per cent of the total workforce received redundancy payments and an astonishing nine per cent of the manufacturing workforce did so. Within the manufacturing sector the individual industries that were hit hardest were metal manufacture, mechanical engineering, vehicle manufacturing, other metal working industries and textiles, clothing and footwear.

The system of management that made possible the apparently peaceful and orderly acceptance of the scales of redundancy and extent of net job loss experienced in recent years owes its origins to the Redundancy Payments Act (1965). The effects of that piece of legislation were almost certainly more far reaching and long lasting than any other element in British employment or industrial relations legislation in the post-war period. Its most important consequences were not intended by those who drafted or introduced the legislation. Indeed, the consequences were not foreseen by supporters of the Act. So strong was its influence that subsequent redundancy legislation, introduced with quite different aims and in quite different circumstances proved to have very little effect.

In view of the central role of statutory redundancy payments within the British system of redundancy, this chapter starts with an account of those provisions and continues with the details of subsequent British legislation about redundancy. These introductory sections lead on to a summary of the main features of the distinctive and predominant system of redundancy in Britain together with an analysis of methods used by British employers to cope with falls in the demand for labour. A short critical evaluation is then made of the practice of nominally voluntary redundancy, which is so central to the British system, before a review is made of provisions to help the redundant other than lump sum payments. The chapter ends with an account of a less visible set of redundancy practices adopted by small employers in Britain which contrast sharply with the predominant system.

Details of the Redundancy Payments Act (1965)

The chief provision of the Redundancy Payments Act (RPA) was to introduce a right to statutory severance payments. That is to say, employees who satisfied certain conditions were entitled to a lump sum cash payment on being displaced from their jobs as a result of redundancy. Redundancy was defined as loss of employment because the job being done no longer existed owing to a reduction or a cessation in the employer's need for work of a particular kind to be done. Here it should be emphasised that the definition included reductions in jobs for any reason including, for instance, reorganisation, relocation, and the introduction of new machinery or methods as well as loss of demand for products or services.

The size of the payment specified in the statute was geared to age and length of service. First, in order to qualify for any payment people needed to have had a minimum of two years' continuous service and to be of working age. The service requirement was a very important condition for, as I show later in the chapter, large numbers of people who become unemployed owing to redundancy do not have the necessary length of service to qualify for a statutory redundancy payment. Secondly, where people did qualify, they were entitled to one-and-a-half week's pay for each year of service over the age of 40; one week's pay for each year of service while aged 22 to 40; and one-half of a week's pay for each year of service when aged 18 to 21. To these arrangements were added two ceilings. A ceiling of 20 years was imposed upon the number of years over the age of 40 that were counted. A ceiling of £40 (1965 rates) was set upon the level of the weekly payment that could be used for the calculation.

The payments were to be made partly from a national redundancy fund to which all employers contributed and partly from the particular employer's own resources. An employer who made a redundancy payment as required by the Act could claim a rebate from the fund. The rate at which rebates have been made has varied over the years but most recently it has been at about 40 per cent. The main provisions of the Act have remained in operation up to the present time, with the ceiling on the size of weekly earnings to be included in the calculations being adjusted over the years until it is now £140.

Despite any limitations upon the people who qualified for statutory payments and ceilings upon the sums they could receive, there is no doubt that the RPA extended entitlement to severance payments much more widely and increased the general level of payments. It was calculated that before the Act only about 17 per cent of employees were covered by any arrangements for redundancy payments based on collective agreements or made on a voluntary basis.[1] The size of payments made within such arrangements was often very modest. Public sector employees were very much more likely to be covered than their private sector counterparts. In effect the RPA changed the situation from one in which employees in a minority of workplaces could expect a modest lump sum payment if they were made redundant to one in which the majority of employees in all workplaces were entitled to a substantial payment.

Two main types of justification for the RPA were put forward by its supporters. The first was economic, the second social. There is little doubt that the predominant influence was economic.[2] There was a consensus among British economists that a major weakness in the British economy was lack of adaptability in British industry. One important element in that lack of adaptability was the reluctance of workers to change, and especially to accept change that involved movement from one employer to another or one sector to another. The RPA was needed in that context to reduce resistance to change and encourage the movement of labour from declining to expanding industries. In relation to its economic objectives critics of the legislation made the charge that the RPA was a late substitute for a national manpower policy. As Britain had failed to develop the active labour market policies which had proved so successful in helping to manage change in such countries as Sweden and Germany, so the argument went, we now needed belatedly to introduce cash incentives to encourage acceptance of change. The fear was expressed that although lump sum payments might help in getting people out of old jobs, they were unlikely to make any contribution to equipping people for new jobs or getting them into new jobs. The criticisms, in this context, were not directed at the principle or practice of redundancy payments as such, nor at redundancy payments as one component in a set of national manpower provisions and policies. The criticism was that too much importance was attached to redundancy payments compared with other measures.

The social case for the RPA was that it was required by natural justice to compensate workers for the losses involved in being deprived of their jobs through no fault of their own and to cushion them against the costs involved in any ensuing unemployment. The case for cash compensation for job loss was often argued on the basis that employees developed property rights in their jobs that were analogous to the rights that property owners had over their property. Critics of the RPA on social grounds argued that while severance payments might provide compensation for job loss they did not provide equitable or adequate compensation. The compensation was only indirectly and imperfectly associated with the costs. Higher weekly unemployment benefit while out of work and improved provisions to equip people for new jobs and find them new jobs would represent more equitable and effective national provisions. Arguments about property rights over jobs were more relevant to arrangements that might be made through collective bargaining between employers and workers' representatives than to the national provisions appropriate for the state to make for people as a whole. The most powerful argument against the provisions of the RPA on social grounds, however, was that it placed people who suffered most from redundancy at greater risk of becoming redundant. That consequence became apparent only after the Act had started to have substantial impact and it is considered more fully in the later account of current redundancy practices.

The Redundancy Procedures Provisions in the Employment Protection Act (1975)

Ten years after the RPA the economic climate in Britain had changed substantially, as it had in the rest of Western Europe. In the early 1960s unemployment was still at the low levels that had characterised the post-war period. One of the principal concerns of public policy so far as manpower was concerned was how to achieve the shake-out of labour that was felt to be needed to promote structural adaption. By the mid-1970s unemployment was already rising and increasing concern was being expressed about the need for job protection. It was in this new climate that a new Labour administration introduced its Employment Protection Act (1975). The EPA included new statutes relating to redundancy. The principal requirement was that employers planning redundancies should consult with trade unions over the proposed dismissals. If an employer planned to dismiss 10-99 people then he had to notify any union recognised in relation to those people at least 60 days before the first dismissal was planned. If 100 or more people were to be dismissed then the period of notice was increased to 90 days. (The periods of notice were subsequently, in 1979, reduced to 30 days and 60 days respectively, following a change of government.) During the period between notification and the first dismissal, employers were required to give information to the union on reasons for the redundancy; the number and nature of the employees scheduled for redundancy; the proposed method of selection for dismissal; and the proposed methods for carrying out the dismissals. After having provided such information the employer was required to respond to any reply that the union might produce. The provisions in the EPA concerning redundancy were part of a package of measures introduced around that time to promote security of employment. The chief criticism directed at the measures was that they over-protected the worker. The argument was that employment protection measures would make it so difficult for employers to shed labour when they needed to that they would become reluctant to recruit labour. In consequence, the measures would be counterproductive and result in increased unemployment rather than increased employment. That view was heavily promoted during the early life of the EPA to the extent that it became part of conventional wisdom. In fact, the evidence provides little support for that conventional wisdom and suggests that the 1975 redundancy provisions had remarkably little impact.[3] Part of the explanation for that lack of impact lay in the distinctive British system for managing redundancy that was fostered by the 1965 RPA.

The British System for Managing Redundancy

I argue later in this chapter that there are a number of systems for managing redundancy in Britain which vary in relation to sectors and levels of employment. The most marked contrasts are between, first, the small firm sector and the large firm and public sectors and, secondly, policies and practices adopted towards manual employees as compared with non-manual employees. On the other hand, despite this diversity, it remains legitimate to talk about a distinctively British system for managing redundancy. That is because there is a set of policies and practices that is widely used in Britain, which differs from systems in other advanced countries and which, although it is not universal, almost certainly covers a larger group of employees than any other system in Britain.

Following the introduction of the 1965 RPA, major changes quickly occurred in redundancy policies and practices. Managers found that when lump sum payments were available to workers then many individual workers were not averse to the idea of redundancy. When there was the prospect of redundancy some would come forward and ask if they might be chosen. One or two companies, notably the Shell Oil Company, Hoover in South Wales and Esso at Fawley, experimented with formal voluntary redundancy schemes. Such schemes characteristically involved three chief components: first, the specification of a target number of jobs to be lost; secondly, the announcement of the inducements available to those who volunteered for redundancy; and thirdly, the definition of categories to whom the offer of voluntary redundancy would not apply. Generally, the voluntary redundancy terms involved increasing the size of severance payments above the statutory minima. Initially, the chief fear among managements was that voluntary redundancy would result in loss of managerial control over the people displaced. In particular, managers feared that they would lose their most skilled, able and enterprising workers. Such workers, they feared, would know that they could readily find alternative employment and be tempted by the prospect of a lump sum payment plus a good job elsewhere. In practice, such managerial doubts proved unfounded.[4] The gearing of the size of statutory payments to age and length of service meant that the largest payments were available to the oldest workers. In consequence, there was a tendency for older workers to volunteer for redundancy rather than those in the prime age group whom managers most valued. Some employers were consciously gearing discretionary extra-statutory payments further to promote that tendency. A judicious mixture of such inducements added to the bias built into the statutory scheme, combined with the specification of categories to whom the offer of voluntary redundancy did not apply, soon meant that employers were exercising more control over redundancy than at any previous period in modern times.

Prior to the development of voluntary redundancy schemes the characteristic trade union response had been to oppose and resist the need for redundancies. If, ultimately, they had to accept the need for a number of redundancies, they would insist upon the traditional criterion of 'last in — first out' as the criterion for selection. That is to say trade unions normally insisted that length of service should be the basis upon which people were selected for service and that the shorter was someone's length of service the earlier that person should be selected. Whatever their initial feelings might have been, trade unions soon found themselves to be powerless in the face of the growth of voluntary redundancy schemes. If they tried to challenge and oppose the need for redundancies, they were undermined by individual members eager to accept voluntary redundancy terms. In consequence, caught in a pincer movement between managerial strategy and individualist opportunism upon the part of members, trade union representatives had no alternative but to adopt two stances in relation to redundancy. The first was to insist upon, 'No redundancy other than voluntary redundancy'. The second was to bargain over the inducements to volunteer and, in particular, to try to bid up the size of the employer's supplement to the statutory minimum payments.

Some of the features and implications of the British system for managing redundancy fostered by the RPA, and especially the way in which it reduced the impact of the redundancy provisions in the 1975 EPA, were revealed by a survey that I did of redundancy policy and practice in manufacturing workplaces employing 50 or more people.[5] Of particular interest in that survey were its findings on measures taken to avoid redundancy, on methods used to run down workforces, on criteria adopted to select people for redundancy and on the impact of the 1975 legislation.

Measures Taken to Avoid Redundancy

The survey was carried out at a time when employers had generally been experiencing a decline in the demand for their products. About two-thirds of the workplaces at which we carried out interviewing said that they had experienced some fall in demand for their products in the previous year. We asked managers in places where demand had been falling whether they took any measures to avoid having to make employees redundant. The large majority (81 per cent) said that they had and there was little variation in the extent to which different types of workplace reported having taken action. The chief variation lay in the nature of the initiatives adopted and the apparent effectiveness of the preventative action. There were two main types of response. One could be styled a marketing approach and the other a manpower reaction. The marketing approach involved efforts to promote sales through identifying new markets or becoming more competitive in existing markets by cutting prices or other means. The manpower reaction involved steps to adjust the size of the workforce or the supply of labour without having to declare redundancies. The individual manpower measures most commonly mentioned were, in order of frequency, natural wastage (or attrition); internal redeployment; short-time working or temporary layoffs; voluntary early retirement or redundancy; reducing the number of part-time workers; and simply labour hoarding or carrying the surplus complement during the period of the reduction in demand.

The manpower response was substantially more common than the marketing approach and was characteristically adopted by larger workplaces and those that were parts of corporations. The less common marketing approach typified the response of smaller workplaces, particularly independent enterprises. It also proved less effective in avoiding redundancy. We looked at the extent to which workplaces had actually implemented enforced redundancies in relation to whether they had taken precautionary measures and if so of what type. We found that where managements had implemented relatively large reductions in manpower over short periods of time, and used enforced redundancy as one of the measures, then they tended to have taken no measures to avoid redundancy or, where they had taken any precaution, the position adopted was a marketing one. The differences were very marked. For instance, enforced redundancies were subsequently implemented in one-half of the cases where a marketing approach to avoiding redundancy was adopted. In contrast, where a well-developed manpower approach was adopted, enforced redundancy occurred in only about one in every ten cases.

Methods Used to Reduce Workforces
We asked managers in our survey, who had brought about reduc-

tions in manpower at their workplaces in the previous period, how the reduction had been achieved. Their most common answers, in order of frequency were: natural wastage (or attrition); redeployment; voluntary redundancy; early retirement; and enforced redundancy. It was apparent that voluntary redundancy (mentioned in 49 per cent of cases where there had been manpower reductions) was practised substantially more frequently than enforced redundancy (35 per cent). An initial interpretation of that difference, combined with the general rank order in the frequency with which different measures were used, might be that managements used progressively more severe methods the greater was the size of the reduction they had to achieve. That interpretation was not supported by our analysis, however, certainly so far as the comparative frequency with which voluntary redundancy and enforced redundancy were operated. There was little tendency for the balance between voluntary and enforced redundancy to vary in relation to the size of the manpower reduction brought about. There was a very strong tendency for that balance to change in relation to the size of the workplace and the level of union influence within workplaces. In larger workplaces voluntary redundancy was very much more common than enforced redundancy. In smaller workplaces the reverse was the case. The contrast was even stronger so far as trade union organisation was concerned. In places where a very high proportion of workers were union members, or where managers rated the influence of unions as strong, voluntary redundancy was more than twice as common as enforced redundancy. Where relatively few workers were union members, or where managers felt that unions had little influence, then enforced redundancy was more common than voluntary redundancy. The implication of the pattern was clear. In larger workplaces, especially ones where unions were highly organised, redundancy was largely brought about through voluntary schemes when it proved unavoidable through other means.

Two other sets of findings were relevant to the implications of voluntary as compared with enforced redundancy. The findings concerned the categories affected by the respective methods. In cases where managers reported that they had had voluntary redundancies, we asked whether the arrangements had been designed or operated to attract particular categories of workers to volunteer and, if so, which categories. We found that in one-half of cases managers said that schemes had been designed to attract particular categories. By far the most common category mentioned as a target group was 'older workers'. The second most common target group was workers who were less than fully fit or had a poor health record. In cases where managers had operated enforced redundancies we asked what criteria had been used as the basis for selection. We found that length of service or 'last in — first out' was by far the most common criterion in such circumstances.

Short-time and Temporary Layoffs

There is little doubt that the effectiveness and popularity of voluntary redundancy schemes have reduced interest in work-sharing in Britain even during the period when unemployment has risen to its current very high levels. In practice, the most common forms of work-sharing have been short-time working and temporary layoffs.

The results of our survey of manufacturing industry showed that 11 per cent of workplaces had operated short-time working in the previous year and nearly one-quarter had done so in the previous three years. Temporary layoffs were substantially less frequent and had occurred in about one in every ten workplaces over the previous three years. Overall, our analysis led us to the conclusion that short-time working and temporary layoffs were generally operated as a method of coping with an identifiably short-term fall in the amount of work to be done, rather than as a means of work sharing in circumstances where management identified a longer-term decline in the need for manpower. It is true, as I indicated earlier, that short-term working, temporary layoffs and work-sharing were among the different measures mentioned by managers as steps they took to avoid redundancies. But they were mentioned very much less frequently among such measures than steps to reduce the size of the work force without enforced redundancy, such as natural wastage, voluntary redundancy and early retirement. Moreover, it was very rare for workplaces to have operated short-time working without having also instituted specific measures to reduce the workforce, while it was very common for managements to have declared redundancies without having had any short-time working. In the large majority of cases where workplaces had operated short-time working, redundancies had also been declared, voluntary, enforced or both. When we asked managers about the reasons for introducing short-time working, the large majority said it had been set up to deal with an identifiably temporary contingency. More recent research on work-sharing in Britain confirms that not only is it an option that rarely features in discussions between managements and unions, but also that the normal processes of collective bargaining leave little scope for it to be considered.[6]

Impact of the 1975 Legislation on Redundancy Procedures

As I have already suggested, while the chief provision of the RPA was intended to encourage movement between jobs, the redundancy provisions in the EPA ten years later were more concerned with job security and the joint regulation of issues concerning redundancy. But in view of the way that redundancy policy and practice developed in Britain following the RPA, it is hardly surprising that the provisions relating to redundancy procedures had little impact. We talked to managers some 16 months after the procedures became operative. We found that two-thirds of the managers who had experienced loss of product demand over that period said that redundancy procedures legislation had had *no* impact upon their policies or practices. Very few said that the requirements had had a major impact. Accordingly, there was little sign of any substantial effect even among workplaces where, in principle, the provisions should have been most relevant. Where managers did say that the provisions had influenced them, they chiefly reported that it had taken them longer to implement the redundancies.

It is not difficult to explain this lack of impact in view of the prevailing pattern of redundancy policy and practice. As I have described, in larger workplaces and particularly those where trade unions were strong, managements had already developed sophisticated manpower practices for running down their workforces, if necessary, before the introduction of the 1975 legislation. Among those manpower practices, voluntary redundancy schemes, encouraged by the previous phase of legislation, played a major part. That was most likely to be the case where trade unions were strongest. In those circumstances, legislation designed to promote job protection by giving trade unions greater opportunity jointly to regulate issues concerning redundancy was much too late. As I have described earlier, trade unions had already opted for or been manoeuvred into a position where the principal points of their attention were insistence upon voluntary redundancy and bargaining over the size of lump sum payments.

On the other hand the workplaces which did not have well-developed redundancy policies and practices, and where enforced redundancy was more common than voluntary redundancy, tended to be small and characterised by poor or weak trade union organisation. The medium through which the redundancy procedure provisions were intended to have an influence was statutory consultation with recognised trade unions. There was little scope for the provisions to have an influence where there was no effective trade union representation.

In short, where trade unions were well organised, policies and practices had already been developed which made the redundancy procedure provisions largely irrelevant. In circumstances where such policies and practices did not exist and there was scope for influencing events, the agent of influence built into the legislation tended not to be strong. Accordingly, for anyone familiar with the development of redundancy policies and practices in Britain it was not at all surprising that the 1975 measures had little impact. The only surprising feature about the response to that legislation was how quickly the view became established that the legislation of the mid-1970s resulted in the worker becoming over-protected and that the consequent difficulty that employers had in shedding labour made them reluctant to recruit. Apart from analyses such as that reported in this chapter, the whole pattern of events since 1975 runs counter to the argument that it has been difficult for employers to shed labour. Since the end of the 1970s unemployment rose from one million to over three million. As outlined earlier, employment in manufacturing industry was reduced by one-quarter. Those changes were brought about with very little organised resistance, dispute or disruption. Again, the explanation, according to my analysis, would seem to be that the public and corporate sectors have been able to run down their workforces through their sophisticated manpower practices in which voluntary redundancy has played a major part. Smaller and non-unionised workplaces have been able to continue declaring enforced redundancies because there has been no organised force to resist or to invoke the legislation that could have made life more difficult for managements.

One feature of employee protection legislation which has had a major impact upon employers and is sometimes confused with redundancy legislation is that concerned with unfair dismissals. Legislation designed to provide employees with protection against dismissal for reasons other than redundancy unless that dismissal could be showed to be justified and justifiable was first introduced in the Industrial Relations Act (1971). All our research upon the effects of the employment legislation of the 1970s shows that the unfair dismissals provisions were among the measures to have had the greatest impact.[7] The majority of managers in our survey of manufacturing industry reported that unfair dismissals legislation had had an effect upon their policies and practices. Many reported that it had had a major impact. The chief effect reported was the Act had led them to reform their procedures, chiefly their disciplinary and dismissals procedure but also in many cases their arrangements for selection, induction and review of performance. In terms of selection the chief message to emerge was that unfair dismissals legislation had led employers to be more concerned about who they took on, rather than how many people they took on. That is to say, it was apparent that prior to unfair dismissals legislation some employers had paid little regard to initial selection for certain levels of job. They just took people on and then got rid of them if they proved to be unsatisfactory. Legislation on dismissals encouraged such employers and others to pay much more attention to whether or not people were likely to be right for the job at initial selection.

It was also clear from our discussions with managers that, for them, employment protection legislation was almost synonymous with unfair dismissals legislations. Their views about the EPA largely reflected their views about unfair dismissals provisions. As statutory arrangements relating to unfair dismissals were introduced some time before the EPA by a government of another colour, it is ironic that managerial evaluations of the second should be so strongly influenced by their experience of the first. The equating of unfair dismissals with the EPA in the minds of managers and many others, however, goes some way to explaining the widespread but mistaken belief that the employment protection legislation of the mid-1970s had a major impact and made it more difficult for employers to declare redundancies and less disposed to recruit.

Some Observations on the General Implications of Voluntary Redundancy Schemes

On the face of things the British system for managing redundancy in the corporate and trade union organised sectors would appear to represent a highly satisfactory system for the parties involved.

Managers are able to run down workforces in a way that is acceptable to its workforces, unions and local community while exercising control over the categories affected. Unions comply and justify their role by insisting upon no redundancy but voluntary redundancy and seeking to maximise the level of cash compensation. Where individual employees lose their jobs, it is, in some sense of the phrase, because they choose to do so.

Three types of qualification need to be made about the apparent attractiveness of voluntary redundancy schemes. The first refers to the sense in which and the extent to which they can be described as 'voluntary'. It is clear that in some cases pressure is placed upon individuals to opt for redundancy within nominally voluntary schemes. That appears to be especially the case when schemes are extended to managerial and specialist staff. Under such circumstances people may be subject to substantial, prolonged stress. In addition, even when no pressure is applied to volunteers, the voluntary component in schemes refers only to the criteria according to which people are selected for redundancy and not to the decisions about whether the number of jobs needs to be reduced and by how many. The schemes place that choice much more firmly and unilaterally in the hands of managements. At the collective level schemes also provide managements with substantially more choice over the categories to be made redundant although within categories they may also give more choice to individuals.

Secondly, because nominally voluntary schemes have made it possible for managements to decide unilaterally whether redundancies are necessary and on what scale, they have reduced the level of job protection to workers. For instance, I have already described how the existence of voluntary schemes largely thwarted the objectives of the Employment Protection Act so far as redundancy was concerned.

The third and most substantial qualification that has to be made about voluntary schemes is whether arrangements that appear so satisfactory to the parties engaged in enterprises and establishments achieve their goals by displacing the social and economic costs on to the wider community. That question is highlighted by a consideration of the categories affected by voluntary schemes. The initial design of the RPA was such that older workers received higher lump sum payments. There was early evidence that the age composition of the redundant quickly changed following the introduction of the Act.[8] Subsequently, it is clear that employers built upon that initial feature of the Act and consciously accentuated it in order to attract older workers and the less fit to volunteer. In contrast, 'last in — first out', the principal criterion according to which people were selected for redundancy prior to the Act (and according to which they are still most likely to be selected where enforced redundancy is practised), ensured that younger workers were more likely to be displaced.

There has been a large number of surveys of the redundant in Britain starting in the 1950s and continuing through the 1970s.[9] Such surveys have repeatedly produced one main finding: the chief influence upon what happens to people who lose their jobs as a result of collective redundancies is their age. The older they are the greater the costs they experience.[10] The older people are when displaced, the longer it takes them to find a new job and the more likely it is that they will not work again. Where they find jobs, the older they are the more likely it is that any job they find will be inferior to the one they lost in terms of skill, level of earnings and other characteristics. In addition, older workers are least likely to engage in training or re-training following redundancy and least likely to move geographically for new jobs. In brief, older workers experience the greatest personal cost as a result of redundancy and they are the group who are most difficult to redeploy. The chief reservation that has to be made about the RPA, then, is that directly and indirectly through the voluntary redundancy schemes it fostered, the Act has encouraged redundancy to fall more upon those who, in social terms, suffer most in consequence and who, in economic terms, are least mobile and adaptable.

Measures to Help the Redundant other than Lump Sum Payments

As outlined earlier in this chapter, one of the major initial criticisms of the RPA was that the introduction of statutory severance payments represented an inadequate and belated substitute for effective labour market policies. For instance, the analysis of the closure of a works in Sweden around the time that the RPA was introduced here revealed that nearly everyone affected by the closure could be accounted for by the public manpower service (or labour market board).[11] One proportion was placed in new jobs by the public employment service. A second proportion was placed in training centres run by the public service. A third proportion was helped to move geographically to take up new jobs in new locations. A final and fourth proportion was maintained by special public funded works until alternative work could be found for them. Through these different means the public service ensured that very few if any of those made redundant by a works closure actually became unemployed. In contrast, the penetration of all the British public manpower services in providing for people made redundant by closures at about the same time was likely to be less than 20 per cent. That penetration represented the impact of the three different types of service: the employment service; the training service; and geographical transfer.

When Hilda Kahn carried out a pioneering study of 6,000 people displaced by a mass motor industry redundancy in 1954, she was astonished to find that only 15 per cent of those displaced were helped to find new jobs by the public employment service.[12] Her main policy conclusion was that that figure represented a wholly inadequate level of help to the redundant to find jobs from the public service. Over ten years later, when the Government Social Survey carried out a national study of the redundant following the introduction of the RPA, it found that the proportion placed remained very similar.[13] At around that period reforms were made to the service and one particular innovation made was the introduction of on-site offices in the event of major redundancies. That is to say, the public employment service set up an office in the workplace where workers were scheduled for redundancy. Officers of the service could then register, counsel and inform workers about alternative job opportunities open to them before they lost their jobs. There was clear evidence that where such offices were established the public service achieved substantially more impact than when it waited for people to come to its local permanent offices. For instance, in a large-scale works closure in South East London, where on-site services were provided, one-quarter of the workers were found new jobs by the service.[14] That proportion was substantially higher than any recorded by previous studies of the redundant.

Early in the 1970s the Manpower Services Commission was established partly on the model of the Swedish Labour Market Board. It set about completing the reform and modernisation of the public employment service through its Job Centre programme. There was clear evidence through the 1970s that it had increasing impact upon the labour market. By the end of the decade, it was helping about one-quarter of all those becoming unemployed to find jobs, a proportion which was substantially higher than the general level a decade earlier and similar to the level achieved by its special on-site service at that stage.[15]

Since the end of the decade, however, there has been a tendency for the progress of the public employment service to be checked if not reversed. Staff have been cut. Emphasis has been placed upon the less labour intensive self-service provisions rather than the labour intensive special services.[16] It is not yet apparent how far those developments have reduced the value of the service for the redundant generally or for particular categories among the redundant.

While the public employment service in Britain has never found jobs for more than a minority of the redundant, it has helped far more than the public training and transfer services. Public re-training and transfer provisions peaked towards the end of the 1970s but even at that stage their combined efforts were helping fewer than five per cent of the redundant. Accordingly, it is likely that, even at their peak, the public employment training and transfer services were helping no more than one-third of the unemployed. Most recently there has been a decline from the peak.

Apart from provisions of the public service it has been normal for employers confronted with the decision to declare closures or large-scale redundancies to announce that they will do everything they can to help workers affected by the redundancies to find new jobs. Despite the fact that such employers have made arrangements designed to help, the indications are that in the majority of cases their efforts have made little impact and, in terms of their practical benefits, represented an industrial relations or public relations gesture rather than a substantial provision. For instance, employers have often set up their own employment service for the period of the redundancy, trawling other local employers for vacancies, publicising these among their threatened workforce and counselling employees on alternative jobs. In the event, though, the evidence has shown that very few have found jobs through their employer's efforts on their behalf. For instance, the figure in South East London was four per cent and that proportion was heavily concentrated among the higher occupational levels.[17]

In contrast to the general experience, however, there have been cases where employers have made effective provisions for displaced employees. A notable example in the public sector is the resettlement service for people leaving the armed forces which has to place about 10,000 people each year. Two features contribute to the effectiveness of these services. First, it involves the investment of substantial resources. Secondly, they are long-term services which have been able to amass very considerable experience and expertise and become established in appropriate networks. A parallel type of development in private business has concerned what some large corporations have identified as obsolete scientists or managers in mid-career. They have developed packages to help the redundant become established in new occupations. The packages have included substantial lump sum payments and also help in identifying and exploiting new opportunities. Again, such services have tended to become established as part of the corporation's normal system of personnel management. That is very different from the setting up of *ad hoc* provisions in the event of a decision to make a large number of manual workers redundant over a short period of time. It is in such circumstances that employers' services have proved to be least effective.

Where employers have managed to help in redeployment, two conditions have been satisfied. First, a long-term resource has been established. Secondly, there has been a major investment of specialist staff, commitment and resources. For instance, where an employer is closing a unit and making reductions in manpower at one location but has operating units at other locations, it has been normal for the redundant to have the opportunity to transfer geographically to a new location. In practice, very few have taken up such opportunities even though housing has been offered to go with jobs. Those who have moved have tended to be in the higher occupational groups. To bring about substantial movements of manual workers between different geographical locations requires the kind of investment that the National Coal Board has made in Britain during periods when it has been closing pits in some areas but opening or expanding them in others. That investment has involved attention to family, social and community considerations that go far beyond the offer of housing to go with a new job. The attention has included guarantees of maintenance of earnings and seniority in any new job; visits for workers and their families to inspect new houses, schools and communities during the period when they are considering moves; and regard for established work groups and neighbourhood patterns when people are being deployed in new workplaces and housed in new areas.

Similarly, when British Steel was beginning its programme of closures and manpower reductions it made a number of substantial and innovative investments to help displaced workers. Two of these were of particular note. The first involved establishing its own operation to try and attract new businesses to set up in areas where it was running down. The indications are that through an imaginative mixture of financial inducements and entrepreneurial flair that initiative was very successful. Its operations compared very favourably with the work of established public agencies for attracting industries partly because the managers running it proved more convincing to businessmen than public servants as advocates of relocation in a particular place. The second initiative involved the provision of training by the steel corporation for jobs outside the industry while people were still employed by the corporation. Critics have suggested, however, that as the pressure on British Steel to reduce manpower rose so emphasis switched from positive measures to help displaced workers to policies that were most effective in getting workers quickly out of the industry in an acceptable way. For that purpose raising the size of redundancy payments proved more effective than practical provisions to improve the labour market prospects of the displaced. That tendency illustrates the way in which, for a business, however well-intentioned it may be and however enlightened it may be in promoting its self-interest, the policies and practices it adopts in running down its labour force will owe more to the needs of the business than the longer-term interests of displaced workers or the labour market. In consequence, those longer-term interests have to be a major concern of the public authorities.

A Different Perspective on the British System of Redundancy Derived from the Study of the Unemployed

A common view of the British system of redundancy is that it has three distinctive features. First, statutory provision is made for lump sum severance payments. Secondly, the characteristic British way of running down workforces is through voluntary redundancy schemes within which employers supplement the statutory minimum payments. Thirdly and consequently, British workers displaced from their jobs as a result of redundancy tend to receive substantial cash payments. Such a view is fostered by the official statistics on redundancies and the size of redundancy payments.

These figures are based only upon those people who do receive a statutory payment when they lose their jobs through redundancy. They ignore the large number of people who do not qualify for lump sum payments. A quite different picture is presented by looking at all those who become unemployed as a result of redundancy.

In common usage it often appears to be assumed that the redundant and the unemployed are the same people. In fact, a number of surveys of the unemployed show that the overlap between the two groups is only slight and many common assumptions about unemployment and the redundant are false.

First, it is assumed that unemployment rises because more people become redundant. Secondly, redundancy is thought of in terms of the consequences of major reductions in manpower or closure by major employers such as those that have occurred in the steel industry, the motor car industry and shipyards in recent years. Thirdly and consequently it is assumed that the redundant and hence the unemployed in general receive substantial redundancy payments. Studies of the unemployed show just how far from the truth these assumptions are. The redundant make up only a minority of the unemployed. People displaced by major collective dismissals represent only a minority of the redundant. Few of the redundant receive even a modest redundancy payment and, in consequence, very few of the unemployed do so. These conclusions may be illustrated by reference to a longitudinal survey that I have currently in progress on *the unemployed flow*.[18] The initial sample was 8,000 people joining the register of the unemployed in May of 1980. We interviewed people for the first time just over a month after they registered. Subsequently, we have interviewed them at intervals on five different occasions. The present results refer to the first wave of interviewing.

First, only about one third of people coming into unemployment did so as a result of redundancy even when people who came to the end of fixed term contracts were included. Twenty-two per cent were not in work prior to registration. Eleven per cent were dismissed for reasons other than redundancy. The remaining one-third reported that they left their previous job because there was some aspect that they could not tolerate. There was clear internal evidence from the survey that in areas of high unemployment the proportion who were redundant from their previous job rose. That is consistent with information from other sources showing that when the proportion of the redundant among the unemployed is plotted over time then the proportion rises as unemployment increases and falls as unemployment drops.[19] Nevertheless, despite that tendency and despite the fact that our sample was selected at a time of high and rising unemployment, it remained the case that only one-third of people becoming unemployed lost their previous jobs through redundancy.

Secondly, only about one-half of those who were made redundant received any redundancy payment. In cases where they did receive payments, sums were generally very modest. Even among men, where payments were higher, the median figure for those who did receive payments was slightly over £500. Of all men becoming unemployed only four per cent received sums of £2,000 or more. Where men did receive such payments they were heavily concentrated in the oldest age group and their unemployment frequently represented early retirement. The actual sums received by the unemployed put into perspective the headline figures that have been quoted to illustrate very high redundancy payments. Such headline sums have promoted the impression generally that the unemployed received substantial redundancy payments and encouraged the British Prime Minister, in particular, to argue that the unemployed should spend their redundancy payments to set themselves up in business. When, in fact, only one in every six of the unemployed men receives any payment and only one in every 25 receives a sum of £2,000 or more and their average age is about 60, such advice does not appear very realistic as a general prescription for the unemployed.

The reason why so many of the redundant do not qualify for any payment is because they do not have the qualifying service of two years or more. That may be surprising in view of the redundancy policies and practices that have been described in earlier parts of the chapter. Such policies and practices encourage redundancy to fall upon the older and, by implication, longer service employees. But as I made clear such policies and practices were characteristic of larger employers. The striking feature about the unemployed is that they come disproportionately from small firms and workplaces. One-quarter of men entering unemployment worked at establishments that employed fewer than ten people. Forty-one per cent worked at places where there were fewer than 25 people. At about the same time, in the British economy generally, one-half of men worked at establishments employing 125 people or more. As emphasised earlier, small workplaces were more likely to operate traditional enforced redundancy practices where people were selected on the criterion of 'last in — first out'. In addition, our research demonstrated that many unemployed people were caught on the treadmill of recurrent unemployment which is characteristic of the small firm sector during recession. We followed up those of our sample who found new jobs within ten months of losing their last. We found that nearly two-thirds lost or changed the initial job they had following unemployment within the subsequent ten months and 39 per cent were made redundant from those initial jobs.[20] The image conjured up is of people jumping from disappearing iceberg to disappearing iceberg in a rapidly thawing arctic sea.

The other picture conjured up by our analysis overall is that, alongside the predominant system of redundancy for manual workers in Britain, practised by the corporate and public sectors, there is a second less visible and much less favourable system. That second system is reflected in the policies and practices of small firms and workplaces. Employment is very much more precarious generally. Periods of service are short. Redundancy and particularly enforced redundancy are much more common. They are concentrated upon short-service employees. The redundant frequently receive no statutory payment and rarely receive any additional discretionary payment.

The dual system means that employees of small firms fare comparatively ill when they lose their jobs. Their position illustrates one of the main criticisms of the RPA when it was initially introduced. That criticism was that statutory payments would be received by only some of the unemployed and be only indirectly related to the costs of job loss. Public policy, in contrast, required measures that we applied to the unemployed as a whole and were directly related to the costs of being out of work.

Notes

1. S.R. Parker, C.G. Thomas, N.D. Ellis and W.E.J. McCarthy (1971), *Effects of the Redundancy Payments Act*, HMSO, London.

2. Santosh Mukherjee (1973), *Through No Fault of Their Own*, Macdonald, London.

3. W.W. Daniel (1978), *The Impact of Employment Protection Laws*, PSI No. 577, London.

4. W.W. Daniel (1970), *Strategies for Displaced Employees*, PEP No. 517, London.

5. W.W. Daniel (1978), *The Impact of Employment Protection Laws*.

6. Michael White (1980), *Shorter Working Time*, PSI No. 589, London.

7. See W.W. Daniel (1981), *Maternity Rights, the Experience of Employers*, PSI No. 596, London; as well as W.W. Daniel (1978), *The Impact of Employment Protection Laws*.

8. Santosh Mukherjee (1973), *Through No Fault of Their Own*.

9. Acton Society Trust (1958), *Redundancy — Three Studies* and *Redundancy — A Survey*, Acton Society Trust, London; W.W. Daniel (1972), *Whatever happened to the workers in Woolwich?*, PEP Broadsheet No. 537, London; F. Herron (1972), *Labour Market in Crisis. Redundancy at Upper Clyde Shipbuilders*, Macmillan, London; H.R. Kahn (1964), *Repercussions of redundancy. A local survey*, Allen and Unwin, London; D.I. Mackay (1972), 'Redundancy and Re-engagement: A Study of Car Workers', *Manchester School of Economic and Social Studies*, vol. 80, pp. 295-312; R. Martin and R.H. Fryer (1973), *Redundancy and Paternalist Capitalism. A Study in the Sociology of Work*, Allen and Unwin, London; S.R. Parker *et al.* (1971), *Effects of the Redundancy Payments Act*; D. Wedderburn (1965), *Redundancy and the Railwaymen*, Cambridge University Press, Cambridge.

10. The general trend for people to fare worse following redundancy the older they are may seem to be odd in relation to the tendency over the past ten years for young adults to have become heavily over-represented among the unemployed stock. That apparent inconsistency is accounted for in two ways. First, until very recently it remained the case that the youngest group among adult workers found new jobs more quickly than other age groups. Their representation among the unemployed stock was a consequence of the fact that they were much more likely to become unemployed than other age groups rather than that they spent longer out of work when they became unemployed. Most recently, however, there has been a tendency for even the youngest age group to take longer to find work than prime age groups. Secondly, studies of the redundant have tended to concentrate upon people displaced by large scale layoffs or closures. Frequently, in such cases, workplaces will not have been recruiting for some time and the age structure of the workforce will have become skewed towards the upper end. In such circumstances few of the youngest age group will be included for study.

11. W.W. Daniel (1970), *Strategies for Displaced Employees*.

12. Hilda Kahn (1964), *Repercussions of Redundancy*.

13. Parker et al. (1971), *Effects of the Redundancy Payments Act*.

14. W.W. Daniel (1972), *Whatever Happened to the Workers in Woolwich*.

15. W.W. Daniel (1981), *The Unemployed Flow*, PSI, London.

16. W.W. Daniel (1981), 'The Employment Service and the Unemployed Flow.' *Policy Studies*, volume 2, part 1.

17. W.W. Daniel (1972), *Whatever Happened to the Workers in Woolwich*.

18. W.W. Daniel (1981), *The Unemployed Flow*.

19. The annual General Household Survey asks unemployed respondents how they lost their previous job. Although the categorisation of answers is less informative than it might be, there is a clear tendency for the proportion of involuntary leavers to rise with the level of unemployment.

20. W.W. Daniel (1983), 'How the Unemployed Fare after they Find New Jobs', *Policy Studies*, volume 3, part 4.

4 JAPAN

Douglas Anthony

Introduction — Unemployment in the Japanese Economy

It is a truism that there are contradictory elements which are difficult to reconcile in developing any policy for managing redundancies. The 'efficient' operation of the labour market within a free enterprise economy means that workforce reductions and the consequent redeployment of labour between occupations, firms or sectors of the economy should take place as quickly and smoothly as possible. This is true *a fortiori* when, as at present, the pace of technological innovation has made one of its periodic spurts, so disturbing established patterns of comparative advantage in international trade and sharpening the edge of international competition. It is frequently deemed desirable to increase the 'efficiency' of the labour market in this respect by, for example, measures designed to increase geographic mobility, improve the flow of information about job vacancies, subsidise re-training, and so on.

On the other hand, civilised societies recognise the need for measures to mitigate and attenuate the effects on workers of the sudden loss of their livelihoods. Some of these measures (for example subsidies paid to firms to retain workers they might otherwise discard) inevitably reduce the speed with which adjustments are made. At the same time legal restraints on the freedom of action of employers to dismiss workers may raise the cost and lengthen the time needed to adapt firms' cost structures in the way they deem necessary.

The difficulties posed by the need to reconcile these contrasting elements have an added piquancy in Japan's case, both because of the suddenness of the onset of the problem on any significant scale, and because of certain features of the employment system which, though older in origin, were strengthened during her period of very rapid economic growth which lasted for nearly two decades from the mid-1950s to about 1973. Until the first oil crisis of the autumn of 1973 which signalled the start of a period of downward adjustment in rates of growth of output and employment, the chief preoccupation of most Japanese firms had been to secure an adequate supply of labour. Couched in broad terms, the constantly growing requirements for labour were not met out of a growth in population, for after a short-lived surge in the birth rate soon after the war, associated with demobilisation and repatriation, Japan's rate of increase in population fell to a level that is amongst the lowest in the industrialised world.[1] Instead a massive intersectoral shift in the working population mainly provided for the labour needs of the large-scale, technologically advanced firms in manufacturing and commerce which led Japan's industrial advance and won her her export markets. Even in 1970, after a continuous drop in the number of its gainfully employed population which began in the 1950s, the primary sector (agriculture, forestry and fisheries) still employed over 17 per cent of the working population. By 1981 the proportion had fallen to under 10 per cent, and given the small-scale, owner-farmer structure of agriculture and the fact that a majority of farmers already have other occupations and only farm part-time, the scope for further transfers from this sector is very small. In fact, since the early- to mid-1970s a similar intersectoral transfer has begun between the secondary (mainly manufacturing) sector and the tertiary sector where services have proliferated and the activities of government have grown, so leading to a demand for more labour.[2]

However, even these marked and prolonged intersectoral movements of the labour force were insufficient to provide for the needs for labour in certain key sectors of the economy, and by the mid- to late-1960s there were clear indications of labour shortages. In this period the proportion of those registered as wholly unemployed rarely exceeded 1.1–1.2 per cent of the total labour force, whilst the job offers to applicants ratio generally exceeded 1.00, also indicating that those wishing to find employment were on the whole able to do so. (In many cases, of course, this meant being prepared to move one's place of residence, and this was the period of a marked rise in the urban and metropolitan population and a declining rural population.) As a broad generalisation it is fair to conclude that unemployment, and with it the problem of managing redundancies, only achieved serious proportions in the 1970s after the first oil crisis. Its magnitude has continued to increase in the first few years of the present decade.

Moreover, it seems clear that the true size of the problem has not been officially recognised. Whilst this is not the proper occasion for a detailed discussion of the peculiarities of official Japanese unemployment statistics and the way they are compiled, it is necessary to note the following points. First, figures for the wholly unemployed (see Table 4.1) include only those who register as actually seeking employment at one of the Public Employment Security Offices. It is well known that a large number of people do not register. This is partly because of the traditional opprobrium which still attaches to being without work, but there are other reasons. For example, Douglas pointed out that participation of women in the labour force tends to vary inversely with the income of the head of the household (although positively with their own earning capacity).[3] This certainly caused a decline in the participation rate of women in Japan's labour force between 1960 and 1972, many of whom simply failed to register; but in recent years lower rates of growth in incomes of the heads of households have worked in the opposite direction, causing an increase in the participation of women in work. Nevertheless, the extent of a form of disguised unemployment stemming from failure to register by women and other workers must be considerable. Second, a person 'totally unemployed' by the definition of the Ministry of Labour is one who has not worked at all during any given week. Therefore, day labourers and others who obtain short-term employment for a few days or even a few hours during that week are not counted. This is a further source of a good deal of disguised unemployment,

Table 4.1: Numbers of Wholly Unemployed and Unemployment Rates, 1970–83

Year	Number of wholly unemployed	Per cent of total labour force
1970	590,000	1.1
1974	730,000	1.4
1975	1,000,000	1.9
1976	1,090,000	2.0
1977	1,100,000	2.0
1978	1,240,000	2.2
1979	1,170,000	2.1
1980	1,140,000	2.0
1981	1,260,000	2.2
1982	1,360,000	2.4
1983	1,560,000	2.6

Source: *Rōdō Undō Hakusho* (*White Paper on the Labour Movement*), Ministry of Labour, Labour Administration Bureau, Statistical Appendix, various issues.

as is the fact that new graduates from schools, colleges and universities seeking their first jobs are not counted amongst the unemployed.

Lastly, and most importantly as far as managing layoffs is concerned, the denominator used in calculating the ratio of the wholly unemployed to the working population is very broadly defined. Not only does it include those registered as actively seeking employment, but also unpaid family workers in Japan's vast small business sector, as well as the many self-employed. Although not as numerous as they once were, these latter two categories of workers totalled 1,594,000 in 1979 or over 29 per cent of all those gainfully occupied in one way or another that year. Most of these will not become unemployed even if job opportunities of the kind which concern us in our study diminish.

Factors such as these have prompted many in Japan to call for a more realistic appraisal of the true level of unemployment.[4] As we shall see later this has very important implications not only for the choice of the government's macro-economic policy, but also for measures specifically outlined for alleviating unemployment under the Employment Insurance Law.[5]

Some Key Characteristics of Japan's Employment System

It may be a helpful way to proceed if we postulate that in Japan enforced redundancies are seen as the very last resort, and then to test what concrete evidence we can adduce against this hypothesis. Accordingly, the following is a list of measures directly affecting levels and conditions of employment (i.e. other than means of cutting firms' cost which are alternatives to savings on labour costs) which are substitutes, to a greater or lesser degree, for outright dismissals. These are:

1. Cutting back on recruits not taken directly from school or university (i.e. mid-career recruits).
2. Loaning or transferring staff to affiliated or subsidiary companies (*shukkō*).
3. Regulating (reducing) overtime work.
4. Temporary shut-downs or layoffs.
5. Introducing additional non-working days each week.
6. Increasing other 'holidays'.

7. Asking for voluntary leavers (*kibō taishoku*).

However, before we go on to discuss if and how far this 'ideal' pattern departs from reality, we must first describe briefly and discuss some important characteristics of Japan's employment system.

Employment Status

For a full understanding of how redundancies have been managed in Japan it is essential to remember that the labour force is divided into two broad categories. There are regular employees (*jōyō rōdōsha*) and temporary employees (*rinji rōdōsha*). There are, however, also seasonal workers (*kisetsu rōdōsha*) and day labourers (*hiyatoi rōdōsha*). The latter have constituted on average between 3 and 3.5 per cent of employed persons (excluding the self-employed and family workers) between 1976 and 1983. Unsurprisingly, the construction industry is the major source of employment for this category of worker, employing nearly a half of them, but this category is also fairly numerous in the small-scale sector of wholesaling and retailing and in the service sector. We will return briefly to the subject later, but suffice it to say for now that there is little certainty of employment for these workers and their lot is frequently unenviable.[6]

In the compilation of employment statistics, seasonal workers

Table 4.2: Regular and Temporary Employees: Numbers and Percentages

Year	Total employees[b]	Regular employees	%	Temporary employees	%
1976	37,120,000	34,020,000	(91.6)	1,860,000	(5.0)
1977	37,690,000	34,260,000	(90.9)	2,110,000	(5.6)
1978	37,990,000	34,360,000	(90.4)	2,260,000	(5.9)
1979	38,760,000	35,050,000	(90.4)	2,360,000	(6.1)
1980	39,710,000	35,860,000	(90.3)	2,560,000	(6.4)
1981	40,370,000	36,460,000	(90.3)	2,640,000	(6.5)
1982	40,980,000	36,920,000	(90.1)	2,740,000	(6.7)
1983[a]	41,980,000	37,687,000	(89.8)	3,020,000	(7.2)

a. Figures for 1983 are averages for January to October.

b. The remaining members of the gainfully employed population are made up of the self-employed and family workers.

Source: *Nihon Tōkei Geppō* (*Monthly Statistics of Japan*), Bureau of Statistics, Office of the Prime Minister, No. 270, December 1983, p. 16.

are included in the figures for temporary workers. Table 4.2 gives an indication of the numbers of regular and temporary workers since the mid-1970s and the proportion of the employed population which they respectively constitute. It should be noted that there has been a steady upward trend in the proportion of temporary workers.[7] It may also be that official figures somewhat underestimate the proportion of temporary workers. Certainly one distinguished Japanese scholar of labour relations and the labour market, whilst agreeing that the proportion of regular workers is overwhelmingly the greater, estimates indirectly that in the early 1970s temporary workers accounted for between 19 and 20 per cent of the total.[8]

Moreover, Hanami is certainly correct when he concludes that the proportion of temporary employees is much higher in small enterprises.[9] This is of considerable significance because small firms predominate in nearly all sectors of Japanese industry to an extent that is probably not widely realised outside Japan, and in consequence they are, taken as a whole, overwhelmingly the most important employers of labour. As their title suggests, and as will be explained in more detail later, the temporary worker is more vulnerable to dismissal than the regular employee. In so far as he is found in larger numbers in the small firm sector which is largely non-unionised, he is doubly disadvantaged in that he has no organisation to which he can turn for help in the event that he wishes to contest a dismissal.[10]

Perhaps the greatest significance of this division of employed labour into two groups is that it is much easier for an employer to dismiss temporary workers than regular workers. Indeed it has been widely claimed that for a long period of time, from about 1960 to the late-1970s, dismissals as a result of redundancy were only to be found amongst temporary workers. Whilst this claim may not do too much damage to the truth in the period up to the first oil crisis of 1973, it is certainly a gross distortion thereafter.[11] However, during this period of very rapid economic growth when the demand for labour was very buoyant, the occasional need to reduce labour costs in the face of short-lived falls in the rate of growth of output and employment was met chiefly by not renewing the contracts of temporary workers. Contracts for temporary workers are generally for one or two weeks, and seldom for more than two months. They were simply not renewed when cuts in manpower were felt to be necessary, whilst at other times they were renewed for period after period. This situation could only persist as long as no major structural alteration was needed in Japanese industry, which was broadly the case in the 1960s. But even then the idea that the dismissal of temporary workers alone was used as a cushion against recession (slower growth) was only really applicable to the relatively small number of firms in the large-scale, technically-advanced sectors of industry, and was never an apt description of the more volatile, economically and financially less secure small firm sector where the distinction between temporary and regular employee was not so clear cut.

Lifetime Employment

This leads us on to the subject of the much discussed lifetime employment system which is so often treated as the cornerstone of 'Japanese-style management'. It is still a vexed question how far within Japanese industry lifetime employment extends, or indeed how well it succeeds in fulfilling the guarantee of security of employment to the worker that the words seem to contain. It developed as a practice amongst certain large firms during and after the First World War as a means of securing a source of certain labour skills which were in short supply. It appears to have spread in the period of rapid economic growth from the mid-1950s when once again there was a seller's market for many kinds of labour. However, those who blithely treat it as a 'traditional' feature of the Japanese employment system would do well to heed the following cautionary note sounded by an American observer. 'The rapid economic growth of post-war Japan clouds the issue of whether employees have permanent employment or whether employers are simply in a better position to guarantee continuous employment.'[12] Moreover, the burden of proof lies with those who claim not only that the lifetime employment system (and the feature so often associated with it — rates of remuneration of employees based chiefly on seniority) has remained largely intact in the face of structural adjustments in industry and the switch to a buyer's market for labour caused by raw material and fuel shortages and by technological change and recession, but also that these features of the employment system will aid in the process of adjustment occasioned by slower growth.[13]

It is hoped that the present study of how redundancies have been managed in the last decade will help forward this very interesting discussion, for the existence of anything resembling a formal and comprehensive guarantee of job security is bound significantly to affect firms' behaviour towards the problem of adjusting their cost structures. Indeed, if the system is as widespread as has often been suggested, wages are better analysed as a component of the fixed costs of firms. It is unnecessary — and probably impossible — to pin down exactly what proportion of the employed labour force receives a guarantee of employment for life, if indeed such it is. It goes without saying that it is a guarantee only given to regular workers. It must also be stressed that it is chiefly a feature of the employment system of large firms and far less common amongst small- and medium-sized firms. Since only roughly 30 per cent of all workers are employed in firms which are not officially classified as small- or medium-sized, it is likely that this figure represents something like the absolute upper limit to the number of employees who can possibly be given such a guarantee. In addition, since large firms also employ temporary workers it would seem more likely that the actual proportion who could in any way be described as being employed under a 'lifetime employment system' is in the range of 20 to 25 per cent of all employees.[14]

Other Characteristics

The point has already been made that Japan's economy was suddenly confronted with the need for marked change and rapid adaptation in the early 1970s. The oil crisis of late 1973 was the clear signal for this transition, and the pattern of change is best followed through what happened to rates of growth of the gross national product. After a decade of real rates of growth which averaged over 10 per cent there followed several years of zero or minimal growth in the mid-1970s. In the last years of the 1970s growth rates were in the region of 5 to 6 per cent, whilst the downward revision has continued in the early 1980s so that rates of increase in the range of 3 to 4 per cent now appear to be the best that can be expected in the short- to medium-term. This has put extreme pressure to adapt on various sectors of the national economy (for example, on government monetary and fiscal management, especially in the face of growing problems over social security and the financing of government debt), and not least on the labour market and the employment system.[15]

Practices and institutions which developed and adapted gradually in the benign climate produced by a high rate of economic growth were quite suddenly confronted with the need for rapid change. In practical terms this meant that firms had to find a way of lowering costs and raising productivity. To do so entailed, *inter alia*, lowering labour costs. In the 1960s the ability to discard temporary workers with relative ease may generally have provided firms with sufficient flexibility in this respect; but in the last decade it has become clear that much more flexibility was needed, and that to obtain it would involve changes in other, seemingly permanent features of the employment system. This was especially true since some of these features imparted to the total wage costs an element of fixity or rigidity which proved intolerable as markets at home and overseas contracted, stagnated or grew at much slower rates.

We have already dealt briefly with one of the chief of these features: namely, lifetime employment.[16] But the 'cultural' commitment to lifetime employment was considerable. Perhaps more importantly Japan's trade unions were deeply committed to its retention, and they were at their strongest amongst the large firms in industry and commerce where the practice was most widespread. Eventually the unions, faced with the choice of fighting an all-out war to try to protect the jobs of all their members or settling for a compromise which would allow them to maximise the incomes of a smaller membership, reluctantly settled for the latter course.[17] However, they naturally saw this as a last resort, and so too, it must be said, did most employers in the large firm sector of the economy. For there were other measures which could precede redundancies and still introduce some of the desired flexibility in total wage costs, especially if the outlook for future economic prospects was regarded as being optimistic and setbacks only temporary.

Some of these measures, while not amounting to redundancies as such (e.g. voluntary severances, permanent transfers to subsidiaries, etc.) are best dealt with in detail in conjunction with our description of redundancy procedures. However, it may be as well to deal with two inter-related steps often taken to reduce the degree of inflexibility in the total wage bill of firms at this juncture.

How Labour is Recruited

'Each enterprise recruits most of its regular employees in April right after graduation from high school or college.'[18] This is a widely held and frequently encountered view of the way in which Japanese firms recruit new labour. Unqualified, it gives a somewhat misleading picture; and the confusion it causes is compounded by the fact that, in discussing this and other aspects of Japan's employment system, writers like the originator of the above quotation fail to make explicit the distinction which exists (and which doubtless they make in their own minds) between the myriad of small firms and the comparatively few large firms in Japan. What follows is a brief attempt to give a more complete picture of recruitment by firms, the way the pattern has changed over the last decade or so and what the differences are in this respect between different sizes of firm.

Cutting down on the rate of recruitment, or ceasing to recruit altogether for a period of time, is obviously a substitute for enforcing redundancies, given that workers regularly leave employment through old age, ill-health and so on. In so far as new recruits do come from the ranks of school-leavers and college and university graduates, it is not a policy which can be long continued, for the average age of the workforce will rise as a result with consequent effects on receptivity to new technology amongst the workforce and so on. Its effect on reducing the total wage bill will also be partly offset as time passes so long as there is any positive correlation between wages and salaries and length of service. (I will return to this and other effects under Japan's seniority wage system in what follows.) Similarly, the total of wage costs may be reduced by replacing one kind of worker with another. For example, the proportion of women in a firm's workforce may be increased since their wages are substantially lower than those for men.[19] However, this measure too can be no more than a partial substitute for enforced redundancies, since there are many areas of work from which women are excluded in Japan (as elsewhere) for reasons of tradition, types and level of education, etc. In addition, distortions and inefficiencies in the structure of the workforce will also result.

Nevertheless, both alterations in the structure of the workforce and cut-backs in or the cessation of recruiting direct from schools and colleges have occurred in an attempt to reduce labour costs in the face of slower growth and hence obviate the necessity for redundancies.[20] Tables 4.3 and 4.4 represent an attempt, albeit partial and incomplete, to show how and to what extent this has occurred, and as such merits some comment.

It is clear from Table 4.3 that over the decade from 1970 to 1980 more than a half of new recruits taken on by firms in the sectors surveyed came from jobs in other firms. It is true that the pro-

Table 4.3: Recruitment in the Labour Force, 1970–80[a]

Year	Total of all recruits (1000 workers)[b,c,d]	Of whom those with previous job experience[e] (%)	Total recruits newly entering employment (1000 workers)	Of whom middle school graduates (%)	Of whom high school graduates (%)	Of whom college and university graduates[f] (%)	Of whom others (%)
1970	4916.6	57.1	2109.2	10.2	31.5	10.9	47.4
1974	3901.1	60.0	1561.6	6.4	32.1	16.8	44.7
1975	3361.8	55.4	1499.0	4.8	30.9	16.5	47.8
1976	3519.4	53.7	1628.5	4.3	25.8	15.8	54.0
1977	3397.9	52.1	1628.4	4.2	28.8	17.0	50.0
1978	3218.7	50.4	1595.9	3.8	28.2	17.9	50.2
1979	3689.9	49.8	1851.7	3.2	27.0	16.8	52.0
1980	3812.3	50.6	1882.9	3.5	27.2	17.9	51.3

a. The figures are based on the Employment Trends Survey conducted by the Statistics and Information Department, Ministry of Labour. The survey covers nine major industries excluding agriculture, forestry and fisheries, construction and government. They are mining, manufacturing, wholesaling, retailing, finance and insurance, real estate, transport and communications, electricity, gas, water and heat supply and services. Only establishments with five or more regular workers were surveyed.

b. New recruits and those who changed jobs.

c. The figures cover only *regular* workers. (See text for the usage of this term.)

d. The figures in no sense represent net additions to the labour force, since no account is taken here of those who left the workforce over the same period.

e. That is, job changers.

f. Colleges refer to educational institutions where the length of course is normally two years (*Tanki Daigaku*). University courses are generally of four years' duration and graduates of the latter would normally expect to advance into managerial positions.

Source: *Nihon Tōkei Nenkan (Japan Statistical Yearbook)*, 1982, Bureau of Statistics, Office of the Prime Minister, p. 70.

portion fell gradually over the decade, particularly from 1974
onwards, since workers tend to become less mobile between jobs
as economic conditions worsen. Nevertheless, inter-firm mobility
has been greater than we have often been led to believe. As for

Table 4.4: The Pattern of Recruitment by Size of Firm 1971-80
(units : per cent)

| Year | Recruits with work experience | New entrants to the labour market by educational qualification | | |
		Middle school	High school	College or university	Other
No. of workers: 5–29					
1971	64.0	2.7	6.4	2.0	24.9
1975	66.9	1.6	4.8	2.3	24.4
1976	63.4	2.0	6.0	3.8	24.8
1978	62.7	1.4	6.6	3.8	25.2
1980	59.9	2.4	7.2	4.9	25.5
No. of workers 30–99					
1971	61.4	3.3	8.8	3.4	23.0
1975	62.6	2.0	8.5	4.4	22.5
1976	59.4	1.6	8.9	5.8	24.3
1978	56.2	1.9	10.0	7.0	24.9
1980	57.9	1.7	10.0	5.1	25.3
No. of workers: 100–299					
1971	59.5	4.5	12.9	6.4	16.8
1975	57.6	2.6	15.8	6.3	17.7
1976	53.2	2.2	13.5	8.2	22.9
1978	49.1	2.3	16.2	8.6	23.8
1980	52.1	1.2	13.9	8.4	24.4
No. of workers: 300–999					
1971	50.8	5.5	17.1	8.8	17.8
1975	46.0	3.2	19.0	15.3	16.4
1976	46.1	2.4	18.0	11.5	21.9
1978	42.1	2.4	21.7	14.7	19.1
1980	41.6	1.5	18.8	15.3	22.7
No. of workers: 1000 +					
1971	37.4	5.2	23.6	9.1	24.7
1975	30.1	2.3	30.2	15.5	21.8
1976	37.2	2.3	20.0	10.6	30.0
1978	29.2	2.6	25.5	14.6	28.1
1980	35.6	1.8	22.3	13.1	27.2

Notes a, c, d and f to Table 4.3 also apply to this table. There is however a difference
in the total number of employees covered in that the figures upon which calculations
in this table are based do not include employees newly joining national or public
corporations.

Source: *Nihon Tōkei Nenkan (Japan Statistical Yearbook)*, various years, Bureau of
Statistics, Office of the Prime Minister.

new recruits to the labour force, we note firstly that those finding jobs immediately upon completion of the period of compulsory education (leaving middle school at age 16 years) have declined as a percentage, whilst those going on into high school education or beyond have increased in number. This is probably both a function of the higher level of basic educational attainment required of new employees, and the steadily tightening conditions in the labour market.

Secondly, we should note the patchy increase and, in addition, the high overall level of entrants into the labour force who are neither new school-leavers nor new graduates from colleges or the universities (the final column of Table 4.3). These are people who have never previously worked, or those for whom a substantial period of time has elapsed since they last worked. Needless to say the majority of people in this category are women.[21] Very tentatively we may conclude from this evidence that some attempt has been made both to substitute cheaper labour for dearer where possible, and that school-leaver and graduate intake has fallen to be replaced by other kinds of labour in years of particularly bad recession (notably 1976 and 1979).

Table 4.4 is an attempt to show how the pattern of recruitment has varied by size of firm over the years of stagnation, slower growth and recession of the decade up to 1980. To clear away the obvious points: first, the proportion of recruits who already have work experience (job changers) clearly declines as the size of firms increases, which tends to support the contention that larger firms resort more readily to recruiting from amongst school-leavers or college or university graduates. Second, as previously shown, those entering the workforce directly they have finished their compulsory education have declined in number, but those who still do so on the whole join very small firms. Third, the proportion of high school graduates in the intake to small firms (particularly those with under 30 employees but also those in the size categories of 100 workers or fewer, or 300 or fewer) has tended to increase over the period surveyed. This is partly a comment on the dynamic state of parts of the small-firm sector; but perhaps more a reflection of the greater reluctance to offer regular worker status/lifetime employment on the part of larger firms in the face of a more uncertain economic future.

The reason for the sharp dip in the intake of college and university graduates into medium-sized and large firms in the mid-

1970s (particularly 1976) is also fairly obvious. This was the period when larger firms were forced to adjust to changes in their cost structures due to higher raw material and fuel costs, and to turn away from their habits of recruiting and using labour in fairly profligate fashion established in the era of very rapid economic growth. A sharp drop in the intake of such people into large firms was partly reflected in a rise in the unemployment rate, and partly through a decline in their relative price, in the increase in the numbers of them who entered small- or medium-sized firms.

It is clear from Table 4.4 that the proportion of other workers (notably women) recruited into firms of all sizes has increased over the period, but most markedly in the medium-sized firm (399–999 workers) and large firm (1000+ workers). Over the same period recruits with recent job experience have tended to decline as a proportion in all but the largest size category we have been able to identify from the data. This tends to suggest that in small- and medium-sized firms they have been substituted, where possible, by other workers (women) whose wages were lower. In the largest size category of firms these workers have been substituted for high school-leavers and college or university graduates (that is, those with a fair guarantee of continuity of employment) most noticeably in years of acute recession (1976 and again in the years from 1980 onwards, though not shown in the figures presented here). The same is true of workers with immediate experience in other firms who, although commanding fairly high starting wages, were less likely to lay claim to the kind of regular employee status or automatic wage and salary increases which would render nugatory the very reason for employing them in greater numbers; namely, to introduce greater flexibility to total wage costs than would otherwise be possible.

However, although we have identified certain important changes in the pattern of recruitment to Japanese firms, it seems fair to conclude that the upheavals of the 1970s and the recession of the early-1980s have produced few radical changes in those parts of the employment system we have so far examined. It seems to have proved more resilient and flexible in the face of a changing economic environment and changed less in its basic characteristics than sceptics might have anticipated.

The Seniority Wage System

The changes in the pattern of recruitment have also had quite serious implications for the seniority wage system in Japan, to which we must now briefly turn. For example, the fact that in some years many firms reduced or ceased altogether to recruit from amongst school-leavers or those newly graduated from colleges and universities has obviously disturbed the established age structure of their workforces. As we have seen, this method of economising on labour costs was quite widely used in the mid-1970s, and is again being used extensively in the recessionary years of the present decade, as I shall show later. However, in so far as there is any positive correlation, as there undoubtedly is, between the level of wages and salaries and years of service, the increase in the average age of the workforce that this measure has tended to produce has in part tended to offset the reduction made in total wage costs to the firm.

Recognising this fact, firms have been tempted to react by calling for more workers to 'volunteer' for early retirement, whilst at the same time being under pressure to alter the age at which retirement occurs. Strictly speaking the formal retirement age was always low, being as early as 55 years in the public sector and in very many firms in the large company component of the private sector of industry. However, in the days before large reductions in the workforce became necessary, regular workers, both blue collar and white collar, were frequently re-engaged, although under different, short-term contracts with lower rates of remuneration and subject to successfully passing periodical medical checks. Therefore, in practice, retirement was often postponed well beyond the official retiring age, and the worrisome gap between the age when employment ceased and eligibility for a state pension began was bridged or at least narrowed. (The state pension scheme covering employees is paid from age 60 for men and age 55 for women.) This practice is less frequently adopted now that conditions in the labour market are tighter.

Instead pressure has been brought to bear to raise the official retirement age and thus *guarantee* security of employment until the pensionable age is reached. The labour unions have naturally pressed for this change, but pressure for it within society as a whole has also built up. This is chiefly because both the number of people and the proportion of the population in the age range affected by arrangements regarding retirement are increasing, and will increase further as the population of Japan ages at a rate unprecedented amongst advanced industrial nations. (The government, too, is not unaware of the implications this has for the cost of the social security system, and not least the cost of pensions.)

However, firms have not been willing to concede a change of this kind without compensating alterations in the seniority wage payment system. Changes would have had to have occurred in any case, since the reductions in young recruits described above have left firms with too many workers in the middle age range. For example, amongst white collar workers there has developed a surplus of personnel, generally recruited before the first oil crisis and the slow-down in economic growth, who would now have expected to have attained positions within middle management, had the favourable economic conditions of the 1960s and early-1970s continued. What was once a semi-automatic progression for regular white collar workers to middle manager status — broadly defined in ascending order as *kakari-chō* (assistant section chief), *ka-chō* (section chief) or *bu-chō* (department chief) — is now by no means guaranteed. A smaller number of personnel in this age range can now expect promotion of this kind before retirement, and therefore the rationale behind payment based mainly on seniority has also been eroded.[22]

This sort of skewness in the age structure of the workforce in many firms has added to the desire of firms to reduce the determining force of seniority in wage and salary payments caused by the extension of the retirement age described above. The exact response has varied as between firms and in different sectors of the economy, therefore what follows can only be an outline summary of the main changes that have taken place.

First, as far as age categories of personnel are concerned, whilst seniority/length of service continues to be the single most important factor in determining remuneration, strenuous attempts have been made to introduce new systems for middle-aged workers (particularly middle managers) which reduce the seniority element as far as is practicably possible. In other words, remuneration for managers is now much more often found to be task and ability oriented than was the case in the past, whilst eventual advancement to managerial rank semi-automatically is no longer so prevalent and advancement on average takes longer.

Secondly, after a certain age has been attained the cost-of-living component in the determination of wages and salaries is frequently given less emphasis than was formerly the case. For example, national data on the age range when the cost of living is at its highest suggest that in the early-1970s it was in the range 45 to 49 years, whereas data for the early-1980s indicate it to be in the 50 to 54 age range. Taking this into account, payment systems have been adapted to eradicate increments based on cost-of-living increases from the age of about 50 years onwards, depending on the firm and sector of industry.

Thirdly, salary differentials between managerial ranks have been reduced, so that promotion does not always bring with it the increase in monetary rewards that would once have been expected.[23]

These are the main ways in which the wage and salary system has been adapted so as to increase the flexibility with which firms can alter their total wage costs in the face of a deteriorating economic environment. The degree of success with which such adaptation takes place will, of course, partly determine the level of redundancies.

Our treatment has necessarily been both general and cursory, and the subject merits a more detailed study than has been attempted here.[24] Nevertheless, it is the author's opinion that the system by which wages and salaries are determined has exhibited a marked flexibility of response to the changing and often difficult economic conditions of the last decade, and that this flexibility has been largely responsible for the remarkably low level of redundancies seen in Japan. Whilst remaining unconvinced that Magota has fully established his contention that the *nenkō* (seniority-based) element has been expunged from the method of wage and salary determination in Japan, much of the evidence he has presented supports the above conclusion.

For example, the rate at which wage and salary increases have occurred has slowed in recognition of the changing age structure of the workforce. Table 4.5 shows this for the case of civil servants, but in recommending each year to the Diet to what extent the salaries of civil servants should be raised, the National Personnel Authority compares the various grades within the civil service with comparable jobs in the private sector, taking into account such things as the degrees of responsibility and difficulty and so on. Therefore the tendency revealed in the table does mirror that found in the private sector. In addition, Magota quotes data from the National Personnel Authority to show how, in large firms (over 1000 workers) in the private sector, middle managers have had to come to accept lower real rates of increase in their salaries than

Table 4.5: Civil Service Salaries after Selected Intervals as a
Multiple of Starting Salaries

Year	After 5 years	After 10 years	After 20 years
1962	1.24	1.71	3.40
1967	1.24	1.59	2.62
1972	1.20	1.50	2.31
1977	1.17	1.45	2.17

Source: R. Magota, 'The End of the Seniority-Related (Nenkō) Wage System',
Japanese Economic Studies, vol. VIII, no. 3, Spring 1979, p.72.

other categories of worker, particularly high school graduates who
would rarely aspire to reach managerial status.[25]

Collective Bargaining, Allowances and Bonuses

It is also generally accepted that these and other adjustments to the
wage and salary system have taken place within a collective bargaining context which has not, by and large, given organised labour
the upper hand. Over-simplifications are unavoidable with so little
space to deal with this question, but company-based unions and
divisions at the national level between confederations of unions
have contributed to this result. The nature of Japanese unionism
has, in the opinion of many observers, made union negotiators too
ready to accept the managements' assessment of the appropriate
annual increase in wages for firms. Weakness and political divisions at the national level have done little to counteract this seemingly inevitable feature of unions which are not craft or job based.
The result has been that in difficult years for the corporate sector,
such as the mid-1970s for example, not only did rates of wage
increases lag behind the rate of price inflation, but also behind
average rates of increase in the productivity of labour.[26]

Unlike most advanced industrial nations where wages generally
refer to base rates only, wages in Japan are often a composite of
the base rate, group incentive rates, individual efficiency rates, etc.,
on top of which are added allowances for the size of family, variation in living costs between areas, travel and housing allowances.
All of these elements are to some extent negotiable and have, in
general, responded to changes in economic conditions in the
manner described above. But in addition there are also important
fringe benefits, notably bonus payments, retirement allowances
and of course, welfare facilities.[27] In the last decade, these too have

tended to vary in size with the degree of difficulty facing Japanese corporations. Magota provides some evidence of the methods by which firms have adjusted lump sum retirement payments and the extent to which they have declined over time.[28] However, more important quantitatively in determining the degree of flexibility with which firms can vary their wage costs is what has happened to bonuses in recent years.

The bonus is paid at midsummer and again at the end of the year. It is separate from wage payments and originally (before the Second World War) it was in part paid to supplement low wages and in part as a kind of reward for achievement and loyalty. After the war these features of the system were eroded and the bonus came to be regarded as an established part of the guaranteed income of personnel. It is difficult to interpret with any exactness from the aggregate data provided by the Ministry of Labour exactly how the bonus has varied as a proportion of the basic wage.[29] Nevertheless it appears that bonuses rose steadily up to 1975 when they approached one-third of the annual basic wage. Bonuses as a proportion of the basic salary dipped quite sharply in 1976 and 1977, and thereafter have appeared to vary in relation to general business conditions.

Fortunately these tentative conclusions can be confirmed from other sources. At the end of 1982, *Nihon Keizai Shimbun (The Japan Economic Journal)*, Japan's most respected financial newspaper, conducted a survey of offers and settlements of year-end bonuses. Six hundred and ninety-three of Japan's major quoted companies were surveyed, 578 of which had reached agreement with their workforces on the size of the bonus. The weighted average increase was 2.97 per cent over the year-end bonus of 1981, which was roughly half the 5.56 per cent increase in the year-end bonus between 1980 and 1981. A similar survey conducted by the *Japan Economic Journal* in mid-1983 to which 516 firms replied reported an increase in the midsummer bonus of only 2.28 per cent. This was the lowest increase recorded since 1978.[30] Thus it is clear that with bonuses forming such a large component of total wage and salary incomes (although the proportion differs by sector and by firm size), and since they are clearly capable of being adjusted by significant amounts (cases have been recorded where a firm in particular difficulties paid no bonuses for a time), their presence in the system allows firms to vary real wage costs in accordance with current business conditions. They are accordingly a measure which is contemplated well before enforced redundancies are considered.

Recent Approaches to the Problem of Surplus Labour

Using data from a large number of firms gathered in a survey conducted by the Ministry of International Trade and Industry, we can obtain a very good idea of the range of measures adopted by firms in Japan in adjusting to the recent recession, and we can also see where measures affecting company personnel in the attempt to reduce wage costs fits into the spectrum of measures taken by firms. In addition, we can compare measures taken in 1982 and 1983 with the methods firms used to adjust their cost structures in the recession precipitated by the first oil crisis of the autumn of 1973. Even more revealingly, we are able to gain a very good idea of the ways firms have sought to adjust wage costs and the order of priority given to the different categories of measure.

Table 4.6 summarises the panoply of measures taken to reduce costs by broad category of industry. As in the mid-1970s, the proportion of firms attempting to adjust to recession by increasing managerial efficiency and reducing their selling costs is very great, whilst a smaller proportion, similar in size to the previous recession, have attempted to reduce their financial costs. The same is broadly true of stock reductions. However, fewer firms appear to have thought it necessary to reduce their stocks of assets or capital equipment or even to cut back on new investment. Indeed, a larger proportion of firms appear to be seeking a way through the recession by devoting more resources to research and development, finding new marketable products and to finding ways of saving on power and energy, even though this involves new capital investment. For example, this has involved a greater emphasis on applying the new technologies of numerical control, etc., to assembly processes, and in non-manufacturing in particular, Japan appears to be on the verge of a large-scale application of techniques of office automation.

Partly as a result of these and other lessons learned in the recession of the mid-1970s, fewer firms (with the exception of those in commerce and services) appear to feel the need to reduce their manning levels, whilst more emphasis is being placed on what is somewhat euphemistically referred to as adjusting the conditions

Table 4.6: Measures of Adjustment in Times of Recession by Category of Industry (unit: monthly average: percentage of surveyed firms carrying out or planning such measures) A = after the first oil crisis, %; B = carried out in 1982, %; C = planned for 1983, %

Industry and period	All industry			Raw material and intermediate goods producing sector (of manufacturing)			Finished goods assembling sector (of manufacturing)			Non-manufacturing)		
	A	B	C	A	B	C	A	B	C	A	B	C
Adjusting numbers employed	67.0	57.1	58.5	76.3	60.0	61.8	69.0	54.3	55.0	52.3	56.8	58.5
Adjusting conditions of employment	30.2	43.2	48.2	35.1	45.5	49.1	35.3	38.1	44.0	17.0	46.9	52.4
Restricting capital investment and investment in R & D	42.8	32.1	36.5	47.4	33.6	36.4	42.2	30.5	40.4	37.5	32.1	31.7
Selling assets	27.7	19.6	13.6	37.7	30.0	22.7	22.4	12.4	7.3	21.6	14.8	9.8
Mothballing or scrapping equipment	16.4	11.8	9.6	31.6	23.6	18.2	11.2	2.7	2.8	3.4	7.4	7.3
Separating off (from the parent firm) or reducing in size unprofitable sectors	20.1	13.9	14.0	27.1	19.1	13.6	17.2	7.6	11.0	14.8	14.8	18.3
Reducing stocks	45.9	49.6	48.8	57.0	68.2	64.5	51.7	44.8	48.6	23.9	28.4	28.0
Economising on general administrative costs and selling costs	80.2	83.4	84.1	75.4	78.2	85.5	86.2	88.6	85.3	78.4	84.0	80.5
Reducing borrowing	38.6	38.5	38.2	41.2	43.6	43.6	33.6	32.4	29.4	35.2	39.5	42.7
Increasing investment in power and energy-saving equipment	48.1	52.0	55.1	61.4	60.9	61.8	45.7	55.2	56.0	34.0	35.8	45.0
Increasing investment in R & D and developing new products	18.6	37.8	46.2	21.1	41.8	54.5	27.6	55.2	58.7	3.4	9.9	18.3
Increasing the proportion of goods and components bought in or sub-contracted out	7.5	6.8	7.6	10.5	6.4	8.2	5.2	5.7	4.6	6.8	8.6	11.0

The survey covers only firms with capital of over 100 million yen. That is to say, firms large enough to be excluded from the small- and medium-size firm category according to the official definition of such firms. All firms with capital of 10,000 million yen or over were surveyed; a sample of 360 firms was taken from firms in the size category 100 million yen to 9,990 million yen.

Source: Ministry of International Trade and Industry, *Shuyō Gyōshu Keiki Dōkō Chōsa (Survey of Business Trends in Major Sectors of Industry)*, 1983 quoted in K. Kobayashi, *'Dainiji Genryōka to Rōdō Shijo no Tenbō'* ('The Second Period of Reduction in Output and Employment and Prospects for the Labour Market'), *Keizai Hyōron*, no. 8, August 1983.

Table 4.7: Methods of Adjusting Levels of Employment by Sector, 1982 and 1983 (unit: monthly average: percentage of firms carrying out or planning such methods)

A = Carried out in 1982, %   B = Planned for 1983, %

Industry and year	All industry		Raw material and inter-mediate goods producing sector (of manufacturing)		Finished goods assembling sector (of manufacturing)		Non-manufacturing	
	A	B	A	B	A	B	A	B
Ceasing or restricting recruitment from amongst school-leavers or college and university graduates	69.0	81.7	64.6	85.1	71.9	83.3	71.7	75.0
Ceasing or restricting recruitment from amongst those changing jobs	48.8	52.0	50.8	52.2	57.9	63.3	34.8	37.5
Allowing natural wastage (not replacing retiring workers etc)	60.1	63.4	70.8	70.1	66.7	70.0	37.0	45.8
Changing or lowering the age of retirement	3.6	5.1	4.6	4.5	1.8	6.7	4.3	4.2
Ceasing or restricting recruitment of temporary or seasonal workers	24.4	29.7	27.7	34.3	40.4	46.7	—	2.1
Ceasing or restricting recruitment of vacational or part-time workers	29.2	29.1	21.5	23.9	43.9	41.7	21.7	20.8
Seconding workers to affiliated or subsidiary companies (*Shukkō*)	51.2	52.0	61.5	68.7	36.8	40.0	54.3	43.8
Laying off workers for stipulated periods	6.5	5.7	15.4	14.9	1.8	—	—	—
Asking for volunteers for early retirement	6.0	3.4	9.2	1.5	7.0	1.7	—	8.3
Enforced redundancies	0.6	0.6	1.5	—	—	1.7	—	—

Source: As for Table 4.6.

of employment (*koyō jōken chōsei*). Table 4.7 enables us to get a fairly clear idea of how firms have set about adjusting levels of employment in practice, though not of course about actual numbers of employees involved.

By far the most widespread practices are those which involve slowing down or stopping recruitment altogether of new school-leavers, new graduates and those changing jobs. This, coupled with natural wastage, appears to have borne the brunt of the adjustment in numbers employed in large firms. As a result very few firms have reported having to resort to enforced redundancies, whilst only a relatively small proportion of firms have had to seek out those willing to be persuaded (volunteer) to retire early. The degree of voluntariness in this process varies from company to company and may not always be very high. The Japanese frequently use the word *katatataki* (the tap on the shoulder) to describe what happens, a process akin to that adopted by the legendary British Army sergeant who obtains the same effect with the words: 'Right, I want three volunteers. You, you and you!' However, this is by no means the whole of the story, since companies often pay a special retirement premium which is 20 to 50 per cent higher than the normal severance allowance included in companies' work rules. Companies may also give the retiring employee considerable help with finding alternative employment. We shall return to this subject in the final section of this chapter, but it is clear that in the large firm sector at least, whilst enforced redundancies are rare, voluntary redundancies are less so, but are still regarded as coming into the category of measures of last resort.[31]

Turning now to Table 4.8 we see that by far the most widely adopted measure is to restrict the amount of overtime, which must generally be regarded as a relatively painless measure for firms, although of considerable importance to individual employees. In addition, as was argued in the previous section, the promise of continuity of employment for the regular worker in the large-scale sector of industry would seem to carry with it a *quid pro quo* which involves widespread willingness to accept at the very least reduced or nil rates of increase in the various components making up wages or salaries. Indeed, in the case of salaried officers of firms even at senior directorial level, a cut in salary may often be the precondition for restraint on the part of other employees.

Next in this section we should explain briefly the practice of

Table 4.8: Methods of Adjusting Conditions of Employment by Sector, 1982 and 1983 (unit: monthly average: percentage of firms carrying out or planning such measures)

A = Carried out in 1982, %   B = Planned for 1983, %

Industry and year	All industry		Raw material and inter- mediate goods producing sector (of manufacturing)		Finished goods assembling sector (of manufacturing)		Non- manufacturing	
	A	B	A	B	A	B	A	B
Cutting officers' remuneration	44.9	47.2	62.0	67.3	45.0	44.7	21.6	28.2
Freezing or cutting manager's salaries	28.3	35.2	36.0	44.2	35.0	38.3	10.8	23.1
Freezing or reducing automatic annual increments in wages or salaries	10.2	16.9	10.0	17.3	7.5	14.9	13.5	20.5
Reducing or freezing rises in the basic wage rate	37.8	54.2	38.0	63.5	20.0	34.0	56.8	71.8
Restricting or suspending bonuses	36.2	41.5	38.0	50.0	32.5	31.9	37.8	46.2
Restricting the amount of overtime worked	74.0	73.9	74.0	78.8	95.0	87.2	51.4	59.0
Reassigning employees within the company	44.9	49.3	48.0	55.8	47.5	59.6	37.8	33.3
Increasing the number of holidays	3.9	2.8	2.0	3.8	7.5	4.3	2.7	—

Source: As for Table 4.6.

reassigning employees within a company, and the practice of *Shukkō* or secondment to affiliated companies. (The English words transfer or loaning of personnel are also included in the meaning of the standard Japanese term *Shukkō*.) It is clear from Table 4.8 that a considerable number of firms have reassigned employees to different tasks. At the managerial level the well-known practice of training potential managers as 'generalists' (as opposed to specialists in a single area of management) has undoubtedly enabled this process to work more smoothly. However, there is much evidence to show that at the blue collar level, too, the Japanese worker, with the albeit sometimes reluctant acquiescence of his union, has been more willing to re-train or even to switch to jobs for which he is unsuited than his western counterpart. This is true not only in response to depressed market conditions, but also in cases where the introduction of new technology has rendered certain jobs unnecessary.

Shukkō or secondment is equally widespread, as is evident from Table 4.7, but somewhat more complicated. It has to be appreciated first of all that most large Japanese companies have a large number of wholly- or majority-owned subsidiary companies, or affiliated companies in which they own a considerable equity stake. In the case of large firms in manufacturing for example, a very large proportion of the component parts of a product may be produced by subsidiary firms, and not infrequently the finished product itself, to which is then attached the name of the parent company. It is this which justifies the dubbing of many of Japan's best-known firms, in consumer durables for example, assemblers (*kumitate kigyō*) or assembly makers. Such firms will also have a large number of subsidiaries who act as exclusive licensed sales outlets, both in the domestic and in foreign markets.[32]

The very widespread nature of such arrangements and the disposition of power between controller and controlled (both monopoly and monopsony power) that they entail, gives large firms considerable power to pass on to subsidiary or affiliated companies employees of all grades who become surplus to their own immediate requirements. The details of arrangements made may differ from company to company. Secondment in some cases is often tantamount to permanent transfer; the employee may remain officially on the books of the company from which he has been seconded, but the recall may never come. In other cases, the recall will come when the anticipated economic recovery materialises.[33] Rights and benefits accumulated over years of service are more often than not protected and retained by the transferee.

A point often overlooked in descriptions of this process is the effect it may have on the firm to which workers are seconded or loaned. Almost by definition, they are smaller firms and frequently the major part of their business is sub-contracting. They do not normally, except in the case of first-line sub-contractors to the very large assembly firms, have subsidiaries to whom they in turn can second or transfer personnel. Hence they must take other measures to reduce labour costs, and in general they have no choice other than to cease or cut-back recruiting, or else divest themselves of staff, whether temporary or regular employees. In so far as the proportion of regular employees is smaller in these firms the task may be administratively easier and less costly. Nevertheless, one is tempted to conclude that this process represents an unfair transfer of the burden of adjusting labour costs in time of recession, and that the price of maintaining the 'lifetime' employment system is in part borne by many firms who are not themselves a party to it.[34]

Lastly in this section, we must refer briefly to the practice of lay-offs which are temporary and generally for a fixed period (*ichiji kikyū*. According to Table 4.7 not very many firms have made use of this method of postponing the problem of over-manning, although in certain sectors of the economy, for example the cement industry, greater recourse has been made to it. During the period for which it is agreed the worker should be laid off he receives a proportion of his normal wage or salary (the average in the 1970s was said to be approximately 90 per cent); nor does he relinquish his other entitlements. It is, therefore, a relatively expensive method of reducing firms' temporary surpluses of labour, and is naturally only resorted to when economic conditions are expected to improve, and as a measure which takes chronological priority over those other measures through which longer-term structural alterations in wage costs are sought. It goes without saying that the practice disguises the true extent of underemployment, if not unemployment.

The Law, Labour Relations Commissions and Redundancies

It used widely to be thought that there was no country in the world where, in the legal sense, dismissals were more difficult to carry through than in Japan. Indeed complaints about excessive legalism in all aspects of Japanese labour–management relations are frequently encountered. Although, historically, the roots of the tradition may go deeper, the greater part of the basis of truth in the claim must surely be traceable to legislation of the early post-war period — the period of the Allied Occupation of Japan. It was then that, mainly under American influence, a series of measures were enacted to redress the balance of legislation and practice which clearly operated against labour and the labour movement in pre-war Japan.

For the individual worker and for employee-employer relationships, the basic policy is delineated in the post-war constitution, which guarantees everyone the right to minimum standards of civilised living — the right to a livelihood provision of Article 25. Article 27, section 1 declares that everyone has the right to work, as well as the obligation to do so, but this too is no more than a general declaration of intent. The Trade Union Law enacted in December 1945 formally guaranteed the right of workers to organise, engage in labour disputes and bargain collectively (although this right was soon to be withdrawn for civil servants and other public sector workers).

A clause in the Trade Union Law, similar in intent to the provisions of the Wagner Act in the United States, established in law the concept of unfair labour practices. To administer this aspect of the Law, a Central Labour Relations Commission was set up in Tokyo, together with local Commissions in each prefecture. When the Labour Relations Adjustment Law was enacted in 1946 with the intention of dealing with labour disputes, the Labour Relations Commissions were given powers to conciliate, mediate and arbitrate in labour disputes. As the years passed their decisions on the merits of cases of dismissals from employment helped establish attitudes towards dismissals (although not legal precedents) and came to have a powerful influence over the rights of employers to declare workers redundant. We shall return to this subject later in this section.

Minimum standards governing wages, working hours, safety and hygiene, the rights of women and minors, accident compensation for workers and so on were established by the third great pillar of labour legislation — the Labour Standards Law passed in 1947. This Law also contains a provision covering the rights of dismissal, and, as such, it appears to supersede Article 627 of the Civil Code covering contracts of employment, which merely states that either party to an employment contract of no fixed term may give notice of termination, which can then take place after two weeks have elapsed. Article 20 of the Labour Standards Law states that an employer must give at least 30 days prior notice of dismissal, or pay the equivalent of 30 days' wages. However, the law does allow this condition to be waived in the case of gross misconduct on the part of the employee or when the economic state of the company is such that placing any barriers in the way of dismissals would be likely to signal the demise of the company.

All this would seem to be fairly clear-cut, but of course the picture is complicated by the fact that there are different categories of worker, as we have already seen.

(a) Let us take the case of workers recruited directly from school or upon graduating from college or university. After a period of probation which may vary in length, according to the firm, from 2 weeks to as long as six months, the worker generally achieves the status of regular worker. His contract will not then stipulate that he be employed for any set period, and the general expectation was, and still largely is, that he will remain with the firm for a long period, and, in perhaps the majority of cases, until he retires. In cases, where dismissals of workers in this category occurred and were contested in law, the courts tended on the whole towards a very narrow definition of what constituted gross misconduct on the part of the worker; they were equally stringent in their interpretation of the other 'gateway' clause, especially in the case of collective dismissals. The courts had to be thoroughly satisfied that all other reasonable measures had been attempted to stave off economic disaster, and that only dismissals could enable the firm to avoid collapse, before they would sanction them. Thus it became part of Japanese industrial lore that only gross dereliction of duty or imminent bankruptcy could deprive a regular worker of his employment.

Of course, even regular workers did change their jobs. Mobility increased as the 1960s wore on and labour became short in this period of sustained and rapid economic growth. In these circumstances mid-career recruits, too, were able to attain the status of regular employees with their new companies in a large number of cases. Thus even up to the supreme court it would seem that Japanese courts have done their best to give substantive meaning to the idea of lifetime employment.

(b) However, there are, as we know, several other categories of worker. The law does not appear to define dismissal in Japan, but it has come to be interpreted to mean the termination of an employee's contract by the employer. The term does *not*, however, cover fixed-term contracts, and it is a fixed-term contract of one kind or another that temporary and seasonal workers obtain. In these cases simple non-renewal of a contract does not qualify as a dismissal, and the situation facing the employer wishing to rid himself of workers in these categories appears to be an easy one, provided he is careful as to his procedures.

This is because Article 21 of the Labour Standards Law defines the following cases as representing the equivalent of a dismissal: (i) day workers (casual workers) who have been employed by the same firm on consecutive days for a period of more than one month (30 days); (ii) workers (temporary employees) employed on two-month contracts who are still employed after two months on the same contract; (iii) seasonal workers engaged for periods of not more than four months whose employment has continued for longer; (iv) workers on probation who have been employed for more than 14 days and then dismissed. In all these cases employers have to prove to the courts, when challenged, that the same conditions apply; namely, gross misconduct on the part of the employee or imminent and dire economic danger to the firm.[35] Even if the courts are satisfied or the dismissals not contested, the employer still has to obtain permission from the Labour Standards Office.

In these circumstances it is hardly surprising that employers prefer to persuade workers voluntarily to take early retirement. However, if the employee brings an action to the effect that he was in fact dismissed because undue pressure was brought to bear upon him, in the majority of cases he is likely to get a favourable verdict from the courts.

Before discussing the work of the Labour Relations Commissions we should refer briefly to the question of work rules and dismissals and the position regarding women. Under the Labour Standards Law employers are obliged to make rules regarding such things as the time of arrival and the time of leaving work, and also regarding contract termination. They are obliged to submit these rules to the competent government agency for agreement, and to post them in the place of employment. However, they are not obliged to obtain the approval of their workers in advance, although they must consult their representatives. Therefore, the employer has a good deal of power over the determination of what might broadly be termed the conditions of employment and its termination. However, if dismissals are made for reasons which fall outside the company work rules; or if violation of these rules merits not dismissal but only suspension of some form of reprimand, then in cases of dispute the courts are most likely to rule for the employee.

Women appear to have a somewhat lower level of protection under the law as regards dismissals. Article 3 of the Labour Standards Law does not appear to prohibit discrimination by sex, although it does prohibit it by race or creed. Women are guaranteed equal payment for equal work, but it is generally accepted that there are still many cases where women are obliged to quit their employment upon marriage or upon the birth of a child. It is equally well known that women part-time workers often perform tasks equal to women full-time workers. These are social issues in which politicians and organised labour should take the lead, and it is only fair to say that the courts have always upheld appeals for reinstatement by women whose employment was terminated upon marriage. Nevertheless, it is still possible for the employer to regulate his wage bill by methods which are discriminatory as between the sexes.

The Labour Relations Commissions are tripartite commissions with an equal number of members representing labour, management and the public at large. The public representatives are appointed by the Minister of Labour in the case of the Central Commission, and by prefectural governors in other cases. The Commissions can make judgements which are binding in law, or they can pursue agreement through conciliation, arbitration and mediation. One criticism of them is that, in cases where the fairness of dismissals is at issue, they have relied too much on the latter approach and have been too concerned with reaching an agreed level of compensation, instead of pressing for reinstatement with the vigour often shown by the courts. However, it should be noted that emphasis on reaching an accommodation by 'adjusting' the positions of the parties in a dispute has a long and hallowed tradition in Japan.[36]

Lastly, it should be noted that much of the work of the Commissions, chiefly in cases of contested dismissals but also in other areas of dispute, is carried on amongst small- and medium-sized firms. This is mainly because the procedures of the Commissions are simpler and cheaper than those of the courts, and their operations in this sector of industry does something to compensate for the undeveloped state of the union movement amongst smaller firms.[37]

Government Attempts to Mitigate the Effects of Redundancies

Although there is private sector involvement in the business of placing workers in employment through companies which run employment introduction agencies (*Shokugyō Shōkui-jo*), these tend to specialise in certain areas of employment (e.g. casual work in Japan's docks). More important is the extensive network of government Public Employment Security Offices (*Kōkyō Shokugyō Antei-jo*). It is with these that workers register in order to receive unemployment benefits due to them under the Employment Insurance Law. Those offices are also charged with the task of helping the unemployed to find new jobs by providing information on vacancies, etc.

As we explained earlier, those newly entering the job market on completing their education rely on their school, college or university to help in obtaining employment for them, or on the direct recruiting activities of firms through contact with the institutions of education. Family or other personal contacts with people already employed in firms is also an important factor in placing new entrants to the labour force. For these reasons the Employment Security Offices deal only with those workers who have become unemployed for whatever reason (of which middle-aged and elderly workers have come to form an increasingly large proportion), or with temporary or seasonal workers, or with those wishing to re-enter employment after a lapse of time (married women form a very substantial proportion of those in this category).

The Employment Security Offices were hard pressed to cope with the extent of unemployment in the recession of the mid-1970s, and have again become hard pressed in the early 1980s. Active or outstanding applications for jobs from amongst regular, temporary and seasonal workers have risen steadily since 1974 (with the exception of 1979 and 1980), whilst the same pattern is seen in new additions to applications from the above categories of workers, with only 1978 and 1979 providing a pause in the steadily upward movement in the numbers. Another worrying feature has been the unbroken rise in the number of outstanding applications and new applications from middle-aged and elderly workers. Table 4.9 gives an indication of the magnitude of the problem, and from it we can also infer that the chances of finding employment are declining, particularly for middle-aged and elderly workers.

These trends have prompted the government to take a number

Table 4.9: Trends in the Main Activities of the Public Employment Security Offices (Unit: 1000, monthly averages, per cent)

Year	Outstanding applications	New applications	Ratio of placements to outstanding applications (%)[b]	Outstanding applications from middle-aged and elderly workers (45 years and over)	New applications	Ratio of placements to outstanding applications (%)
1975	1553	343	–	584	94	5.0
1980	1531	373	7.9	630	121	6.3
1981	1661	394	7.1	695	128	5.5
1982	1744	401	6.6	738	129	4.7
1983[a]	1821	415	6.7	786	129	4.8

a. Figures for 1983 are the average for the first 10 months only.

b. The figures in column 4 give a somewhat exaggerated picture of the success the offices have in placing workers in jobs. This is because no distinction is made between temporary workers and seasonal workers on the one hand, and regular workers who have become unemployed on the other. Whilst as a proportion of outstanding applications those from the former category form only approximately 15 per cent of the total, the ratio of placements for these workers is as high as 20 per cent or more, for obvious reasons. A corollary of this is, of course, that those not seeking seasonal employment, and those who have become unemployed after having held the status of regular employees, will on the average have to wait longer for a new appointment and have a smaller chance of obtaining one than these figures indicate.

Source: Calculated from *Nihon Tōkei Nenkan* (*Japan Statistical Yearbook*), 1983, Bureau of Statistics, Office of the Prime Minister, p. 74, and *Nihon Tōkei Geppō* (*Monthly Statistics of Japan*), Bureau of Statistics, Office of the Prime Minister, No. 270, December 1983.

of additional measures to try and cope with the increasing level of redundancies. The tendency has been to introduce specific pieces of legislation to help specified industries which are considered to be suffering particularly severely from fluctuations in economic activity but where the supposition is that recovery will eventually come. The aid comes in the form of grants to companies who continue to pay the wages of staff who are temporarily laid off (*ichiji kikyū*), and help in paying the wages of staff who are 'seconded' or 'loaned' to subsidiaries or elsewhere. Under the employment adjustment scheme so introduced, up to one half of the wages of employees laid off are paid for a period of up to 75 days. In smaller firms (fewer than 300 employees) the proportion may reach two-thirds. Under the Law Relating to Manpower Organisation, employers in industries designated as belonging in the category entitled to receive this help have to report reductions in their workforces to Public Employment Security Offices, and the help they receive is channelled through these offices.

Similar measures have been taken in the case of industries where the problem is seen as structural rather than temporary, so that something far short of complete recovery is expected. (Examples are textiles and chemical fibres, and shipbuilding.) In these cases, firms are not only eligible for the same degree of help with temporary layoffs and transfers, but are also entitled to government help to scrap excess capital equipment. In addition, firms designated as belonging in industries of this category who intend to dismiss 30 or more employees (excluding those retiring at or beyond the retirement age fixed in the firm's work rules, but including those who retire voluntarily) must draw up a re-employment assistance plan and submit it to a Public Employment Security Office for approval. The same applies to firms 'seconding' (*Shukkō*) 100 or more workers. Those who are actually dismissed then receive from the Office a job-seeker's notebook which entitles them to special assistance. This assistance is in addition to ordinary unemployment insurance benefits and takes the form of travel and subsistence allowances where the worker has to live away from home in order to undergo officially sponsored programmes of re-training. In addition, workers dismissed from specified depressed industries have become eligible for assistance with transport and subsistence costs when seeking work in another area. So too do certain other workers referred to the Employment Security Offices under the Employment Insurance Law.

At roughly the same period the government realised that there was a close relationship between industries which were fundamentally ailing, and geographical areas with particularly marked employment problems. (Shipbuilding and textiles, for example, tend to be geographically concentrated and figure very prominently in local economies.) Consequently, these measures of assistance to the unemployed were extended so that workers dismissed from any industry in designated geographical areas became eligible to receive them.[38]

The numbers of workers covered by these various measures has, of course, varied with the severity of the recession, but at times numbers affected have been large, and consequently the system has become very costly.[39] A part of the cost is borne by the Employment Insurance System which was revised in 1975 in part in recognition of the increasing severity of the problem. The employment insurance premium, out of which unemployment benefits are paid, now amounts to five-thousandths of the employees' remuneration, while the equivalent of eight-thousandths is paid by the employer (the proportions were equal before 1975 at five-thousandths by each party). At the same time a further premium which is the equivalent of three-thousandths of the firm's total payroll is paid by the firm under the Employment Insurance Law. This money is used to finance the schemes described above, which are intended to help firms in difficulties and employees who are made redundant. However, the amount collected in this fashion has been insufficient to cover the full cost, and the government has had to provide supplementary funds on a large scale. Moreover, if the rate of unemployed (as defined earlier) were to exceed four per cent, the government is committed under the Employment Insurance Law to raise rates of unemployment benefit, so increasing the already considerable costs of unemployment.

Conclusion

Broadly speaking the problem of redundancies and the management of them did not assume major importance until about 1974. Before that sufficient flexibility in the labour market was ensured by the presence of certain categories of workers who were, in some senses, not part of the mainstream (seasonal and temporary workers), and whose origins were to be found amongst those whose educational attainment was below average, or who were in some other way 'under-privileged'. These persons were to be found in disproportionately large numbers in the small and very small firm sectors of industry.

This generalisation does not hold for the recession of the mid-1970s, nor for the early 1980s. Whilst lifetime employment may have been secured (although one must be careful when defining the term), it has become increasingly clear that it is the privilege of a small and favoured elite whose numerical importance as a proportion of the workforce is probably diminishing. Moreover, it has not been sustained without considerable adjustments in the system of payments and promotion which were once regarded as being almost equally as 'traditional' and sacrosanct as lifetime employment.

Now the risk of unemployment (even long-term unemployment) has spread much further throughout the Japanese workforce, even though Japanese firms have evolved a system of graded steps for reducing labour costs which enables them to stop short of dismissing workers in all but the most stringent of circumstances. The law and the government have in their several ways prodded and encouraged firms to follow this pattern. One is left with the impression that, so far, the problem has been well-managed by international standards; but that, without a change of heart in Japan and other countries towards the macro-economic management of economies, the costs of unemployment at the personal level for firms and for the government can only increase.

Notes

1. From the mid-1950s until the late 1970s crude rate of increase averaged around 1.1–1.2 per annum. Since then it has dropped below 1 per cent per annum to a level of around 0.7 per cent per annum and the rapid ageing of the population will undoubtedly prove one of Japan's major economic and social problems in the coming decades. Figures calculated from: *Nihon Tokei Nenkan* (*Japan Statistical Yearbook*), Bureau of Statistics, Office of the Prime Minister, 1983, pp. 14-15.

2. In 1970, the secondary sector (mining, construction and manufacturing) employed 35.2 per cent of Japan's nearly 51 million workers, whilst the tertiary sector (wholesaling and retailing, finance, the public utilities, services and government) employed 47.3 per cent. In 1981 the proportions were 34.7 per cent and 51.6 per cent respectively. Figures calculated from: *Nihon Tokei Nenkan* (*Japan Statistical Yearbook*), 1983, p. 61.

3. Paul H. Douglas, *The Theory of Wages* (Macmillan, New York, 1934).

4. For example, A. Mizuno, *Chingin Kozo Hendo Ron (The Changing Structure of Wages)* (Tokyo, Shin Hyoronsha, 1973), who would have raised the then official unemployment rate from 1.4 to 1.96 per cent. A crude allowance of the same kind for the present time would put the unemployment rate in the range of 3 to 4 per cent, or perhaps as many as 2.25 million people.

5. The sensitivity of female workers to changes in labour market conditions, and the appropriateness of official measures of unemployment in Japan, are discussed by S. Nishikawa and H. Shimada in S. Nishikawa (ed.), *The Labor Market in Japan: Selected Readings* (University of Tokyo Press, 1980), pp. 128-41.

6. Figures are calculated from *Nihon Tokei Geppo (Monthly Statistics of Japan)*, Bureau of Statistics, the Prime Minister's Office, no. 270, December 1983, p. 16; and from *Nihon Tokei Nenkan (Japan Statistical Yearbook)*, 1983, p. 65.

7. Moreover the trend seems of even longer duration. The proportions for 1968 and 1971 are both under 5.0 per cent, as calculated from figures given in *Nihon Tokei Nenkan (Japan Statistical Yearbook)*, 1982, although it must be admitted that where years overlap figures differ slightly from those given in the source cited in note 6 above, despite the fact that both sets of figures emanate from the Bureau of Statistics of the Office of the Prime Minister, and ultimately from surveys carried out by the Ministry of Labour.

8. T. Hanami, *Labor Relations in Japan Today* (Kodansha International Ltd., Tokyo, 1979), p. 25.

9. Ibid., p. 25.

10. For a detailed description of the importance and the role of small firms in the Japanese economy, see D. Anthony, Chapter 4, 'Japan' in D.J. Storey (ed.), *The Small Firm: An International Survey* (Croom Helm, London, 1983), especially pages 46-63.

11. See, for example, V.T.J. Schenk, 'Redundancy and Redeployment in the Synthetic Fibre Industry 1973–1979', a Master's thesis presented to the University of Sheffield, Centre of Japanese Studies, December 1980.

12. R.E. Cole, *Japanese Blue Collar* (Los Angeles, 1971), p. 114.

13. See, for example, T. Inagami, *Japan Labor Bulletin*, 1st April 1976, p. 16.

14. Under the Basic Law Relating to Small- and Medium-sized Firms, small-and medium-sized firms are defined as those employing fewer than 300 workers. There are, however, variations in the definition for different sectors of the economy. For a discussion of this and for figures on the proportion of workers employed in small- and medium-sized firms see D. Anthony, 'Japan', pp. 46-8 and pp. 51-7.

15. Those interested in Japan's financial problems might like to consult D. Anthony, 'Japanese Fiscal and Financial Problems' in R. Shiratori (ed.), *Japan in the 1980s* (Kodansha International Ltd., Tokyo, 1982), pp. 147-64.

16. A brief and simple description of lifetime employment and its accompanying features, such as lifetime welfare may be found in T. Hanami, *Labor Relations in Japan Today*, pp. 25-35.

17. For a detailed account of the union response to the need to reduce labour costs in a major firm in dire economic peril, see R. Pascale and T.P. Rohlen, 'The Mazda Turnaround', *The Journal of Japanese Studies*, vol. 9, no. 2, Summer 1983, pp. 219-63. This article is also illuminating on other aspects of the management of redundancies in this single firm, Toyo Kogvo (the makers of Mazda cars).

Union membership as a whole has naturally suffered over the last decade. The number of union members fell from 12,590,000 in 1975 to 12,471,000 in 1981, whilst the percentage of all workers belonging to a union has fallen steadily from 35.4 per cent in 1971 to 30.8 per cent in 1981. The equivalent proportions for the United Kingdom, West Germany and the United States in 1981 were 59.4, 41.5 and 23.6 per cent respectively. The decline in membership in Japan still continues and the figure is now below 30 per cent. Source: Ministry of Labour, *Labour Statistics Handbook, 1982.*

18. T. Hanami, *Labor Relations in Japan Today*, p. 25.

19. For example, the average monthly payments to regular male workers in five electrical and electronics manufacturers as of March 31st 1983 was ¥270,360, ranging from the highest (Mitsubishi Electrical Corporation) with ¥292,484, to the lowest (Sharp Corporation) with ¥245,562. (The five firms were Mitsubishi Electrical Corporation, Toshiba Corporation, Hitachi Ltd., Sharp Corporation and The General Corporation.) The average wage for female workers per month in these companies was ¥135,883, ranging from the highest of ¥147,200 (Toshiba Corporation) to the lowest of ¥115,501 (The General Corporation). Thus female workers on average received 50.3 per cent of the payments made to male workers. Of course, this does not take into account such things as length of service (males on average had worked 7.75 years longer) and average age (males were older by 9.75 years on average) as well as qualifications. Nevertheless, in so far as substitution by females for males was possible, there were probably substantial savings to be made in the total wages bill. There is no reason to suppose that the experience of these firms is a typical of firms in many sectors of manufacturing/assembly industries. Figures are from *Yuka Shoken Hokokusho* (*Financial Reports of Quoted Companies to the Ministry of Finance*), covering the financial year April 1st 1982 to March 31st 1983.

20. For example, in the autumn of 1982 it was announced by several of Japan's largest firms in the iron and steel industry, where large numbers of school-leavers used customarily to be taken on each spring, that fewer or no graduates would be taken on in the spring of 1983. For example, Nippon Kokan — no male high school graduates to be taken on; Kawasaki Steel and Sumitomo Metal Industries — to reduce recruits to less than one-third of those taken on in April 1982. Similar announcements came from various shipbuilding and heavy machinery companies. See Japan Institute of Labour, *Japan Labor Bulletin*, vol. 21, no. 10, October 1982. In September 1983 it was announced that the five major steel producers in Japan would take on no regular blue collar workers from amongst high school graduates in the spring of 1984, and the intake of male college/university graduates would be cut by ten per cent. See *Japan Labor Bulletin*, vol. 22, no. 9, September 1983. In July of 1983 Japan National Railways announced it would discard more than the 22,600 workers lost in the previous year, while at the same time it would take on no new recruits, a move which would have a serious effect on employment opportunities for high school graduates. In 'normal' years the recruitment level would be in the range of 12,000–15,000 workers. See *Japan Labor Bulletin*, vol. 22, no. 7, July 1983.

21. In the Japan Institute of Labour, *Japan Labor Bulletin*, vol. 22, no. 9, September 1983, p. 2, it was reported that a survey conducted by the Prime Minister's Office showed that for the first time since 1956 over a half of wives in Japan (50.8 per cent), measured by normal status over the course of the year, participated in the labour force, and that this confirmed the already known fact that women's participation in the labour force was steadily increasing.

22. In fact the wage and salary system in Japan has not been as static and uniform as it is sometimes portrayed. Whilst it is true that until the mid-1970s seniority was by far the most important factor in determining remuneration, the determining forces of ability and achievement were never absent and had grown in importance even in the 1960s. For a discussion of these changes and for further references see: M. Oda, 'Compensation and Promotion: the Plight of Middle Managers', *Bulletin* of Sophia University Institute of Comparative Culture, Business Series No. 95, Tokyo, 1983.

23. The above summary of changes in the system of determining payment to

personnel owes much to M. Oda, 'Compensation and Promotion'. His work is particularly valuable in that he summarises case studies of specific changes negotiated in some well-known Japanese companies which are not otherwise accessible to those who do not read Japanese. In addition, his work contains a discussion of how the concept of specialists of one kind or another has been introduced into Japanese firms to try to provide status and incentive to those who cannot expect advancement to more traditional managerial level positions, and how it has been adapted to Japanese conditions.

24. Those wishing to pursue the subject further are recommended to see Y. Sano, 'Seniority-based Wages in Japan — A Survey', *Japanese Economic Studies*, vol. V, no. 3, Spring 1977; and R. Magota, 'The End of the Seniority-Related (*Nenko*) Wage System', *Japanese Economic Studies*, vol. VII, no. 3, Spring 1979. As the title of his article suggests, Magota takes what many would regard as an extreme position, stating at one point that: '... it is already possible to assert not that "*nenko* wages are vanishing" but that they have already vanished.' Nevertheless he makes out a powerful case for his position, and demontrates that the cost of introducing flexibility into the total wage costs of firms has fallen chiefly on the middle-aged and the elderly worker. Both groups have been more prone to become unemployed than other age groups in the workforce, and both groups have had to accept either lower and more widely spaced increments in their salaries, or more serious cuts than was customary in the past.

25. Ibid., pp. 74-5.

26. Those interested in Japan's singular system of collective bargaining are recommended to see T. Shirai, 'Collective Bargaining', Chapter 8 in K. Okochi, B. Karsh and S.B. Levine (eds.), *Workers and Employers in Japan* (Princeton University Press, 1974); and T. Hanami, Chapter 4, 'Enterprise Unionism and the National Setting', *Labor Relations in Japan Today*, pp. 88-113. For the determination of salaries see: Robert J. Ballon, 'Salaries in Japan: the System', *Bulletin* of Sophia University Institute of Comparative Culture, Business Series No. 93, Tokyo, 1982.

27. For a full, though by now slightly dated description of the system as a whole, see: N. Funahashi, 'The Industrial Reward System: Wages and Benefits', Chapter 10 in Okochi, Karsh and Levine (eds.), *Workers and Employers in Japan*. A detailed analysis of the *nenko* system and other features of personnel administration is contained in M. Tsuda, 'Personnel Administration at the Industrial Plant Level', Chapter 11 in Okochi, Karsh and Levine (eds.), *Workers and Employers in Japan*. Details of the way the bonus is determined are also contained in Robert J. Ballon, 'Japan's Salary System: the Bonus', *Bulletin* of Sophia University Institute of Comparative Culture, Business Series No. 57, Tokyo, 1977.

28. R. Magota, 'The End of the Seniority-related (*Nenko*) Wage System', pp. 97-101.

29. This is chiefly because figures are only given for 'special annual payments' which include other allowances besides the twice yearly bonus. In addition, there is some confusion about what constitutes the basic wage. However, the calculations reported in the main text follow the same pattern whether basic annual wages are calculated from average monthly contract cash earnings, which contain allowances, or 'prescribed' or 'regular' (*shoteinai no kyuyo*) wages. Nevertheless the conclusions drawn must be regarded as somewhat tentative although the general pattern is clear. Source: *Basic Statistical Survey of the Structure of Wages (Chingin Kozo Kihon Tokei Chosa)*, as reported in *Japan Statistical Yearbook (Nihon Tokei Nenkan)*, 1983, Bureau of Statistics, Office of the Prime Minister, pp. 432-3.

30. Source: *Japan Labor Bulletin*, vol. 22, no. 2, February 1983, and vol. 22, no. 8, August 1983.

31. The Japanese use the English words 'hard' and 'soft' to describe measures taken to make adjustments in wage costs. None of the measures in Table 4.8 is 'hard', whilst only those indicated in the last three, or possibly four, columns of Table 4.7 would generally be regarded as belonging in the 'hard' category.

32. This is a feature of the way oligopolistic competition has developed in large sections of Japanese industry. To take the electrical machinery, electrical appliance and electronics industry as an example, Mitsubishi Electric Corporation listed 22 consolidated subsidiaries and a further 78 unconsolidated subsidiaries. For Toshiba Corporation the figures were 32 and 400 respectively. For Hitachi Limited, the figures were 45 and 384. A similar pattern will be found in the automobile industry and elsewhere; and, in the non-assembly sector of manufacturing, vertical integration is frequently accompanied by a pattern of equity ownership which results in subsidiary or affiliate status for the majority of firms. Source: *Yuka Shoken Hokokusho (Financial Reports of Quoted Companies)*, Ministry of Finance, various companies, 1983.

33. For a detailed analysis of the process as it operated before the recession became general from 1974 onwards, see H. Inohara, '*Shukko*: Loan of Personnel in Japanese Industry', *Bulletin*, Sophia University Institute of Comparative Culture, Tokyo, 1972. For an analysis of the practice in the textile and chemical fibre industries where *shukko* was first utilised widely, see V.T.J. Schenk, 'Redundancy and Redeployment'. Pascale and Roehlen's description of how Toyo Kogyo, the makers of Mazda cars, used the system is particularly detailed. Workers not needed for production work were transferred in large numbers to subsidiaries (dealers) to act as car salesmen. Although in part paid by the firm to whom they were transferred, Toyo Kogyo continued to pay a proportion of their wages, as well as bonuses and fringe benefits. Workers would be recalled after a fixed tour of duty and lose none of their seniority. Pascale and Roehlen, 'The Natda Turnaround', pp. 239-42.

34. There are other ways in which the burden of adjusting to recessionary conditions is passed from larger to smaller firms (the term frequently used in Japan is *shiwayose*), such as delaying payments to sub-contractors, raising the price of materials sent to sub-contractors, etc. For more details of this see D. Anthony, 'Japan', pp. 63-72.

35. However, there are recorded instances where a court has ruled that the right to dismiss has been abused by the employer, and thus that the dismissal was illegal, even in cases which do not seem to fall into the above category. For examples see T. Fukui, 'Labor–Management Relations and the Law in Japan: III Dismissal', *Bulletin*, Sophia University Institute of Comparative Culture, Tokyo, 1973.

36. It should be noted that only the public representatives on the Commissions can reach decisions, and that it is not infrequently the case that the task is left to the chairman, who is often very experienced in the matters at issue.

37. For a more thorough discussion of Labour Relations Commissions, readers are recommended to see T. Ariizumi, 'The Legal Framework: Past and Present', Chapter 4 in Okochi, Karsh and Levine (eds.), *Workers and Employers in Japan.*

38. The amount paid can vary with age, geographical area and the industry from which the worker was dismissed. However, persons under 30 will normally receive this assistance for a maximum of 90 days, whilst those over 55 may qualify for assistance for 300 days.

39. For example, on 1 August, 1979, the number of workers in firms designated as eligible for assistance under (i) above was over $3\frac{1}{2}$ million, whilst those in firms eligible under (ii) was over $2\frac{1}{2}$ million. See V.T.J. Schenk, 'Redundancy and Redeployment', p. 37.

5 AUSTRALIA

Vic Taylor and Di Yerbury

Introduction

Any understanding of current redundancy[1] practices in Australia involves two key related considerations. First, attention must be given to labour market developments in the post-war period, and more particularly over the past decade. Such developments generate pressures among ranks of workers fearful of retrenchment, though how far these pressures grow depends upon policies already in operation and the severity of social and economic impacts. Secondly, account must be taken of institutional and political arrangements which exist to mediate such pressures. This entails a grasp of the Federal framework of government and the industrial relations system and, in particular, some knowledge of how arbitration tribunals deal with redundancy disputes. It is also important to bear in mind the high union density with 57 per cent of wage and salary earners organised in 322 unions at the end of 1982.[2]

The second section of this chapter analyses trends in the labour market, while the third part comprises an overview of the legal framework for managing private sector redundancies, noting in particular Australia's failure to conform with international standards, the meagre protection offered by legislation and approaches adopted by way of award standards in the Federal and New South Wales (NSW) jurisdictions. In the fourth section, we outline the formal policies on technological change adopted by the major national, tripartite consultative committee and survey actual practices and programmes. Given its significance in Australia, employing over a quarter of wage and salary earners, it is appropriate to consider also how public sector redundancies are managed: the fifth section uses Commonwealth and NSW employment as examples.

Labour Market Developments

Recession and Structural Changes

By most criteria the operation of Australian labour markets in the first two-and-a-half post-war decades was unlikely to provoke much interest in redundancy provisions. The rate of unemployment was thought to range between 1.0 and 1.5 per cent and only occasional years saw unemployment climb higher. Retrenched workers, by and large, soon found other jobs, often at better pay, and rarely appeared to show much concern for loss of accrued benefits related to length of service.

The past decade or so has seen labour market characteristics change dramatically, with pressures for redundancy protection intensifying. Two changes dominate this recent period. The first is the significant decline in growth of aggregate demand, and hence for labour power, which took place from around the middle of the decade and is yet to show persistent signs of reversal; the second is the marked degree of structural change in patterns of industrial employment which had become evident some time before the onset of recession, but was clearly compounded by the savage competitive economic climate ushered in by world-wide downturn. The end result has been a sudden upward shift in the number of redundancies as employers in vulnerable industries have progressively exhausted other less drastic forms of labour adjustment in an effort to sustain acceptable levels of profitability.

Even with the relatively bleak economic climate prevailing in the later 1970s, however, unions, industrial tribunals, and governments felt only spasmodic pressures to fashion general protective measures. From the beginning of the 1980s this situation has changed rapidly, with increasing numbers of primary labour market male workers having to contemplate the prospect of extended periods of unemployment in an extremely slack and changing labour market. The leeway provided by secondary workers, and would-be new entrants to the labour force, has been exhausted in many sectors, with the result that recently the pool of unemployment has been swollen by an influx of older male workers.

Both these developments are evident in Tables 5.1 and 5.2. Table 5.1 shows that in the five years November 1977–82, employment growth amounted to a mere 6 per cent, with much of this occurring among those working less than the standard full-time week. Full-time jobs lost through redundancies and attrition

Table 5.1: Distribution of Employment by Industry

Industry	Employed persons November 1982		Movement in employment November 1977 to November 1982
	'000	Share %	%
Agriculture and agricultural services	397.3	6.3	+7
Forestry, fishing and hunting	23.8	0.4	a
Mining	92.4	1.4	a
Manufacturing	1,1162.3	18.3	−7
Electricity, gas and water	145.2	2.3	a
Construction	439.6	6.9	−9
Wholesale and retail trade	1,276.2	20.1	+7
Transport and storage	364.1	5.7	+10
Communication	132.7	2.1	a
Finance, property and business services	563.9	8.9	+22
Public administration and defence	295.2	4.6	+7
Community services	1,047.0	16.5	+14
Recreational, personal and other services	410.7	6.5	+9
Total	6,350.7	100.0	+6

a. Indicates that sampling error is too high to provide reliable estimates.

Source: Australian Bureau of Statistics, Labour Force Surveys, Reference Nos. 6203 and 6202.

in manufacturing and construction have been replaced by part-time jobs in industries such as wholesale and retail trades, finance, community and recreational services. It is indicative of these trends that in terms of absolute numbers employed, wholesale and retail trades now exceed the once dominant manufacturing sector, while the rapidly growing services industry is poised to overtake both in the near future, should current trends continue.

Experience within manufacturing has varied considerably as Table 5.2 illustrates. Comparing annual average employment for 1973–7 with that for 1978–82, four industries shed jobs at a rate significantly greater than the sector as a whole. Food, beverages and tobacco, clothing and footwear, together with transport equipment (which includes motor vehicles and parts, shipbuilding and repair, and railway rolling stock) all experienced labour displacement in excess of the 7–8 per cent realised across all manufacturing industries. Those industries appearing to do relatively better included wood and wood products, paper and printing, chemical, petroleum and coal products, basic and fabricated metal products. More recent reports now indicate that these latter two industries have experienced a severe shakeout from late 1982.[3]

What these data do not clearly show, however, is that many industries experiencing the worst of this phase of the recession are those with a high proportion of male manual workers, high union density and militant traditions. As a result, job security issues have been thrust to centre stage, with particular redundancy situations

Table 5.2: Distribution of Manufacturing Employment

Manufacturing industry (two digit categories)	Employed persons November 1982		Estimated movement in employment, average 1973/77 to average 1977/82
	'000	%	
Food, beverages and tobacco	188.1	16.2	Fall of 15%
Textiles	35.1	3.0	Fall of 20%
Clothing and footwear	76.5	6.6	Fall of 16%
Wood, wood products and furniture	89.4	7.7	Steady
Paper and printing	111.8	9.6	Steady
Chemical, petroleum and coal products	64.8	5.6	Slight decline
Non-metallic mineral products	52.1	4.5	Fall of 9-10%
Basic metal products	91.9	7.9	Steady (significant reductions reported during 1983)
Fabricated metal products	110.8	9.5	Steady
Transport equipment	126.1	10.8	Fall of 11-15%
Other machinery and equipment	148.6	12.8	Fall of 8%
Miscellaneous manufacturing	67.1	5.8	Slight decline
Total	1162.3	100.0	Fall of 7-8%

Source: *Employment Prospects by Industry and Occupation. A Labour Market Analysis*, Department of Employment and Industrial Relations, July 1983.

attracting considerable media attention.[4] Recent figures suggest that job losses peak towards the end of 1982 when, in November and December, employment fell by 92,000 with 85 per cent of workers affected being males.[5] For many, the usual summer vacation was to become the start of an extended period of anguish and despair as members of the rapidly growing corps of long-term unemployed.

Extent of Redundancy

Despite the apparent magnitude of redundancies implied by labour market developments, there are no reliable data as to actual number, nor where they occur industrially, or regionally. Probably the best indication is derived from the official estimates of labour mobility made each February as part of the periodic Labour Force Survey. In that month, respondents who left jobs in the previous twelve months are asked to provide reasons for leaving. Two response categories are relevant here — business closures and lay-offs. Although far from ideal measures of redundancies, the figures seem to be the best available proxies.

As Table 5.3 illustrates, over the year February 1981–2 an estimated total of 315,200 people were retrenched, either because operations ceased, or because of insufficient work.[6] At the time of the survey (February 1982) the male unemployment rate was 5.8 per cent with an average spell of 31.6 weeks, while for females the respective figures were 9.1 per cent and 25.1 weeks. The data show that almost half of those retrenched were married and slightly fewer were aged between 15 and 24. There seems a fairly pronounced tendency for younger employees to experience redundancy, underlining arguments that 'last in — first out' rules are common in unionised labour markets experiencing recession.

The most conspicuous feature of Table 5.3 is the marked difference between the employment status of retrenched males and females at the end of this period. In male ranks, while just on 60 per cent had managed to gain employment, nearly a third remained unemployed, and fewer than 10 per cent had left the labour force. Among females the position was quite different. Fewer than 40 per cent were re-employed, and nearly the same proportion as their male counterparts remained unemployed. However, fully one-third of the female group had left the labour force, suggesting a strong discouragement effect. Certainly the ineligibility of dependent females for unemployment benefits, and

Table 5.3: Selected Characteristics and Employment Status of Persons Retrenched in Australia, February 1981 to February 1982

	Number	Married	Aged 15-24	Employed end February 1982	Unemployed end February 1982	Not in labour force end February 1982
	'000	%	%	%	%	%
Males	192.3	47.8	44.1	59.6	31.9	8.5
Females	122.9	47.6	48.7	39.4	27.1	33.5
Persons	315.2	47.7	45.9	51.7	30.0	18.2

Source: Australian Bureau of Statistics, *Labour Mobility, February 1981 to February 1982*, Catalogue No. 6209.

the associated need to comply with work-test requirements, would inevitably lead to job search strategies varying considerably from those required of males drawing benefits. But there is probably much more to the different experiences. In particular, it would be useful to have data available on specific procedures adopted in redundancy situations to assist employees to locate new positions, and on recruitment criteria adopted in recession, according to gender.

The Legal and Institutional Framework in the Private Sector

The Constitutional Duality of Powers

The Constitution provides for a duality of powers, both Commonwealth and states having capacity to deal with industrial relations and employment. While the legislative powers of the states are largely unconstrained, the powers of the Commonwealth are strictly limited: it cannot act except under a specific head of power in the constitution.

The most relevant power for the private sector is s. 51 (xxxv), which enables it to make laws in relation to 'conciliation and arbitration for the prevention and settlement of industrial disputes extending beyond the limits of any one state'. An important constraint in this placitum, on which the Australian Conciliation and Arbitration Commission (ACAC) is based, is its limiting effect on both subject matter and processes. Unlike the states, the Commonwealth cannot legislate directly on industrial relations, unless it can find a basis under some other power.

One significant such power is s. 52, whereby the Commonwealth can legislate concerning its own employees (as discussed later in this chapter). Section 122 of the Constitution provides power to 'make laws for the government of any territory ...'; and Federal Parliament could also use s. 51 (i), concerning 'Trade and commerce with other countries, and among the states' to support action covering areas such as the airlines and waterfront. Moreover, expansionist decisions of the High Court render it increasingly probable that the Commonwealth could use the 'corporations' power, s. 51 (xx), to regulate conditions of employment in corporations. As discussed below, the High Court would also seem to have opened up the potential of the 'external affairs' power, s. 51 (xxix).

Again, the Commonwealth may make conditional grants to the states to fund welfare programmes beyond its own competence. It can also provide for unemployment benefits (which remain the most significant form of income support for those losing employment) under the 'social security' power, s. 51 (xxiiiA), which would also support — although governments have chosen not to introduce it in the private sector[7] — an income maintenance scheme for retrenched workers as long as they remained unemployed.[8]

Australia's Failure to Meet International Standards

Although the constitutional constraints are no longer as daunting as was once thought, the Commonwealth has not resorted to positive law on employment security in the private sector. The Federal platform of the Australian Labor Party (ALP), which sets out policies committing the Hawke Government (elected in March 1983), provides in Article 20 for the right of employees, through unions, to be notified and consulted about proposed changes in work methods and organisation, including technological change. Article 23 provides for the 'establishment of standards and unions in termination of employment situations ...' and Article 24 provides for the 'establishment of provisions relating to redundancy which identify the rights and obligations of employees, employees and unions ...'. The Article spells out the subject matter of such rights and obligations, but does not indicate the process by which they would be achieved. However, in practice the Hawke Government has so far limited itself to 'in principle' support for general standards on redundancy in Federal awards.

All the states having elected to establish tribunals to deal with industrial disputes, the result is considerable variation in the treatment of employment security. Moreover, the states have chosen not to use their legislative powers to give a statutory basis to redundancy provisions, except to a very limited extent — mainly under Labor governments in NSW, as discussed below. Since the protection provided under awards is also very limited, it remains the case that Australian private sector employees generally fall well behind those of other advanced industrialised nations, in terms of legal protection against job loss and legally based 'cushioning' in the event of job loss. This was highlighted in the 1980 Report of the Committee of Inquiry into Technological Change in Australia (CITCA)[9] established by the previous Federal government in December 1978, in the context of widespread concern about the disemployment potential of technological change and its industrial relations implications.

CITCA pointed (in para. 7.82) to more favourable standards in other Western countries, particularly in respect of periods of notice, information provided to unions and to public authorities, consultation with unions on measures to mitigate the consequences of redundancy (such as attrition, redeployment and re-training) and compensation, whether lump sum payments or income maintenance. It concluded (para. 7.84) that every effort should be made to avoid retrenchment, but that standards and entitlements are desirable for all employees 'laid off through no fault of their own', regardless of whether this retrenchment arises from technological change or for other reasons (para. 7.85). It pointed out that such standards could be applied by legislation, but regarded awards as more flexible (para. 7.40). Specifically, CITCA proposed a two-part retrenchment scheme comprising a publicly funded temporary income maintenance scheme for retrenched workers, plus lump sum severance pay together with generous notice to be sought as general standards in Federal awards in a test case sponsored by the Federal government before the ACAC. The (non-Labor) government then in office endorsed CITCA's enthusiastic espousal of technological change but declined to take up either of these major recommendations. However, test case proceedings were initiated by the Australian Council of Trade Unions (ACTU) in 1981.

In the past, it has been possible to argue that, even were the Commonwealth politically inclined to legislate on redundancy, it would meet with constitutional hurdles. A significant High Court ruling, Koowarta *v.* Bjelke-Petersen (1982) 39 ALR 417, suggests, however, that the Hawke Government could use the 'external affairs' power to ratify ILO Conventions and implement their provisions by legislation. This would be so, theoretically, even without the states agreement, or prior action by the states to bring laws and practices into conformity with the Convention. In December 1983, however, the Minister for Employment and Industrial Relations said that 'it will not be possible to ratify' ILO Convention No. 158, Termination of Employment, because at this time law and practice in Federal and state jurisdictions fail to conform with it. The Commonwealth proposes to continue with usual consultative procedures with the states on ratifications, as well as through the International Labour Affairs Committee of the National Labour

Consultative Council (NLCC), a statutorily-based, tripartite body,[10]

At present, therefore, it seems that the most likely vehicle for improving the legal position of retrenched employees will be the ACTU test case and proceedings before state tribunals, notwithstanding recent legislative initiatives in NSW.

Legislative Provisions

Until December 1982, the primary legislative provisions on redundancy in the private sector were s. 88G of the Industrial Arbitration Act (NSW), which arose from recommendations of an inquiry into technological change,[11] and the similar (albeit less generous) s. 82 in the Industrial Conciliation and Arbitration Act (South Australia). Section 88G relates only to technological change and provides for the mandatory insertion into an award or agreement upon application to the appropriate tribunal of provisions relating to employer's obligations. These obligations are not specified — they are a matter for negotiation or arbitration — except in so far as the employer must give not less than three months' notice to redundant employees and notify appropriate tribunals.[12]

The CITCA Report pointed out (para. 5.247) that while, predictably, unions covering areas most likely to be affected were the ones that had tended to seek the protection provided for, little more than 20 per cent of NSW awards, affecting between 30 and 35 per cent of the workforce covered by NSW awards, actually incorporated such provisions. In South Australia they could be found in less than one clause in ten (para. 5.248).This would seem to reflect, on the one hand, the lulling impact of long years of full employment. On the other, where consciousness of job insecurity had raised job protection higher in priorities, many unions evinced qualms lest legally-based compensation undermined the struggle for preservation of existing jobs. However, it is understood that there was a considerable jump in applications under these statutory provisions when retrenchments started to mount in the early 1980s.

By late 1982, moreover, increasing pressures for legislation were being directed at the NSW Labor government by the NSW Labor Council. These were influenced by widespead retrenchments in the influential steel industry, accompanied by lengthy proceedings before the Industrial Commission of NSW to determine redundancy provisions; and fears of large-scale retrenchments before the end of the year through employers seeking to avoid payment for the Christmas period. The state government hurriedly enacted the rather clumsy Employment Protection Act (1982), with certain other state Labor administrations expected to follow suit. In the event, however, somewhat similar legislation introduced by the Labor government of Victoria was defeated in its Upper House in mid-1983. The South Australian Labor government has committed itself to action in respect of employment protection, but has not yet announced what initiatives it will take; nor has the Western Australian Labor government acted as at end-1983.

All three sets of current legislative provisions — s. 88G (NSW), s. 82 (SA), and the Employment Protection Act (NSW) — are of a procedural rather than a substantive kind, with the result that, in the state and Federal arena, it is generally left to tribunals to impose on employers substantive award obligations on redundancy. Thus, the Employment Protection Act (NSW) requires private sector employers (of no fewer than fifteen employees) to give seven days' notice to the Industrial Registrar of intention to dismiss an employee. This notice must contain comprehensive information including applicable awards or agreements, payments to be made as a consequence of the dismissal, and service with the employer.

The Act does not attempt to define 'redundancy' or 'retrenchments', nor to distinguish between retrenchments arising from different causes. Indeed, in its original terms it applied to terminations generally, with few exceptions. The requirement to notify has never applied in cases of misconduct, or casual employment. Further exceptions were added in early 1983: where employment is for a specified period or specified task; age retirements; employment on a 'trial' basis (limited to six months); transmission of business to another employer (unless retrenchments result); and retrenchments already covered by award or registered agreement provisions. In December 1983 a further regulation exempted employees not covered by state award or industrial agreement;[13] those not continuously employed by the employer for at least twelve months; and those paid severance payments at least equal to those in Table 5.4 below.

Notifications are passed on to the Industrial Commission so that it may investigate and award redundancy provisions where appropriate. There were over 18,000 notifications during 1983, most of them covering multiple retrenchments. These provided ample evidence that many long-term employees including middle-level managers, other white collar personnel and others in career-type employment, were being retrenched in substantial numbers and, in most instances, with very little in the way of redundancy notice and compensation. With respect to personnel not covered by awards — private sector managers are a major example — so far the Commission has merely noted their retrenchments: since they are non-unionised, unions have not initiated proceedings on their behalf and there is no provision for individual employees, not represented by a registered organisation, to put a case to the Commission. Since the December 1983 regulation, moreover, they need no longer be notified.

Even for employees covered by awards, the operation of the legislation has been slow to meet its objectives. The massive incidence of notifications created delays in processing, and also made a case-by-case approach, as originally intended, logistically infeasible. The NSW Labor Council therefore initiated a test case in the NSW Commission,[14] along the same lines as the ACTU case before the ACAC, and joined to it proceedings for redundancy provisions in the retail industry associated with a major organisational merger.

The proceedings were intended to give rise to general standards, the Act empowering the Commission to make orders on matters including severance pay, gratuities, superannuation, preference in re-employment and re-training. Until the December 1983 regulation, which incorporated the President's recommended scale of severance payments, handed down in consequence of the test case in July 1983, the Act provided no standards or criteria.

As the first test case decisions on redundancy, the judgement merits analysis. Fisher P rejected union submissions that redundancies should be dealt with 'in a conglomerate way', and held that three different causes should be considered separately: the recession, technological change and company reconstruction, mergers and takeovers. (He also thought that the Act was not intended to load 'an ordinary and customary turnover of labour' — such as intermittency of work in building, seasonal fluctuations etc. — 'with a significant cost burden in relation to severance'.) Here Fisher P focused only on recession-induced retrenchments, later handing down a more generous decision in the retail proceedings.

Employers argued that union claims would apply redundancy

provisions for the first time to a wide range of often small and vulnerable employers, including in the metal trades (where, as the President had concluded in his Steel Industry decision of January 1983, the level of severance payments was 'very low indeed, with the exception of the steel industry'). Moreover, they argued that 'it is not for the employer to provide the social safety net that the community demands'. Fisher P shared their concern that employers may not have funds in place to meet redundancy payments, and that making such payments during the recession might put survival at risk for some; further, care should be taken not to disadvantage NSW industry, particularly areas hardest hit by recession. He concluded that 'the utmost that industry can accommodate in the current climate is a modest and limited scale of relief ...'. However, workers should not be retrenched with little notice and no compensation. The type of worker encompassed by the proceedings was mainly industrial employees in weekly wage employment who 'often have a settled expectation of continued employment', likely to increase with service, which they should be compensated for; but given their comparative mobility this aspect of loss is less than it would be in 'career' employment.

He recommended a scale of severance payments (see Table 5.4), intended to put more emphasis on needs than 'patterns of past employment', and 'directed towards the amelioration of social hardship by supplementing income from unemployment benefits and so prolonging the maintenance of living standards and extending the period [of job search] ... without serious erosion of family assets ...'. In deference to 'our familiar concept of service-related payment', a short incremental scale was used. The President accepted evidence of increased hardship for those over 45 to be dealt with 'by increasing the rate, not lengthening the scale'.

As at end-1983, the backlog of notifications is still being processed. Unless they are disputed (e.g. on grounds such as capacity to pay, none of which cases has been heard yet) the recommended scale is applied.

The Jurisdiction and Functions of the Federal Commission (ACAC)

The limiting wording of the constitutional power, s. 51 (xxxv), constrains the ACAC in dealing with redundancy. Its only processes are conciliation and arbitration, and it can adjudicate upon redundancy only when it is the subject of an interstate, industrial

Table 5.4: Scale of Severance Payments Recommended in Recession-induced Retrenchments by President of Industrial Commission of New South Wales[a]

Length of continuous service by employee	Rate for calculation of amount of severance payment	
	If employee under 45 years of age	If employee 45 or more years of age
Less than 1 year	Nil	Nil
1 year and more but less than 2 years	4 weeks' pay	5 weeks' pay
2 years and more but less than 3 years	6 weeks' pay	7.5 weeks' pay
3 years and more but less than 4 years	7 weeks' pay	8.75 weeks' pay
4 years and more	8 weeks' pay	10 weeks' pay

a. Recommended in decision of July 1983 on Employment Protection Act Test Case Proceedings.

Source: Employment Protection Regulation 1983 (NSW), enacted December 1983.

dispute. Its decision must fall 'within the ambit' of the subject matter in dispute, and can bind only the parties to the dispute. Since it has no power to make 'common rules', the only way it can prescribe general standards is through 'test case' proceedings which use specific awards to gain a decision: then other unions apply for variation of their own awards to incorporate these standards.[15]

Because of (unnecessarily limited) statutory definitions, the claims must directly involve the relationship of employer and employee. If the employer's right to retrench is at issue, it may be treated as a managerial prerogative and as outside the ACAC's jurisdiction. Thus the High Court held in the Air Pilots case (1971) 127 CLR 11 that the question of whether pilots should be retrenched was a matter for management; but the terms on which they could be retrenched (e.g. notice and compensation) were within the ACAC's powers. Again, claims for employer/union (as opposed to employer/employee) consultation fall outside the ACAC's scope, as it declared when ruling on jurisdiction in the ACTU's test case.[16] A further outcome is a doubt about the ACAC's power to deal with matters having effect after the employment has ended. Finally, questions such as whether a dismissal should have been made and/or a dismissed employee reinstated have been held to be 'judicial' matters and outside the powers of the ACAC, which is solely an arbitral (award-making) body.

Because of these and other constraints,[17] as soon as the ACTU initiated proceedings on job security in October 1981, employers mounted jurisdictional challenges. The ACAC handed down its decision on jurisdiction in October 1982, as a result of which the ACTU revised its claims. Since these comprise an 'ambit' claim, and no one expects benefits of such quantum to be prescribed, it would be misleading to set it out in full. However, the main standards it now seeks would require employers to make 'all efforts . . . to avoid terminations of employment due to redundancy', and provide preference in retention of employment and in respect of all other benefits to unionists. Where retrenchments cannot be avoided, employers would be obliged to observe general standards of notice, lump sum severance pay, payment of leave entitlement and income maintenance; assist with job search; and afford preference in re-employment to retrenched workers. Where redundant workers are transferred, the employer would have to provide income maintenance, relocation expenses and re-training. What is sought is a set of minimum standards, with parties retaining the flexibility to negotiate or seek award provisions beyond these minima, according to the circumstances of particular cases. The claims relate to 'permanent' weekly employees currently entitled to the standard one week's notice.[18]

The ACAC is expected to hand down its decision in early 1984. As for provisions already incorporated in Federal awards, many of them the result of negotiations rather than arbitration, surveys carried out by the Department of Employment and Industrial Relations (DEIR) in August 1978 and May 1982 indicated that, despite the increasing percentage of Federal awards and agreements containing redundancy provisions (from 78 or 10 per cent in 1978, to 147 or 15 per cent of all awards surveyed in 1982), coverage is still very limited, protecting no more than an estimated 122,000 employees. Only six of the top 50 Federal awards (as listed by the ACTU) have redundancy provisions — the metal industry awards (the subject of the test case proceedings) being a notable exception. Industry coverage is uneven, redundancy provisions appearing prominent in awards covering the vehicles, chemical, airline, shipping and municipal employment sectors. Aspects of the content of provisions are shown by the following breakdown: extended notice and/or payment in lieu, 47 awards (1978) and 110 awards (1982); notification and/or consultation with employees and/or unions, 14 (1978) and 40 (1982); redundancy or severance payments, 28 (1978) and 58 (1982). While DEIR was unable to draw firm conclusions as to developments in respect of quantum (reflecting the ad hoc approach of the tribunal hitherto[19]), it did suggest that the content of provisions has become more comprehensive and sophisticated, and that there is also a greater incidence in awards of redundancy-related provisions such as job search assistance, re-training, and criteria for selecting retrenched employees.[20]

The ACAC started off very cautiously in this area, its first major case on redundancy concerning clerks displaced by automation in the oil industry. Their union in 1968 sought 'permanent' employment for most employees with five years' continuous service plus a guarantee that such employees would, unless they consented, 'be continued in employment in the same city, town or locality without reduction of salary or demotion in grade or classifications'. The ACAC considered this to be 'too restrictive . . . in the light of what the employers have already done' and felt that justice would be served by financial compensation. It urged that when employers were contemplating technological change which might cause terminations or transfers interstate, 'it is essential that both the employees and the union concerned should be informed of and involved in the planning as soon as possible'.[21]

The ACAC has generally steered clear of determining whether employees should be retrenched, arbitrating primarily on whether (and, if so, how much) notice and redundancy pay should be provided. It has so far dealt mainly with actual and impending redundancies which can be treated on their own facts, but some general principles can be identified.[22]

Thus arbitrators have looked at causes, being more inclined to provide protection or compensation where retrenchments result from decisions of the employer and are under its control, as in technological change: Vehicle Building case, 1972; and Municipal Officers case, 1978. Capacity to pay has been a factor (as in the NSW jurisdiction): Clothing Trades case, 1983. Moreover, job redundancy where suitable alternative employment can be provided will not normally attract protection or compensation unless it involves hardship such as drops in pay, as decided in the Snowy Mountains Authority case, 1969, which also indicated that there is more likelihood of redundancy provisions being awarded in 'career' type industries where an expectation of continued employment prevails. In the Milk Processing and Cheese redundancy case, 1980, the Industrial Commission of South Australia concluded that employees with a record of long and faithful service have a proper and reasonable expectation that their employers will accept obligations beyond the bare common law requirement to give notice. This approach was adopted by a member of the ACAC in the Clothing Trades case, 1983. Turning to the contrary circumstances, there is reluctance to grant redundancy provisions where redundancy could have been predicted at engagement, especially if remuneration takes this insecurity into account, as in casual work and the anticipated completion of projects: Yallourn W Power Station, 1971; and re. Australian Workers Union (Major Victorian Civil Construction) Redundancy Award, 1978.

However, protection and compensation have sometimes been awarded in respect of closures of collieries or factories, the ACAC specifying in the John Lysaght case, 1973, some of the criteria it considered significant, including: length of notice; length of service; whether alternative employment is available; compensation payable from existing schemes; the loss of long-service and other payments; loss of seniority and security of employment; in some circumstances, the reason for the retrenchments; loss of wages; costs of relocating; and possibly to provide for early retirement.

The two main provisions have been extended notice and lump sum severance pay, although in isolated instances the following have been awarded: preference to unionists; the seniority principle; preference in re-employment to retrenched employees (on a seniority basis); early retirement. In working out the appropriate amounts of notice and/or severance pay, tribunals have normally considered seniority (sometimes imposing a minimum qualifying period and various factors relating to hardship, including age).[23]

The ACAC has tended to regard lengthy notice as a sufficient alleviating factor, sometimes displacing the need for redundancy payments as in the Merchant Service Guild case, 1971. In a more recent case it stressed the provision of notice, to be worked out on the basis of years of service and age (since older persons often find it more difficult to obtain and adapt to comparable work elsewhere and often give up more in terms of seniority). Lump sum severance payments only come into operation as compensation when the prescribed notice is not provided.

This case, handed down in respect of municipal officers in 1978, ten years after the ACAC's first major statement on redundancy, is also something of a landmark. In most previous cases, the ACAC had been dealing with particular, existing situations of redundancy. Here it concluded that the time had arrived where 'general (as distinct from *ad hoc*) provisions may be awarded, even in the absence of agreement on principle'. However, for the present at least, it concluded, 'general redundancy provisions should be confined to situations which will be within the control of the employer, e.g. a decision to introduce a new technology'. If general standards result from the ACTU test case, which apply regardless of the cause of redundancy, this will therefore constitute a considerable departure by the ACAC from its previous approaches.

Policies, Practices and Procedures

Tripartite Guidelines on Technological Change

The tripartite National Labour Advisory Council (NLAC) now

replaced by the National Labor Consultative Council, adopted guidelines on technological change in 1969 which were supplemented in 1972. Major recommendations are that employees and their representatives should be informed as soon as a firm decision has been taken about the proposed introduction of technological change, consistent with the employer's need to protect business interests. 'Full and early' consultation on consequences should include details of implementation and expected effects on employees such as re-training, redeployment, transfers and retrenchments. Employers are urged to provide adequate notice to redundant personnel, notify the Commonwealth Employment Services and permit time off for interviews without loss of pay. Reflecting the prevailing view of employer bodies, the guidelines did not incorporate any recommendations on compensation.

In its 1980 Report, CITCA commended in principle the NLAC guidelines as to consultation and notification (para. 5.22).[24] Drawing on surveys, however, including the Department of Productivity and Australian Bureau of Statistics (ABS) surveys summarised below, CITCA concluded (para. 5.250)[25] that, although many large private employers and public enterprises conformed to the guidelines or went considerably further, 'most employers' are not aware of or are unfamiliar with [their] provisions'. CITCA recommended (para. 5.261)[26] that the guidelines, 'supplemented by more recent awards and agreements, should form the basis of a prescribed minimum standard of consultation in all industries'.

The then government found itself able to strongly endorse CITCA's emphasis on 'adequate notification and consultation' about technological change, but not to the point of espousing obligations enforceable at law (notwithstanding its acknowledgement that observance of the NLAC proposals had been very patchy). It invited the NLCC to form a committee to update and promote the guidelines, together with a review of guidelines on notice and assistance to employees seeking alternative employment.[27] The NLCC committee met only once, (in May 1981), however, the ACTU making it clear that it was prepared to be involved in the revision only if the outcome would be incorporated in Federal awards, while the Confederation of Australian Industry expressed opposition to the concept of award obligations on notification and consultation.[28]

Consultative procedures on technological change have received considerable emphasis in the public sector, however, as highlighted by policies in Commonwealth employment, particularly those involving the Public Service Board or the monopolies providing tele-communications and postal services. Features of relevant guide-lines stress:

— involvement of unions from pre-feasibility to operational phases;
— supply of information to unions, including existing systems and existing staff arrangements, reasons for changing, details of new equipment, evidence of benefits, etc.;
— evaluation including changes to staff required, impact on working environment, requirements for re-training, redeploy-ment or relocation of staff, etc.

The Public Service Board's guidelines also note that the timing and rate of technological changes 'should be decided against a back-ground of the need to enable proper and effective redeployment of staff and to minimise the likelihood of any retrenchment of existing staff'.

Enterprise Policies and Practices

Insights into redundancy policies and practices recently followed by Australian companies can be derived from three relevant sur-veys. Pauncz[29] reports the findings of a 1977 study by the then Department of Productivity (DEP), involving 450 companies operating in four industrial sectors susceptible to a variety of eco-nomic and technological changes likely to reduce labour require-ments. Drawing on responses supplied by the 282 organisations which had experienced redundancy it is possible to isolate some features of practices at that time.

Considerable attempts were made by firms to avoid retrench-ment through various means, the most popular being natural wastage, transfers and measures aimed at spreading workloads. Early retirement schemes and re-training directed towards rede-ployment were less popular approaches, although, on average, each firm indicated that it used three specific methods to alleviate the need for redundancies. Where dismissals were initiated, most firms (65 per cent) gave notice of one week or less to manual employees, whereas managerial staff received over three week's notice in 77 per cent of cases. Typically, employees were formally advised of retrenchments in individual interviews, though in a few instances work site meetings, personal letters or company bulletins were the preferred means.

The survey demonstrated that management considerations were more important in deciding which employees to retrench. The most frequently mentioned factor was the worker's employment record assessed on criteria such as attitude, and contribution to output in quantitative and qualitative terms. Management's concern to retain employees with specific skills and experience was reflected in the fact that this was the second most important criterion. Length of service and age were relatively less popular, suggesting that union prescriptions, commonly emphasising such considerations, were heeded less than one might expect. This view is reinforced by the finding that only a handful of respondents listed union membership as a factor in choosing between employees.

An attempt was made to ascertain the extent and determinants of lump sum payments in excess of award provisions. Replies indicated that 45 per cent of firms did make such payments and that a positive association existed between size of firm and their incidence. Common ingredients were *pro rata* annual leave loadings, service related gratuities and some component of employer's superannuation fund contributions. Payment for sick leave credits, and age-based formulae, were unusual.

In keeping with the overall content of policies followed it was hardly surprising that in 63 per cent of cases management autonomously determined policies and only in 17 per cent were employees consulted before determining procedures. This is consistent with the results of a later survey undertaken by the Australian Bureau of Statistics[30] for CITCA, which estimated that only 5 per cent of enterprises introducing technological change over the three years to 1979 had entered into consultation with employees or their representatives. This situation was more pronounced in smaller non-manufacturing firms than in large manufacturing undertakings (employing more than 80 persons), where an estimated 42 per cent engaged in consultation of some type. The same survey found that retrenchments were carried out more frequently in larger manufacturing firms (21 per cent of cases) than in other sectors and this perhaps explains why more managements turned to consultation in these cases.

A third more recent survey was carried out in 1982 by the consultants, Cullen, Egan and Dell (CED).[31] Their research was based on information received from 200 larger firms operating in Australia, embracing a broad industrial spread including manufacturing, construction, financial, service and extractive sectors, and provides a useful contrast to the earlier work. In total, employment at respondent firms accounted for just on 5 per cent of the labour force, with the treatment accorded to award and award-exempt employees reported separately. Australian-owned organisations constituted 34 per cent of the sample with the remainder having overseas parentage, mainly United States (35 per cent) and United Kingdom (20 per cent).

Just about half the firms had reduced the number of award-covered employees during 1982. Smaller losses were recorded for award-free employees with reductions in senior management numbers occurring in only 23 per cent of cases. While 'natural wastage' was the most common expression of reduced demand for labour (89 per cent), two-thirds of respondents indicated that they had implemented retrenchments for award-covered staff, while over half had promoted early retirements. At the same time, firms also adopted a wide range of measures short of encouraging voluntary quits and compulsory retrenchments to effect reductions in labour utilisation. Over 60 per cent of organisations required employees to take accrued annual and long service leave while 16 per cent admitted that hours and pay were reduced (which would generally have been an award breach — albeit one which many unions have chosen to 'overlook' in the present climate); further, a fifth indicated that they had implemented temporary layoffs (leave without pay) during the year. The 60 per cent who had made use of early retirement schemes to effect cutbacks (commonly at age 55) said that scope had been greatest in 1981 and 1982 and many therefore expected the numbers exiting by this means to stabilise, or even decrease, from 1983.

Formal redundancy policies existed for award-covered employees in 42 per cent of firms, but only in 35 per cent for award-free staff. Policies were in the process of being developed for these two categories by a further 12 per cent of respondents. The most important considerations shaping policies were 'general business practices', award provisions, together with length of service and age. Surprisingly, less than 10 per cent of firms indicated that they were directly influenced by international parent company policies. It might be, however, that international practices found their way into policies by less direct means.

The data suggest considerable diversity in redundancy schemes. Considering only those companies with formal policies, average notice given to award-covered employees was 4.5 weeks, while their award-free colleagues received 5.8 weeks. The majority of firms, however, did not require employees to work out their notice to be eligible for redundancy payments, though 10 per cent of firms did offer an incentive bonus to workers who stayed for the entire period.

Each respondent company was asked to indicate the most important factor in selecting workers to be retrenched. Here there was a distinct contrast. Award-covered employees were most commonly selected for retrenchment on the basis of 'last in — first out', a situation at odds with the earlier DEP survey, whereas those not subject to award regulation were chosen most frequently on the basis of assessed performance. Generally speaking, however, management still seemed to retain considerable discretion in both instances.

Compared with earlier practice, lump sum payments seemed more prevalent in 1982, as indicated in Table 5.5. Some payments such as accrued annual leave and long service leave must be paid out in accordance with relevant awards and statutes; other payments can be discretionary. However, few companies made only statutory payments. Besides formula-based components related to either service or age, or both, over 50 per cent indicated that they made *pro rata* payments to employees for accrued long service

Table 5.5: Percentage of Companies with Formal Redundancy Policies Making Specific Non-statutory Payments to Retrenched Employees

Employee category	Lump sum payment determined by formula based on service, age, etc.	Accrued sick leave credit	*Pro-rata* long service leave credits paid prior to eligibility	*Pro-rata* annual leave loading credits paid prior to eligibility	Superannuation payments in excess of formal entitlement
	%	%	%	%	%
Award covered employees	96	33	56	50	28
Non-award employees	89	24	56	49	26

Source: Cullen, Egan and Dell Survey, p. 4.22.

leave credits before eligibility was reached. These can be significant sums, though the typical practice of applying a maximum number of weeks to lump sum payouts can moderate overall costs.

At the time of writing (December 1983), a fourth survey, of hundreds of redundancy packages, is being completed by the Amalgamated Metals, Foundry and Shipwright's Union. It seems that this highlights as one of the most generous in terms of redundancy payments the package provided by ACI Plastics PL, namely: 'one year's service: one week's pay; one to five year's service: four weeks' pay plus three weeks' pay for each completed year of service, plus $1,000; more than five years' service: four weeks' pay plus three weeks' pay for each year of service, plus $2,000. If notice is not given there will be payment in lieu of notice. *Pro rata* annual leave with $17\frac{1}{2}$ per cent loading; *pro rata* long service leave with five years' service; $17\frac{1}{2}$ per cent loading on long service leave after 1 April 1976.[32] The published CED[33] survey suggests that a more typical *ex gratia* payment is likely to be between one and two weeks' pay per year of service.

Whether retrenched or encouraged to retire early, a former employee is likely to experience a variety of emotional and financial pressures as a result of the change. This is particularly true of those with long service and expectations of a continuous career until normal retirement. Two-thirds of companies indicated that they provided some form of counselling. As in other countries, specialist consultants have emerged in Australia. Their services vary, ranging from euphemistically termed 'dehiring' or 'outplacement' packages, to specific services such as job search assistance, or help to reorganise finances. In a number of major centres the Commonwealth Employment Service offers individual and group counselling services for redundant workers to assist them to come to grips with the emotional trauma so many experience. Some employers encourage their workers to make use of these government-funded facilities, though often large-scale redundancies can stretch the limited capacity of such labour intensive activities, despite the willingness of committed staff.

Interestingly, the CED[34] survey disclosed that among award-exempt employees (mostly managers), over half the companies gave an option to purchase a company car. Rare cases went so far as to offer an option on the company home, presumably occupied by the employee, while occasional firms provided extended medical and life insurance cover and made special arrangements for the repayment of loans from the company. About half also offered preference for re-employment should business improve.

What surveys such as these fail to highlight is the impact which industrial action might have on management's approach to redundancy situations. Some disputes have been particularly bitter and drawn-out in recent years, attracting significant media attention and a measure of sympathy for workers involved. Part of the improved standards evident in sections of industry might reasonably be attributed to such action. While it is true that limited workplace union organisation in Australia, multi-unionism in many plants, and the recession have restricted the capacity for strategic industrial leverage at plant level, some cases do exist. One of the more notable disputes took place in mid-1983 at Australian National Industries (ANI) Ltd.'s Comeng rolling stock plant in Sydney, which at the time employed about 650 workers. Although action revolved around the retrenchment of only 83 workers, observers saw it as representative of an aggressive management, intent on using redundancies to break traditional custom and practice, and to generally wrest job control from the shop floor. Unions initiated a number of measures, including strike action and bans on ANI companies. Management retaliated with legal manoeuvres, including action under the Trade Practices Act, which outlawed secondary boycotts. The inevitable compromise, reached after some months and involving the Industrial Commission of NSW, improved redundancy conditions and moderated the company's proposal to reduce over-award payments to retained employees. It appears, too, that ANI did succeed in implementing some of the shop floor changes sought,[35] demonstrating what some had been aware of for some time, namely, that private sector management could gain concessions in work practices in redundancy situations. Post-recession workplace industrial relations may be rather different to what prevailed in the seventies.

Labour Market Programmes

DEIR administers an extensive array of labour market programmes to service particular needs and groups. One of these groups is that of redundant workers. While they may be eligible for various programmes as unemployed persons, four schemes have particular relevance.[36]

Labour Adjustment Training Arrangements (LATA), designed to deal with problems confronting workers involved in large-scale redundancy situations, were introduced late in 1982. Consultation takes place between relevant parties — DEIR, employers, unions and educational authorities, as well as participants themselves — to develop special, mostly full-time, vocational training packages, including tertiary courses, for eligible individuals, to enhance labour market prospects. During training, participants are entitled to unemployment benefits together with weekly training allowances, currently (August 1983) $A46.35 for adults, and half that for juniors; and limited support for study aids. Eligibility depends upon the minister declaring particular large-scale redundancies covered. So far LATA has extended to former steel industry employees in NSW and SA, affected NSW coalminers, and workers retrenched by a large farm equipment manufacturer in Victoria. Budget allocations for 1983–4 indicate scope to assist up to 3,000 people.

Government concern that retrenchments can significantly affect apprentices, and hence future supplies of skilled labour, is demonstrated in a Special Assistance Program. Subsidies are available to employers who otherwise would be forced to retrench an apprentice, or are prepared to take on and re-indenture apprentices already retrenched. Alternatively, training allowances can enable unemployed apprentices to complete a basic trade course under various arrangements. Numbers using this programme grew nearly four-fold in 1982/3 to 4,376, with continued growth predicted.

Unemployed persons, or those threatened with redundancy, may apply for relocation assistance. However, restrictive criteria apply, and only about 2,000 people annually are being assisted. Essentially, applicants need definite job offers in other locations for which no suitable local applicants are available. Budget figures suggest that average relocation assistance amounts to around $A1,000.

In August 1983, the Federal government announced a major job creation initiative which, when in full operation, is expected to create 70,000 new jobs annually. This Community Employment Program (CEP) is designed to help long-term unemployed, defined as those registered for at least three months, but specifies priority for those longest on the register and particular disadvantaged groups such as aboriginals, migrants and disabled persons. This programme concentrates on local employment projects and operates through networks of committees which vet proposals from potential sponsors. These can be local councils, voluntary organisations, or state and Commonwealth departments and authorities. Although those obtaining positions receive award rates, most are likely to be employed at, or near, the minimum wage for unskilled labour, given the type of work. In addition, jobs funded have a limited duration. Thus, whether CEP will help provide access to more stable long-term employment patterns for those currently experiencing great difficulties remains to be seen. In the short term it may at least help some retrenched older workers and females who encounter major barriers gaining re-employment in depressed labour markets.

Managing Excess Staff in Government Employment

While a major attraction of public employment in Australia (operating on a 'career service' model) has been security of employment, attempts by governments to control public expenditure have placed the concept of 'tenure' in jeopardy — although public servants still enjoy much more security than those in the private sector. This section of the chapter provides two case studies, dealing with the introduction by the previous non-Labor government of a new legal framework to manage redundancy in Commonwealth employment; and outlining the provisions and procedures whereby redundancies are managed in the NSW government administration.

Commonwealth Public Employment

Provisions in the Commonwealth Public Service Act before 1979 which related to redeployment and retirement were described by the responsible minister as not providing an adequate legal framework or sufficient staff protection.[37] In addition to the statutory provisions, mention should also be made of the 'Guidelines for Redundancy Situations in Australian Government Employment' issued in 1974 and updated in 1978. These are intended to apply in all redundancy situations in Commonwealth employment except in relation to: staff employed under the Public Service Act; employees of authorities in a statutory relationship with the Public Service Board; employees covered by the Public Service Arbitrator's Determination 509 of 1977 on redundancy; and employees covered by Federal awards incorporating redundancy provisions.

The original Commonwealth Employees (Redeployment and Retirement) Bill (CERR) came before Parliament in 1976. Unions expressed vigorous opposition and complained of inadequate consultation, and the stormy debate was accompanied by acrimonious industrial disputation. This reflected the deteriorating public sector industrial climate, and reactions to what was regarded as the government's 'union-bashing' propensities, as well as growing concern about the likely effects of technological change on jobs in the wake of an unusually high degree of machinery of government dislocation, and heavy cutbacks in staffing imposed through administrative reviews and strict 'staff ceilings'.

Finally enacted in 1979, CERR provided both for voluntary early retirement with superannuation rights and euphemistically-termed 'management-initiated early retirement' — i.e. redundancy — when a department head (or authority electing to come under CERR) identifies staff as eligible for redeployment because their services cannot be used efficiently and economically. Where the board concludes that redeployment is not possible, it issues a certificate and the department head or authority may retire the employee, who may appeal to a special tribunal.

CERR provided for terms of awards made before or after its enactment to prevail over its own provisions. Therefore Determination 509 of 1977, a negotiated instrument providing standards greatly in advance of those in the private sector, remains in existence. It provides for unions to be consulted about redundancies by the Board and for notice of redundancies (six months' notice to permanent officers, with twelve months' notice to those over 45 years of age or with 20 or more years of service; and one month's notice to temporary employees, including industrial workers). If suitable alternative employment has not been found (with training if necessary) when notice runs out, permanent officers are given one month's notice of transfer to a lower salary level or termination, while a temporary employee may be transferred or terminated immediately. The other major provisions prescribe income maintenance, time off for job search and 'reasonable' relocation expenses.

Unions sought a new arbitral determination to improve on this and provide additional safeguards, which the Board strongly opposed on management prerogative grounds. The ACAC concluded, however, that while consultation and time periods between steps might inhibit managerial discretion, it was not a determination upon managerial policy as such.

An interim determination provided consultation rights and preference in retention for unionists. The final Determination, 503 of 1980, largely endorsed provisions drafted by the Board. However, the government in March 1981 used little-used powers to 'disallow' Determination 503, and amended CERR to prohibit further determinations on matters which it covered, to protect 'what are, reasonably and properly, management prerogatives',[38] while leaving Determination 509 still in operation. Future change therefore can be achieved only by amending the Act — which the Hawke Labor Government has promised, in consultation with unions, reflecting the ALP platform on public sector industrial relations. (The joint review commences in January 1984.) The government also submitted in the ACTU case that 'the range of job protection provisions applying to some 350,000–400,000 Federal public service employees strengthens the case in equity for minimum standards for all Federal award employees'.[39]

New South Wales Government Administration

Section 37 of the Public Service Act 1979 (NSW) prescribes that the maximum number of staff in a department shall be determined by the Premier, as necessary for the efficient, effective and economical management of its functions and activities. In August 1981, the Treasurer wrote to ministers emphasising the need for expenditure controls due to sharply rising costs, particularly labour costs. In February 1982 the Premier told all ministers to trim administrative outlays and staff levels and eliminate overtime, and announced a government functions task force to identify low priority activities which could be phased out. Suspensions of recruitment and appointments were announced in May 1981 and again in February 1982.

The Act gave the NSW Public Service Board powers to redeploy and retrench employees and reduce salaries where necessary. In March 1980, the Board announced that these would be used only where staff numbers exceeded staff ceilings. Department heads were to determine 'excess persons' and inform the Board, which would circulate a register of such persons, to be considered for any vacancies. (Redundant temporary employees may be dismissed at any time.)

In February 1982, the Premier wrote to the Combined Public Service Unions of NSW, promising to give the highest priority to ensuring no job loss or 'unreasonable work demands'. Task force deliberations led to two major organisational changes in May 1982, abolishing 105 jobs. A redeployment unit was set up in the Board to consult with unions, and all the personnel were redeployed. In June 1982, the Premier announced a reduction of 2,200 in staff numbers by 30 April through the 'freeze', and predicted a further (task force-related) reduction of 600 jobs during late 1982. Again, unions were assured that 'projected reductions in staff numbers will be achieved by natural attrition' although some staff might have to relocate.

During that month the Board issued the 'Guidelines on Management of Excess Staff'. While amended since, the basic principles remain that the initial responsibility for redeployment rests with department heads, who must try to transfer staff within their own departments; no vacancy is to be filled without considering whether suitable 'excess persons' are available; all staff should be given the maximum possible information, promptly, about any change; and 'excess persons' should be given personal counselling with detailed explanations of policies and provisions. As at September 1983, after 16 months in operation, the redeployment unit seemed to have had considerable success: of over 300 'excess persons', only 34 awaited positions.

Where placement at the same salary is not possible, the Board usually places the officer in a lower-level position, preferably in the same department; reduces the salary; and certifies that the reduction is only because of redundancy. Salaries are normally maintained for up to three years, to help officers adjust financial commitments, and to provide a 'carry over' period during which vacancies may occur. Officers with a certificate, moreover, have a right of preference over others when suitable vacancies emerge.

In the few recent instances where retrenchments have been unavoidable, the government has applied a severance pay package. The main instance was in the State Dockyard. When major shipbuilding ceased in 1976/7, approximately 1,000 personnel were retrenched, with a further 400–500 retrenchments taking place since August 1982. The package applied in 1976/7 provided for four weeks' notice or pay in lieu, with two weeks' severance pay for each year of service up to a maximum of ten years. Employees had the option of accepting severance pay or the retrenchment benefit payable under the Retirement or Superannuation Fund, if applicable. The current package provides for a maximum of 26 weeks severance pay for over 18 years of service with payment of Fund or retrenchment benefit in full. The package does not apply to staff engaged on a temporary or specific task basis, or where an individual unreasonably declines redeployment. It has also been applied in other situations involving comparatively small numbers, as in the closure of country gaols and a grain handling terminal, and cutbacks at a state abattoir and the state brickworks.

In 1980, unions applied for a Government Employees (Redundancy) Award, the Board questioning the jurisdiction of the Industrial Commission of NSW to award some of the terms claimed and arguing that the statutory provisions form a comprehensive code. The matter, which has not been treated as urgent — probably reflecting the fact that most 'excess persons' in NSW employment are not retrenched — is awaiting decision.

Conclusion

With the tempo of labour market change accelerating in recent years as the twin pressures of structural change and recession intersected, increasingly more organisations have been compelled to declare redundancies. From the late 1960s and earlier, attention had been given to the impact of technological change in both private and public sectors. More recently, however, redundancies have reflected more fundamental economic forces with company rationalisation schemes and business decline coming to the fore. In the past, employees depended on the goodwill of employers, or individual unions took up the cudgels for specific groups (mainly through industrial tribunals and usually after the dismissal decisions were taken). Such initiatives appeared to have had only minor impacts on management autonomy. A few unions, it is true, believed that industrial action could help save jobs and induce better redundancy agreements from employers, but the overall outcome was a patchy, uneven, partial and unpredictable coverage in terms of redundancy provisions, with the average private sector employee falling considerably behind internationally accepted standards.

Trends currently evident, however, show that much more attention is now being devoted to the creation of general (minimum) standards of protection, pursued mainly in the form of arbitrated test cases. The awarding of general standards in the ACTU's test case, as expected in 1984, would represent a departure by tribunals from past *ad hoc* approaches, in which they have indicated a wariness about awarding general prospective clauses in the absence of actual retrenchment situations, and a tendency to treat specific redundancy disputes on their own particular facts. Nevertheless, certain fairly consistent principles (if not specific standards) can be extrapolated even from the previous case-by-case approach, such as the tribunals' readiness to recognise, on the ground of industrial justice, a form of quasi-property right (not explicitly indentified as such) which workers develop in jobs to which they have given years of service in the legitimate expectation of stable continued employment: in such cases arbitrators have often regarded compensation as appropriate. In the main, however, tribunals have focused on measures to alleviate hardship to the employees concerned, particularly notice, and have not attempted to interfere with underlying management decisions about the fact of redundancies.

As the President of the Industrial Commission of SA has observed,'... particularly over the last decade, one of the most dynamic developmental areas within the industrial relations scene in Australia has been that which directly or indirectly touches upon job security. What has transpired has been a very interesting product of a blend of legislative change, arbitral evolution, developing stances adopted by employer and employee organisations and general social attitudes.'[40] Tribunals' decisions have assumed a special significance, given the reluctance of governments, including Labor administrations, to provide for substantive redundancy protection or compensation on a legislative or administrative basis. Thus, at both Federal and state levels, employers currently bear the cost of any improvement in redundancy provisions as direct increases in labour costs, rather than the additional liability being shared by the community as a whole.

Acknowledgements

The authors gratefully acknowledge the valuable assistance provided by officers of Federal and state departments and tribunals, and representatives of union and employer councils.

Notes

1. No one definition of 'redundancy' has been favoured in Australia, although that of Bray CJ in the South Australian AMSCOL case (1977) 16 SASR 6, is often quoted, referring to 'a dismissal, not on account of any personal act or default of the employee dismissed or any consideration peculiar to him, but because the employer no longer wishes the job the employee has been doing to be done by anyone'. Where redundancies have been treated differently according to causes, this is indicated in the text.

2. Australian Bureau of Statistics, *Trade Union Statistics*, Catalogue No. 6323, 1982.

3. Redundancies in the NSW steel industry, actual and foreshadowed, achieved such large proportions that the NSW Industrial Commission was asked by the state government to initiate an inquiry in 1982 to investigate the justification for retrenchments and the possibility of alternative action. (D. Yerbury and R. Clark, 'Redundancy and the Law: the Position in Mid-1983', *Journal of Industrial Relations*, vol. 25, no. 3, 353-75, 1983.)

4. Among those mass redundancies attracting particular media attention were the closure of General Motors Holden's Pagewood plant in 1980 (1,200 retrenchments), and the continuing programme of cutbacks within The Broken Hill Proprietary Company Limited steel group at Newcastle and Wollongong during 1982-3.

5. Australian Bureau of Statistics, *The Labour Force, Australia*, various issues, Catalogue Nos. 6202 and 6203, 1983.

6. Where there is an expectation that a job will last for only a limited period of time, as in construction or seasonal industries like food processing, a separate and distinct temporary job code is utilised.

7. The Commonwealth government told the Commission in the ACTU test case proceedings [Transcript (1983) op. cit.] that it did not at that time — June 1983 — contemplate the introduction of an income maintenance scheme. This position reflected 'its concern for broader equity consideration and the comparative protection of those who qualify for retrenchment compensation and those who cannot obtain work'.

8. D. Yerbury, 'Redundancy: The Response of Australian Law', *Australian Journal of Management*, vol 7, no. 1, 77-100, 1982.

9. *Report of the Committee of Inquiry into Technological Change in Australia* (CITCA), Australian Government Publishing Service, Canberra, 1980.

10. R. Willis, 'Ministerial Statement by Minister for Employment and Industrial Relations', *Commonwealth Parliamentary Debates*, H. of R., 8 December 1983.

11. Mr Justice Richards, *Inquiry into Recent Mechanization and other Technological Changes in Industry: Report and Recommendations*, NSW Government Printer, Sydney, 1963.

12. The South Australia provision is not mandatory and does not specify three months' notice.

13. As a result of a successful challenge by employers to the High Court, it was ruled in 1983 that the legislation did not apply to employees working in NSW who are covered by Federal awards.

14. The decision of the President of the NSW Commission in the Steel Industry Redundancy case, January 1983, also encouraged a test case approach. Fisher P noted that collective dismissals have today become 'a commonplace of industrial life ... Under such altered circumstances the view that industrial tribunals are dealing in an *ad hoc* manner with isolated problems amounts to fiction which can profitably be abandoned'.

15. A. Boulton, 'Job Protection and the Test Case Approach', *Industrial Relations Reform*, The University of New South Wales, Occasional Paper, No. 6, 1981.

16. J. Carroll, *Termination of Employment*, CCH Australia Ltd., Sydney, 1983, p. 120.

17. D. Yerbury (1982), op. cit.

18. Transcript of Catalogue No. 3690 of 1981, Amalgamated Metal Workers and Shipwrights Union *v.* BHP and Others, 1983, pp. 245, 256 and 257-8.

19. In the Coal Industry Redundancy case, January 1983, the Coal Industry Tribunal stated as finding of fact that there were no general standards of redundancy protection or compensation, and that most arrangements were negotiated or arbitrated on an *ad hoc* basis.

Department of Employment and Industrial Relations (DEIR), *Employment Prospects by Industry and Occupation: A Labour Market Analysis*, Canberra 1983a.

Department of Employment and Industrial Relations Programs, 1983–4, Canberra, 1983b.

20. Transcript of Catalogue No. 3690 of 1981, op. cit.

21. 122 CAR 330 at 334. Citations of other ACAC decisions are provided (with additional details) in Yerbury (1982), op. cit.

22. L.T. Olsson, 'Job Security — The Australian Scene', *Journal of Industrial Relations*, vol. 23, no. 4, 529-47, 1981.

23. D. Yerbury (1982), op. cit.

24. CITCA (1980), op. cit.

25. Ibid.

26. Ibid.

27. P.R. Lynch, 'Ministerial Statement by Minister for Industry and Commerce', *Commonwealth Parliamentary Debates*, H. of R., 18 September, p. 1519.

28. Transcript (1983), op. cit., pp. 300-1.

29. K. Pauncz, 'A Survey of Redundancy Procedures', *Work and People*. vol. 5, no. 1, 7-12, 1979.

30. Australian Bureau of Statistics, *Technological Change in Private Non-Farm Enterprises in Australia for the Three Years Ending 30 June 1979*, Catalogue Nos. 8106, 1980.

31. Cullen, Egan and Dell (CED), *The Employment Crisis: The Wages Freeze, Loss of Work*, Seminar, Sydney 14 February 1983, Mimeo.

32. *Workforce*, Issue no. 474, Specialist Newsletters Pty. Ltd., Milsons Point, NSW, December 1983.

33. CED (1983), op. cit.

34. Ibid.

35. *Bulletin*, 'Why John Leard Cut the Comeng Payroll', 21 June 1983.

36. DEIR (1983), op. cit.

37. D. Yerbury, 'Recent Developments Affecting Retirement and Redeployment Rights in the Commonwealth Public Sector', *Australian Bulletin of Labour*, vol. 6, no. 3, 1980.

38. R.I. Viner, 'Second Reading of the Commonwealth Employees (Redeployment and Retirement) Amendment Bill', *Commonwealth Parliamentary Debates*, H. of R., 3 March 1981, p. 351.

39. Transcript (1983), op. cit., p. 517.

40. L.T. Olsson (1981), op. cit., p. 529.

6 WEST GERMANY

Gerhard Bosch

Introduction

In a capitalist economy, such as West Germany, the employed live with the constant uncertainty of losing their employment for economic and/or reasons of technological development. In this sense the problem of job loss has always been an essential theme in collective bargaining. The importance of this theme in comparison to other problems depends on the employment situation in general; because in a situation of full employment it is much easier to find a new job than when unemployment is high.

Apart from the immediate post-war years up to 1950, the problem of job loss in West Germany has become the main theme in the last few years in discussions of labour market policies because of the rise in mass unemployment. In the 1950s unemployment was sometimes also very high, but because of the increase in the GNP (Gross National Product) both the unemployed and a great number of refugees could be quickly absorbed and the numbers of employed rose rapidly (see Table 6.1). Trade union policies were mainly concerned in those years with increasing wages and in improving sickness benefits (i.e. continuing wage payments during sickness). The main emphasis of the state's social policy was the improvement of pension schemes.

Between 1960 and 1973 the employment situation improved and the rate of unemployment was sometimes below one per cent. The policies of the state in the period of the social democratic/ liberal coalition (from 1969) were concerned mainly with reforms in education, labour market policies, health and safety, and works council legislation. Although discussions concerned with reform were influenced by labour shortages, the problem of reducing the workforce, in view of the prevailing job situation, played a surprisingly important role. This was probably because of:

(1) some bigger industries, e.g. mining and steel, reduced the' number of their employees considerably;
(2) during the first of the larger economic crises (1966–7) in West

164

Germany it became clear how serious the consequences of a crisis in a particular industry could be, faced with a general reduction in the level of employment (see the fourth section in this chapter); and

(3) the rate of increase in the GNP tended to decline over the period and one could see that in view of the high increase in productivity many jobs in future would be under threat (see Table 6.1).

The trade unions were able, because of their powerful bargaining position due to full employment, to negotiate on an enterprise basis both safeguards dealing with redundancy and rationalisation protection agreements. The coalition government after a period of no reforms (the Dismissal Protection Law was passed in 1951), legislated to deal with the problems that had accumulated meanwhile. The conclusion of social plans became law (Works Council Law, 1972) and the protection in case of mass-dismissals was improved. (Employment Promotion Act, 1969, Amendments to the Dismissal Protection Law, 1969.)

Since the middle of the 1970s the employment problems have become more acute in West Germany. Conflicts concerned with staff reductions have increased. In numerous enterprises which were being closed strikes or sit-ins took place.[1] Job loss caused by the economic crisis and rapid technological change has become the predominant theme in collective bargaining. The protection of the employees could be improved through some agreements, which in contrast with the period of full employment, were only achieved after hard bargaining. The policy of the state supported for some years a reduction in the amount of protective legislation. Through the combination of restrictive economic and social policies of the state and a high degree of unemployment the classical mechanism of the industrial reserve army operates again.

Below it is shown how the most important legal and wage agreements operate in practice in regard to job loss caused by economic and technological changes. It concerns the Dismissal Protection Law (section two), the legal requirements in cases of mass dismissals (section three), social plans (section four) and rationalisation protection agreements (section five). Further we shall examine strategies which on the one hand can prevent dismissals (section six), and on the other can circumvent existing protective legislation (section seven).

Table 6.1: Growth and Unemployment in West Germany, 1950–82

Year	Gross National Product[a]		Productivity increase per working hour[b]		Employees[c]		Unemployed[d]	Unemployed as percentage
	billion DM	%	1976 = 100	%	1000	%	1000	%
1950	143.6		21.6		13963		1869	11.0
1951	158.6	10.4	23.0	+ 6.6	14580	+ 4.4	1714	10.4
1952	172.7	+ 8.9	24.0	+ 4.3	15055	+ 3.3	1652	9.5
1953	186.9	+ 8.2	25.2	+ 4.7	15645	+ 3.9	1491	8.4
1954	200.8	+ 7.4	26.6	+ 5.6	16280	+ 4.1	1411	7.6
1955	224.9	+12.0	28.4	+ 6.7	17160	+ 5.4	1074	5.6
1956	241.3	+ 7.3	29.5	+ 4.0	17805	+ 3.8	876	4.4
1957	255.0	+ 5.7	31.6	+ 7.2	18317	+ 2.9	754	3.7
1958	264.5	+ 3.7	33.3	+ 5.2	18519	+ 1.1	764	3.7
1959	283.8	+ 7.3	36.2	+ 8.8	18865	+ 1.9	540	2.6
1960	613.4	+ 9.0	39.3	+ 8.6	20257		271	1.3
1961	643.1	+ 4.8	41.6	+ 5.8	20730	+ 2.3	181	0.8
1962	671.7	+ 4.4	44.5	+ 7.0	21032	+ 1.5	155	0.7
1963	692.5	+ 3.1	47.4	+ 6.4	21261	+ 1.1	186	0.8
1964	738.5	+ 6.6	51.3	+ 8.4	21484	+ 1.0	169	0.8
1965	778.7	+ 5.4	54.0	+ 5.3	21757	+ 1.3	147	0.7
1966	799.3	+ 2.6	56.5	+ 4.5	21765	+ 0.0	161	0.7
1967	798.9	− 0.1	60.7	+ 7.6	21054	− 3.3	459	2.1
1968	847.9	+ 6.1	64.3	+ 6.0	21183	+ 0.6	323	1.5
1969	911.6	+ 7.5	68.6	+ 6.6	21752	+ 2.7	179	0.9
1970	957.5	+ 5.0	71.1	+ 3.6	22246	+ 2.3	149	0.7
1971	988.1	+ 3.2	75.0	+ 5.5	22606	+ 1.6	185	0.8
1972	1029.0	+ 4.1	80.8	+ 7.7	22633	+ 0.1	246	1.1

Table 6.1 continued:

1973	1075.9	+ 4.6	85.9	+ 6.3	22906	+ 1.2	273	1.2
1974	1080.8	+ 0.5	89.4	+ 4.1	22640	− 1.2	582	2.6
1975	1063.9	− 1.6	93.4	+ 4.5	22014	− 2.8	1074	4.7
1976	1123.0	+ 5.6	100.0	+7.1	21939	− 0.3	1060	4.6
1977	1154.1	+ 2.8	104.3	+ 4.3	22029	+ 0.4	1030	4.5
1978	1194.0	+ 3.5	108.1	+ 3.6	22264	+ 1.1	993	4.3
1979	1241.6	+ 4.0	113.7	+ 5.2	22659	+ 1.8	876	3.8
1980	1265.5	+ 1.9	115.4	+ 1.5	22986e	+ 1.4	889	3.8
1981	1261.1e	− 0.3	119.5	+ 3.6	22877e	− 0.5	1272	5.5
1982	1246.6	− 1.1	122.8	+ 2.8	22455e	− 1.8	1833	8.1

a. 1950-9 without Saarland and West Berlin in prices of 1962; 1960-82 in prices of 1970.
b. 1950-9 without Saarland and West Berlin; 1960-3 without West Berlin.
c. 1950-9 without West Berlin.
d. 1950-8 without Saarland.
e. Preliminary figures.

Source: Statistisches Bundesamt, Fachserie 18. Bundesministerium für Arbeit und Soziales: Statistisches Taschenbuch.

Individual Dismissals

The Legal Situation

There was no legal protection in the Weimar Republic in case of individual dismissal. The only method open to employees was to obtain compensation from the Labour Court by proving their claim.[2] The dismissal protection legislation valid today was passed in 1951, and though there have been several amendments, the basic law has remained unchanged.

According to the Dismissal Protection Law every valid dismissal has to be 'socially justified'. It is 'socially justified' if the dismissal is for the following reasons:

(1) for personal reasons applying to the employee (e.g. loss of ability to work);
(2) for reasons in connection with the behaviour of the employee (e.g. persistent lateness, theft);
(3) compelling economic reasons (e.g. loss of work due to loss of orders or rationalisation) (para. 1: Dismissal Protection Law, *Kündigungsschutzgesetz*).

The dismissal notices are also only valid if the employees cannot be transferred within the workplace or within the firm, or if the dismissal is contrary to an agreed selection list with the works council, or if another employee is less entitled to social protection and should have been dismissed instead of the person who was actually dismissed. The employee has to go to court within three weeks against his dismissal in order to obtain the protection of the dismissal legislation. Should he win his case, the court may nevertheless terminate the contract of employment on application of the employer, should a continuation of 'collaboration in the interest of the firm' not be expected (para. 9: Dismissal Protection Law). In such cases the employee receives compensation which amounts up to twelve months' earnings, and in the case of older employees (e.g. 55 years of age and 20 years of service) it is as high as 18 months' earnings. Should there be a works council in the firm it has to be consulted before the dismissal takes effect. But, the works council may only object to the dismissal if:

(1) 'the employer has not, or not sufficiently taken into consideration in dismissing the employee his social situation;

(2) 'the dismissal is contrary to the agreement of selection;

(3) 'the employee who has been issued with a dismissal notice can be employed elsewhere in the same establishment or in another part of the firm;

(4) 'the continued employment of the employee is possible after having received retraining or further training; or

(5) 'the continued employment of the employee is possible with a changed contract of employment and the employee has given his consent to such a course.' (Para. 102, II: Works Council Constitution Law.) The objection of the works council usually entitles the employee to continuation of employment up to the point when the decision of the court relating to the dismissal case takes effect.

Should the dismissal be 'socially justified', no compensation is payable to the employee. His protection lies in the fixed period of notice which should give him the opportunity, before the dismissal becomes effective, to find a new job. On average white collar workers have a longer period before the dismissal becomes effective than blue collar workers (see Tables 6.2 and 6.3).

The periods of notice laid down by law are a minimum which have been improved upon in a number of collective agreements, and since 1973 improved agreements have been concluded especially for older employees. In factories employing 56 per cent of the working population a valid dismissal for personal or economic reasons is impossible for those employees of at least 50 or 55 years

Table 6.2: Dismissal Periods of White Collar Workers

Years of service	Age of employee after completing the:	Period of notice
at least 5 years	30th year	3 months
at least 8 years	30th year	3 months
	33rd year	4 months
at least 10 years	30th year	3 months
	33rd year	4 months
	35th year	5 months
at least 12 years	30th year	3 months
	33rd year	4 months
	35th year	5 months
	37th year	6 months

Source: White Collar Dismissal Protection Law (*Angestelltenkündigungsschutzgesetz*)

Table 6.3: Dismissal Protection for Blue Collar Workers

Years of service	After completion of years:	Period of notice
from 5 years	40 years	one month to the end of the month
from 10 years	45 years	two months to the end of the month
from 20 years	55 years	three months to the end of the quarter

Source: Codified Civil Law, para. 622 (*Bürgerliches Gesetzbuch*)

and who have a period of service with a company usually of 10 or 15 years.[3] It is not known what percentage of all employees are covered by these agreements and who are therefore protected from dismissal. Should there be special reasons, dismissal without notice is possible. As a rule this would mean a dismissal caused by behaviour possibly because of theft.

The legal situation in relation to the economic dismissals can be summarised as follows: the dismissal protection legislation is based on the principles of a market economy which permits the employer the freedom to reduce the number of employees. An investigation by the court to determine the economic reasons and the necessity for dismissals is in principle not possible. The labour court can only investigate whether the reason given for dismissal (reduction in turnover, lack of orders, etc.) is factually correct, and whether less stringent measures e.g. internal transfers, could have been possible.[4]

About the Practice of Dismissal

The Hamburg Max-Planck Institute for foreign and international civil law conducted a representative investigation into the practice of dismissals in private enterprises in West Germany between 1978 and 1980. In this connection, employers, works councillors, dismissed employees, judges of labour courts, lawyers, legal experts of trade unions as well as representatives of employers organisations were questioned and court records were evaluated.[5] Some of the most important results of this study are summarised in Table 6.4.

An extrapolation of the number of dismissals determined by the research and related to the total number of employees gave a result that showed that in 1978, 1.229 million employees were dismissed

Table 6.4: Total Number of Dismissal Notices, 1978

	Numbers ('000s)	Proportion of the employees of private enterprise %
Dismissal notice by the employer	1,229[a]	7.4
Notice by the employee	1,279[a]	7.7
Dismissal notice due to bankruptcy	250[b]	1.5
Liquidation agreements	150[b]	0.9
Non-extension of fixed term labour contracts	318[b]	1.9
Total	3,226	19.4

a. Extrapolation.
b. Estimate.

Source: B. Klees, 'Ausgewählte Probleme des Kündigungsschutzes in Gegenwart und Zukunft', in R. Ellerman-Witt, H. Rottleuthner and H. Russig (eds.), *Kündigungspraxis, Kündigungsschutz und Probleme der Arbeitsgerichtsbarkeit*, Opladen, 1973, p. 245.

and that 1.279 million employees gave notice on their own accord. In addition there were dismissals resulting from bankruptcy, which have not been considered in the research, as well as from liquidation agreements (*Aufhebungsverträge*), which have usually been instigated by the employer as well as the non-extension fixed-term labour contracts. For the year 1978, a year which was comparatively favourable for employment, the picture emerges (Table 6.4) where 67 per cent of the dismissals were for personal or behavioural reasons, whilst 33 per cent of the dismissals were for economic reasons. In most cases of dismissals several reasons were mentioned (Table 6.5).

The proportion of dismissal notices which are connected with economic conditions are in reality considerably higher than are revealed in the Table 6.5. The majority of dismissed employees (57 per cent) gave, apart from the official reasons, other reasons such as rationalisation, and also added that trade union and political activity played a part. Even 38 per cent of the employers questioned admitted that in dismissal notices for economic reasons the employees with the lowest performance were selected.

Since the 1950s one can observe a change in the practice of dismissals. The proportion of economic dismissals has been reduced in total. This can be seen, for example, in the case of a Bremen shipyard, where the personnel records from 1954 to 1980 can be analysed (Table 6.6).

Table 6.5: Reasons for Dismissals

	%
Absence without excuse	23.3
Inadequate performance	21.2
Frequent or long illness	19.8
Lack of orders	15.8
Lack of ability	12.5
Lateness	11.0
Alcoholism	10.2
Declining ability to perform	10.0
Rationalisation	8.7
Refusal to work	8.5
Other personal or behavioural reasons	20.6
Other economic reasons	15.7

Source: J. Falke, 'Kündigungspraxis und Kündigungsschutz', in R. Ellerman-Witt, H. Rottleuthner and H. Russig (eds.) *Kündigungspraxis, Kündigungsschutz und Probleme der Arbeitsgerichtsbarkeit*, Opladen, 1973, p. 17.

The researchers (Dombois *et al.*) came to the following conclusion:

> The personal or the behavioural reasons for dismissal notices increase in importance as an employment policy instrument and replace during a period of recession to a certain extent the usual reasons for dismissals because of lack of work. From 1967 during periods of decline lists of names of workers were prepared who were, because of their non-attendance or 'lack of suitability', to be dismissed ... The dismissals therefore achieved two aims: they vacate in line with the orderbook workplaces, and serve at the same time as a selection and 'cleaning' exercise. It is aimed to select workers of such behaviour and with characteristics who do not comply with the required norms of discipline and performance ... And also, the tendency for conflicts declines because of dismissals: because dismissals are now justified in individual cases and therefore neither the reduction in workplaces, nor the selection method is a subject for debate. The destruction of workplaces is transformed into an individual guilt problem. The selection is no longer as in the 1950s negotiated as a policy matter; selection on the basis of social criteria recedes behind the criteria of discipline and performance.[6]

Another reason for the change in the dismissal praxis could be that in the case of individual dismissals based on behavioural cri-

Table 6.6: Dismissals by a Bremen Shipyard, 1954–80

	1954–9 %	1960–9 %	1970–4 %	1975–80 %
Proportion of economic dismissals	90	54	—	9
Proportion of behavioural and personal reasons for dismissals	10	46	100	91

Source: R. Dombois, P. Friedmann and P. Gockell, 'Von Heuern und Feuern zur stabilen Mindestbelegschaft', in *Mehrwert, Beiträge zur Kritik der politischen Ökonomie*, vol. 23, Berlin, 1982, p. 15.

teria, the rationalisation protection does not apply. No social plans can be finalised and agreed upon, and a special dismissal can be more easily accomplished without keeping to the period of notice.[7]

The risk of dismissal is distributed very unevenly. Older male white collar workers with long service and high qualifications are unlikely to be dismissed. Foreign women, with few qualifications, run most risk of losing their job. Dismissals are much influenced by which firm you belong to. The rights of seniority in contrast to the USA are only partly formally secured (e.g. through a collective agreement providing dismissal protection) and in some cases seniority rules have been established informally in large enterprises.[8]

Table 6.7: The Percentage of Certain Groups of Workers in relation to Insured Employees and Dismissals in the Private Sector, 1978

Group of workers	Percentage of workers:		Dismissals per 1000 per year
	Employed	Dismissals	
Blue collar workers	59	77	96
White collar workers	41	23	41
Women	36	43	88
Men	64	57	66
Germans	90	80	66
Foreigners	10	20	144
Age (in years)			
below 25	21	26	90
25–34	23	31	100
35–44	27	24	68
45–54	19	15	56
above 54	10	4	27

Source: J. Falke, 'Kündigungspraxis und Kündigungsschutz', op. cit., p. 15.

Seniority arrangements are often disadvantageous especially for women, foreigners and unskilled workers because they have as a rule the shortest period of service with a particular enterprise (Table 6.7).

In small- and medium-sized undertakings dismissals are much more frequent than in large enterprises (Table 6.8). The smaller firms do not usually try, when orders fluctuate, to stabilise their workforce as large firms do, but react at once with dismissals. When a short-lived recovery occurs they are more likely to employ workers than large firms.

The high figures for dismissals in small firms can also be explained by the fact that dismissals protection legislation only covers firms with more than five workers. A works council can only be established in a firm with more than 20 workers. Furthermore, most small- and medium-sized firms with 20 to 200 workers have no works councils which could object to a dismissal.[9]

Only in 20 per cent of all cases do works councils oppose dismissals. In the majority of cases they agree or allow the dismissal to become legal through their silence. The 'consent' is also signed in dismissal cases where a social plan has been agreed (section four). Nevertheless a great proportion of works councils affirm the dismissals and emphasise the legitimacy with their signature. To a great extent they are ready to recognise the reason given by management. This demonstrates the predominating attitude in the works councils of co-operation, certainly at the time of the inquiry (1978). Striking is the greater degree of opposition to dismissals in big firms. This can partly be explained by the fact that, in a larger undertaking, there is a chance of further employment in a different department and possibly after re-training. The legally demarcated

Table 6.8: Frequency of Dismissals and Size of Private Enterprises

Number of employees	Percentage of workers		Dismissals per 1000 employees per year
	Employed	Dismissals	
up to 20	25.7	48.4	135
21-100	22.2	25.4	82
101-300	16.3	12.7	60
301-1000	14.5	6.6	32
above 1000	22.3	6.9	26
Total	100.0	100.0	74

Source: J. Falke, 'Kündigungspraxis und Kündigungsschutz', op. cit., p. 16.

Table 6.9: Attitude of Works Councils according to Size of
Enterprise in Relation to Planned Valid Dismissal Notices

Reaction	5-100	101-300	301-1000	above 1000	n	%
Agreement	52	43	33	32	191	43
Silence	17	23	24	18	91	21
Questioning	18	12	15	21	69	16
Opposition	13	22	28	29	91	20
Total	100	100	100	100	442	10
(n=)	(166)	(136)	(102)	(38)		

Source: A. Höland, 'Das Verhalten von Betriebsräten in der Kündigungssituation', in R. Ellermann-Witt, H. Rottleuthner and H. Russig (eds.), *Kündigungspraxis, Kündigungsschutz und Probleme der Arbeitsgerichtsbarkeit*, Opladen 1973, p. 70.

appeal possibilities of the works councils are primarily designed for the large enterprises (Table 6.9).

The attitude of the works councils is additionally strongly influenced by the reasons given for the dismissal. Dismissals for behavioural reasons (possibly criminal activity, absence without excuse) are very often supported by the works councils. One can assume that in the majority of cases the workforce supports them and in some cases the councils are pressurised by the workforce to agree to the dismissals. The most likely opposition of works councils to dismissals would be in cases of an illness or declining performance because these dismissals are not advocated for reasons which workers could support, i.e. personal faults.

Illness and declining performance are not events for which the individual seems to be guilty; they are possibly the result of wear and tear of the job. Economic causes of dismissals are also more important in regard to conflicts within the enterprise. The workforce in this case becomes a victim collectively of economic developments for which it can not be blamed and against which collective actions of the workforce and the works council can develop (Table 6.10).

Individuals are more likely to challenge the dismissal in the courts if the works council objects. Until their case has been heard only a small proportion of those given a dismissal notice will continue to be employed. Court action was taken against dismissals by about eight per cent of those affected. Principally the actions were taken in cases of personal and behavioural dismissals. Economic dismissals which were 'objectively' necessary were accepted rather than the accusations of bad behaviour or personal failure. In addi-

Table 6.10: Attitude of the Works Councils according to Reasons Given for Dismissals

Reasons for dismissal		Reaction (%)				
	No. of cases	Agreement	Silence	Quest.	Opp.	Total
(a) Personal, behavioural reasons for dismissal						
Absence without excuse	82	56	22	12	10	100
Illness	76	25	10	16	49	100
Alcohol	70	46	23	23	8	100
Inadequate ability	49	41	31	10	18	100
Lack of discipline ·	48	63	17	8	12	100
Lack of performance	45	47	15	18	20	100
Refusal to work	25	44	36	4	16	100
Criminal activity	21	62	19	10	9	100
Quarrel with colleagues	14	50	21	7	22	100
Decline in performance	13	15	15	15	55	100
Conflicts with employer	10	20	20	30	30	100
Total		203	92	64	94	453
%		45	20	14	21	100
(b) Economic dismissals (n = 101)		41	14	18	27	100

Source: A. Höland, 'Das Verhalten von Betriebsräten', op. cit., p. 73.

tion, court action has little chance of success when rationalisation measures are taken or when faced with lack of orders.[10] Only nine per cent of those taking court action were re-employed, while most agreed to be compensated by their former employer through a settlement. In a few cases reinstatement was achieved through a court decision.[11] Most court actions ended with a compensation payment (about 60 per cent of cases). According to the opinion of the judges questioned the employees were unjustifiably dismissed in most cases. Through the compensation payment their workplace was 'purchased' and the notion of job property rights established. Compensation amounts on average are a little more than half (56 per cent) a gross monthly salary per year worked in the particular establishment. In the case of Germans the compensation per year is twice as high, amounting to 66 per cent, as the compensation paid to foreigners (34 per cent of a gross monthly salary per year of service).[12]

In conclusion, the dismissal protection legislation is more advantageous for employees in large enterprises who have a long service record. The risk of dismissal is most acute for 'problem groups' in the labour market, i.e. women, foreigners and unskilled workers. In the case of a dismissal notice the person affected has, as a rule, to leave the establishment immediately and because of the long period a dismissal protection action takes (1974 about seven months from the application to the court to the judgement in the lower court, and on appeal, using all legal possibilities, two to three years), the individual is forced to search for another job. The dismissal notice therefore means dismissal is final. 'It means that a "dismissal protection court action" is — with very few exceptions — not a court action to save the job, but an action to decide upon the amount of compensation.'[13]

Mass Dismissals

For mass dismissal special regulations apply.[14] One speaks of mass dismissal if within one month due to changes within the enterprise the following minimum numbers are dismissed (Table 6.11).

For enterprises with less than 20 employees the following regulations do not apply. Should mass dismissals be contemplated within the next twelve months they must be reported to the Department of Employment by the employer. The reaction of the works councils — provided there is one in existence — must also be included. In a case where the employer does not inform the Department of Employment he is compelled to 'compensate the Department of Employment for the expense incurred by the

Table 6.11: Mass Dismissal Criteria

Numbers employed	Minimum numbers of dismissals
21–59	6
60–250	10% of those employed
251–499	26
500 plus	30

Source: Dismissal Protection Law, para. 17.

Department for re-training the dismissed persons or their being placed into other employment during a period of six months'. (Para. 8, Employment Promotion Act, *Arbeitsförderungsgesetz.*) Mass dismissals only become effective in principle after a month has elapsed from the time they have been reported (the status quo period). In a case where the works council has not been informed, the report of the employer to the Department is considered as having not been received. A commission of the Department of Employment operating locally or regionally, in which both employers and trade unions have equal representation, can call for the 'status quo' to operate for two months. This should offer a possibility for the employees to find a new job. In the case where the employer is unable to employ the workers in the firm during the status quo period, the Department of Employment is empowered to grant short-time working payments. Through this legislation the Department of Employment is given the chance to plan labour market measures early, e.g. re-training, and aim either to prevent dismissals or to soften the impact of the consequences.

The practice of these regulations has, up to now, not been systematically researched. The West German TUC is at the present moment conducting a limited study of the activities of mass-dismissal commissions of the Department of Employment and has come to the following interim conclusion.[15] In many branches of the Department of Employment no local mass-dismissal commissions have been established. Further, the trade union organisations in the localities are in many cases of the opinion that the ability of such commissions to prevent dismissals is small. The opposite has also been found. Sometimes managements and works councils are invited by the commissions and are questioned about the economic position of the enterprise. In some cases it was possible through labour market policy measures (re-training) and economic subsidies (reduction in interest rates, etc.) to prevent closure and dismissals. Sometimes the conditions apertaining to the dismissals could be improved, e.g. by postponing the dismissal date or providing higher rates of compensation. However, these possibilities are little known up to now either by the employers or the trade unions. They are not as in other countries (e.g. Austria) being used to aim for a restoration of firms threatened with bankruptcy.

Social Plans

The Legal Situation

The Works Constitution Act of 1972 which is in force today directs the employer with an establishment of more than 20 employees that he must inform the works council concerning 'planned changes in the establishment' which could result in 'specific disadvantages for the workforce'. The disadvantages may not consist of dismissals, but could refer to loss of income or loss of qualification. Under the concept of 'changes in the establishment' are considered, above all, works closures, removal of works or departments, amalgamations with other works, alterations in the organisation of an establishment and new methods of work or manufacture (para. 111: Works Constitution Act, *Betriebsverfassungsgesetz*).[16] In regard to such alterations the works council can demand the development of a 'social plan' to minimise the disadvantages for the workforce. The Act does not contain any details of what the social plan has to regulate. Its detailed contents are a matter for negotiations between works councils and top management. Should there be no agreement, the social plan is drawn up by the Arbitration Commission. The Arbitration Commission has equal representation and consists of an equal number of representatives of the works council and management, and a 'neutral' chairperson whose appointment must be approved by both sides (para. 76: Works Constitution Act). The arbitrators have 'to take account of the social interest of the employees involved as well as paying attention that their decision, as far as the employer is concerned, can be defended on economic grounds' (para. 112: Works Constitution Act).

The Social Plans in Practice

The first social plans were agreed upon in the Montane industries, i.e. in mining from 1957 and in the steel industry from 1963.[17] Since then social plans have been negotiated for nearly every closure in both branches, although a legal compulsion came about later. The reasons for this development are to be found in the following special conditions of the structural crisis in mining and steel making:

1   Closures occurred mainly in large enterprises where many workers were employed. The closures were confined to very

limited areas containing a mono-industrial structure (Ruhr area and Saarland). The crisis in a particular industry developed into a crisis of the region. In spite of full employment the loss of the workplace meant a high risk that the employees would remain out of work.

2   The closures were concentrated in areas well organised by trade unions, in which — as distinct from agriculture — resistance either developed or was feared. During the economic crisis of 1966 to 1968, the government and the employers feared a 'radicalisation' of the workers and a reappearance of communist traditions within the trade unions affected.

3   Finally, the trade unions in the coal and steel industries possessed a certain influence in regard to personnel policies, due to the co-determination regulations in those industries, within individual enterprises. The trade unions have equal representation on the supervisory board and on the board of directors. The labour director is a trade union appointee. During the structural crisis, the trade unions had to prove that through their influence in regard to personnel policies the severity of the closures for employees could be reduced.

The social plans in the Montane industries were considered a proof by the trade unions of the efficiency of the co-determination regulations in the coal and steel industries. The social plans in the Montane industries provided the example also for other industries and finally in 1972 for the alteration of the Works Constitution Act.[18]

The Institute for Social Research and Social Science in Saarbrücken investigated the contents of the social plans in 1975. Altogether 229 social plans from steel, engineering, textile and clothing, chemical industry and mining were evaluated. The research included all social plans known to the trade unions from the years 1970 to 1974. The majority of social plans negotiated would have been included in the review.[19]

The vast majority (92 per cent) of all the evaluated social plans were drawn-up because of total closures or part closures. Only 5.7 per cent of the social plans were concerned with the other structural alterations in establishments mentioned in the Act (e.g. new manufacturing methods), and a further 2.7 per cent of the social plans were preventative plans which laid down conditions concerned with future expected redundancies, still unknown in every

Figure 6.1: Combination of Personal Measures in Social Plans

Training for the job	Leaving the establishment	Transfers within/ between departments
	284 (95.0)	n = 299
	only leaving the establishment	
		only transfer 14 (4.7)
	leaving and transfers 73 (24.4)	
49 (16.4)		
Training, leaving and transfers 45 (15.1)		

Training, and leaving 4 (7.3)

Source: P. Ochs, *Sozialpläne*, op. cit., p. 81.

detail.[20] Social plans are, therefore, above all a means to overcome closures. The disadvantages for the workforce which are caused daily by the ongoing rationalisation measures, are hardly dealt with by social plans.

The social plans lay down conditions for the following types of measures in cases of redundancy (Table 6.12) and on many occasions we find a combination of measures. However, in more than 50 per cent of all social plans only dismissal is mentioned (compare the bar chart — Figure 6.1).

One can observe considerable differences between industries. In mining and steel making as well as in large enterprises transfers play a bigger role than in small- and medium-sized establishments such as in the textile and clothing industries. The smaller and

Table 6.12: Personnel Measures used in Social Plans

	%
Dismissals	87.8
Removal to other establishments	38.8
Early retirement	17.4
Re-training (connected with removal to other establishments)	17.1
Removal to other departments of the establishment	9.4

Source: P. Ochs, *Analyse betrieblicher Sozialpläne*, Saarbrücken, 1976, p. 82.

medium enterprises were shut down in most cases and as it is usually the only factory the firm possesses it makes transfers impossible. Larger firms were interested, in view of the labour shortages at the time when the social plans were instigated, in keeping the younger and qualified workers. When the workforce did not accept the transfer offer, no compensation was paid following dismissal.[21] At the end of the 1960s foreign workers were in part excluded from social plans,[22] allegedly for the reasons that they had not been employed in the undertaking long enough. These reasons, due to the increasing period of service of the foreign workforce, became less sound. Besides, their number had greatly increased in many establishments, so that the works councillors as elected representatives of the workforce could no longer agree to debar foreigners from the benefits of the social plan.

What were the achievements of the social plans in specific cases? When dismissals took place compensation was paid primarily. In addition, agreements were reached concerning the right to live in company-owned accommodation, jubilee payments, firm-based pensions, payments in kind (e.g. free coal), and Christmas bonuses. The level of compensation was based mainly on the membership of a firm (97.3 per cent of the social plans), on age (64.8 per cent of the social plans), and also earnings, but in considerably fewer cases (25.7 per cent) (see Table 6.13).[23]

The amount of compensation differed considerably according to the financial position of the firms. When a close-down occurs the financial position is usually weak which means that the provisions of the social plans are worse. This applies especially to the textile and clothing industry. Larger firms, even after a closure or a dismissal of workers, will probably continue to exist and can be pressurised to pay larger sums in compensation (Table 6.13).

Table 6.13: Level of Compensation according to the Social Plan

	Closing of establishment	Closing of plant or removal	Part closure	Dismissal
	(n = 65) %	(n = 88) %	(n = 52) %	(n = 20) %
Max. 5 months' earnings	66.2	34.8	55.8	40.0
up to 10 months' earnings	18.5	28.1	26.9	15.0
more than 10 months' earnings	15.4	37.1	17.3	45.0

Source: P. Ochs, *Sozialpläne*, op. cit., pp. 177–80.

In the case of early retirement, a subsidy was paid as a rule to top-up unemployment benefit until a pension was received. In the case of those moving to work, a subsidy was usually paid for a certain time to make up for a loss of income and if necessary fares were paid. The many arrangements differ from firm to firm and cannot be described in this short survey. A common characteristic, however, of these arrangements is that for the disadvantages suffered by employees a monetary compensation only was paid. Most social plans did not give a guarantee that an employee would continue to be employed using his qualifications and maintain his income. This would have required long-term manpower and personnel planning being established within a firm. Such a change in managerial practices cannot be enforced within the parameters laid down by the Works Constitution Act.

A further empirical investigation of social plans established that in bankrupt firms, compensation was only half as large as when dismissals take place from firms which continued to exist.[24] The main reason for this could be the small financial resources remaining within these firms. Social plans were concluded only in 15 per cent of all bankruptcies where the preconditions for a social plan existed (existence of a works council and more than 20 employed persons).[25] In the case of bankruptcy the employees in most cases receive nothing. However, their wages for the last three months they have been employed are safeguarded since 1974. In cases where the firm cannot pay the wages because of lack of finance, they are paid by the Department of Employment. The financing of the 'bankruptcy wages fund' comes from contibutions paid by all firms. In bankrupt undertakings which had developed a social plan, trade union recognition was 60 per cent, which is considerably higher than the average for firms in West Germany (36 per cent).[26] The actual use of legal protection possibilities is, therefore, dependent on a strong trade union organisation within the firm.

The content of the social plan is essentially the result of negotiations with a firm. It is possible to show how much the result of these negotiations was influenced by conditions within the undertaking. With firms in possession of strong financial resources or strong trade union influence (Montane Industries) some favourable results could be obtained. Many employees were transferred and those made redundant received large sums in compensation. In the steel industry the social plans were in some cases considerably improved in the middle and at the end of the 1970s. In the social plans concerned with the restructuring of the steel industry in the Saar region, dismissals for economic reasons were specifically excluded.[27] In smaller undertakings which were closed and had weaker trade union organisations, however, dismissals occurred with definitely smaller sums of compensation being paid. It is unknown (except in bankruptcy cases) in how many instances no social plan is in existence. In conclusion one can say, employees faced with the same risks are served by very unequal social plans.

Rationalisation Protection Agreements (New Technology Agreements)

From the end of the 1960s a number of rationalisation protection agreements have been agreed. Such agreements are at the present time in force for more than half of all blue and white collar employees. The majority have been concluded in industry and affect blue collar workers. However, recently similar agreements have been concluded in service industries and for white collar workers.[28] Rationalisation measures are defined as a rule as those measures brought about by the employer 'which change the technology or organisation in order to increase the productivity of the establishment if those lead to transfers, lowering of status or redundancy'.[29] The agreements are in part confined to 'decisive rationalistion of the work process'.[30] Firms which are rationalising continuously and not by great leaps are, by this method, able to avoid rationalisation agreements. Smaller firms (with fewer than 20 employees) are as a rule not included in the agreements. Excluded are alterations which are the consequences of economic difficulties (e.g. lack of orders) or in the public service, cuts in services.[31] Especially during an economic crisis when rationalisation measures can be justified because of economic problems facing firms, the rationalisation protection based on negotiations is decidedly less effective.

The majority of agreements emphasise the priority of transfers and re-training rather than dismissals. One assumes that the affected workforce is prepared to be transferred. In case they are not prepared to accept a 'suitable' position offered, they forgo all claims arising from the rationalisation agreement. In the case of transfers, the employees continue to be paid the previous earnings according to age and length of service for a specific period of time.

In the engineering industry in Baden-Württemberg all the employees over the age of 55 who have been with the firm at least for one year have their earnings guaranteed until they draw their pension.[32] Re-training has to be arranged and paid for by the firm, should 'the personal and technical ability' exist or should the new workplace require this. Re-training is usually confined to 10 to 13 weeks. In practice, this is more job-familiarisation than additional job training.

Many agreements exclude the dismissal for economic reasons of employees after a certain age and after a certain period of service. However, there are many exceptions as the following example illustrates:

> Employees who are 50 years old and have 10 years' service and in whose case the sum of years of age added to years of service is at least 65 are then entitled to greater protection.
> A valid dismissal for economic reasons is impossible. This does not apply to dismissals (a) in the face of mass dismissals ... (b) in firms with less than 100 employees because of reduction in turnover.[33]

The level of agreed dismissals compensation will differ according to the financial and economic position of the particular industry. Usually the differences are dependent on age and service (Table 6.14).

At the age of 45 and a period of service of 15 years the average compensation amounts to 4.6 months' earnings, and at 55 with 25 years' service to 9.0 months' earnings. On average, the highest possible compensation in the case of dismissal due to rationalisation amounts to 9.7 months' earnings.[34]

In a few cases up to 16 months' salary is paid.

Most agreements compel the employer to give early information about the planned alterations and to consult with the works council. This does not mean that the works council is receiving extended rights in regard to co-determination above that laid down in the Works Council Constitution Act. The agreements only confirm the duties to inform and consult as laid down by law.

In some recent agreements, achieved after a hard struggle, attempts have been made to influence the work process and to reduce the disadvantageous consequences of rationalisation measures.[35] An example of this are the agreements in the printing industry. Eight years after the introduction of computerised systems only 'specialists of the printing industry, especially typesetters' are permitted to exercise certain functions.[36] Also manning regulations have been established, which determine how many printers have to attend to machines of various sizes.[37]

Table 6.14: Rationalisation Protection and Compensation

	Rationalisation Protection Regulation (*Cumulative Percentages*)		
	Economic security in case of rationalisation (n — 52)	Compensation	
		Minimum requirements (n — 75)	Requirements for the highest rate of compensation (n — 72)
Age			
from 40	30.8	70.7	9.7
from 45	71.2	96.0	9.7
from 50	96.2	98.7	23.6
from 55	100.0	100.0	37.5
from 60	100.0	100.0	95.8
Length of service			
from 5	1.9	14.7	0.0
from 10	88.5	97.3	4.2
from 15	94.2	100.0	11.1
from 20	96.2	100.0	20.8
from 25	100.0	100.0	95.8

Source: J. Falke, A. Höland, B. Rhode and G. Zimmermann, *Kündigungspraxis und Kündigungsschutz in der Bundesrepublik Deutschland*, Bonn, 1981, p. 956.

Alternatives to Dismissals within an Enterprise

Cyclical demand fluctuations can hardly be influenced by an individual firm, but they can develop strategies which reduce their influence. Such a possibility exists, for instance, in 'offering a specific product with the aim to only satisfy the demand for the stable product within a differentiated market situation'.[38] Taking the motor industry of West Germany as an example, several investigations showed how Mercedes was hardly touched by the economic crisis of 1974/5 and was, therefore, able to pursue a steady personnel policy taking a long-term view.[39] Such a strategy was conditional upon a considerable power in the market and is, therefore, only possible for firms which have a significant presence (possibly a monopoly) in a sector of the economy. Furthermore, the cyclical risks would be transferred to other undertakings which are subjected to greater fluctuations.

But for these firms dismissals are not the only possibility to reduce the volume of their activities. Other possibilities are the reduction of overtime, cutting out extra shifts, short-time, stopping recruitment, early retirement, re-training, reduction of sub-contracting and agency workers, and mutual agreements to forgo protective legislation. Dismissals have partly become an expensive and not necessarily effective short-term method (from the firm's point of view). As demonstrated, through the dismissal protection legislation and the rationalisation protection agreements as well as the social plans, transfer of employees achieved a preference over dismissals; firms reduce their labour force at first by stopping recruitment in order to facilitate transfers. The works councils have a certain right to participate in deciding on overtime and short-time (para. 87: Works Constitution Act), and a limited right to be consulted in the case of agency workers (para. 99: Works Constitution Act). They therefore possess the means to exert pressure to reduce the number of dismissals.

The questioning of more than 1,600 firms in 1975 by the Institute for Social Research in Munich showed that, when operating a workforce reduction, on average three measures are used. Most widespread were the reduction of overtime, dismissals, cessation of recruitment and short-time working (in that order).[40] Dismissals were more prominent in those firms which reduced their workforce more than the average; obviously the potential for the other measures was inadequate. The investigation also shows that in

Table 6.15: Distribution of Employment Policy Measures according to Size of Firm, 1974/5 (manifold calculations — results in %)

Size of firm (number of employees)	1–10	10–50	50–200	200–500	500–1000	1000–2000	2000–5000	5000 and more	Total weighted (50 and more employees)
(Unweighted base)	(43)	(257)	(788)	(440)	(182)	(98)	(63)	(44)	(1615)
Measures									
1) Bridging through re-training	0.0	2.1	2.5	2.4	4.1	8.2	11.9	22.0	2.8
2) Reduction of outwork	0.0	6.7	10.3	11.7	18.1	18.8	38.1	52.9	11.6
3) Fewer agency workers	0.0	8.1	12.3	15.6	13.0	23.9	26.9	52.5	13.5
4) Reduction of overtime	25.1	63.5	81.6	83.2	92.1	92.7	93.6	100.0	82.8
5) Cancellation of extra shifts	0.0	8.1	11.6	18.5	24.2	24.3	26.9	23.5	13.8
6) Short-time	0.0	18.7	33.5	39.3	50.9	55.6	57.8	71.1	36.3
7) Recruitment stop	41.6	36.7	38.1	48.0	64.8	79.2	75.8	58.1	42.6
8) Contract cancellation	0.0	0.7	3.6	5.7	12.0	21.0	24.9	33.1	5.1
9) Early retirement	8.2	6.0	7.6	17.8	28.5	29.4	43.8	75.4	11.6
10) Dismissals	50.2	52.1	61.5	57.2	68.2	56.0	65.8	38.7	60.9
11) Drafting of a social plan	0.0	1.4	2.7	7.6	8.7	9.8	43.8	21.5	4.7
12) Total measure	125.1	204.1	265.3	307.0	384.6	418.9	509.3	548.8	287.1

Source: R. Schutz-Wild, *Betriebliche Beschäftigungspolitik in der Krise*, Frankfurt, New York, 1980, p. 135.

establishments with an experience of personnel planning, as well as equal representation of management and works councillors in personnel planning commissions, the number of dismissals can be reduced. A long-term personnel plan enlarges the possibilities of action because a necessary reduction of the labour force can be recognised early, and tackled in time. For the works councils, alternatives to dismissal can be recognised earlier where long-term personnel planning exists. The choice of personnel policy measures is most strongly influenced by the size of enterprise. Size is a combined indicator of the financial strength of the firm, the viability of the protection legislation, the manoeuvrability within personnel policies, and the trade union influence within the firm. The larger the firm, the greater the possibility of the measures taken in practice (Table 6.15).[41]

Nearly all measures were used more, with the exceptions of dismissals and the stopping of recruitment, with the increased size of the undertaking. This applies particularly to short-time working and early retirement which are largely financed by the state. Short-time working wages are financed by the Department of Employment and amount to 68 per cent of net earnings. Short-time money can as a rule only be obtained for six months. With high unemployment and for regions with greater than average unemployment and especially endangered sectors of the economy, the payment can be extended to 24 months. The steel industry is able at this moment to receive short-time money for 36 months. Unemployed persons 60 years old who have been unemployed for a year can retire early. Employers dismiss 59-year-old employees on the basis of this regulation and pay them a subsidy making-up their unemployment benefit. The Department of Employment is prepared with the informal understanding of these firms to take these unemployed off the register. Some re-training measures are financed by the Department of Employment. The stabilisation of the personnel policies of the large firms is only made possible through public funds (Table 6.16).

The decline of sub-contracting and restricting agency workers in the large firms shifts the risks of unemployment to smaller firms; the greater degree of dismissals in small firms (see section three) is the compelling mirror image of job security in the larger firms. Internal alternatives instead of dismissals can therefore increase the dismissal risk for other employees considerably. The alternative to raising job security of all employees is, therefore, a matter

Table 6.16: Use of Public Funds for Early Retirement and
Re-training[44]

Has the firm used public funds once previously for ...	Number of employees					
	0–49 (n — 35)	50–99 (n — 43)	100–499 (n — 148)	500–999 (n — 55)	1000 and more (n — 67)	Total (n — 351)
Early retirement	9	9	26	42	70	33
Re-training	31	44	42	47	61	46

Source: Results of a questionnaire sent to works councils by the West German TUC
1980.

for the economy as a whole (work-schemes and reduction of working hours).

Strategies of Evasion Adopted by Firms

During the period of full employment most employers did not per-
ceive problems in extending the protection of the workforce. Job
losses 'produced by new technology could, because of continued
employment growth, usually be absorbed within an establishment.
This changed with the economic crisis of 1974/5 when employers
had to overcome great fluctuations in demand. The protection of
the workforce turned out, from the point of view of the employers,
to be a major obstacle to hiring and firing employees at a moment's
notice without incurring great costs. Changing over to personal
and behavioural dismissals (section two) alone could not produce
the necessary flexibility in the workforce. In the large firms in
which dismissal protection has been furthest developed, a flexible
reserve of employees has been built up. Since most of the legal and
negotiated dismissal regulations apply to those who are full-time
employees, flexibility of the workforce was produced through
unenforceable contractual arrangements. Included in this category
of arrangements are part-time work, short-term contracts and temporary agency employment:

(1) Part-time work has increased considerably in the last few
    years. Twelve per cent of all employed persons (more than 90
    per cent of women) work less than the normal agreed working

hours. Many agreements are only operative for employees above a minimum number of working hours. The rationalisation protection agreements of the insurance industry, the public services, and the post office are, for example, valid only for part-time workers employed for more than 20 hours; besides that, their working conditions are inferior. Dismissal protection is mainly valid after a longer period of service than with full-time employees.[42]

(2) Short-term contracts invalidate the dismissal protection legislation. The contracts terminate automatically and there is no need to provide a dismissal notice. Furthermore, the employee is not entitled to compensation. In the public service where, because of the collective agreements, there are no dismissals for personal or economic reasons, and also in industries subject to economic fluctuations such as the motor industry, short-term contracts have been increasing. In 1979 there were 212,000 employees in the public service with short-term contracts (eight per cent of all employees).[43]

(3) In West Germany, agency employment is increasing. The agency employer employs workers exclusively for the purpose of hiring to other employers on a time-basis. The difference between this and a private labour exchange is that the employee has a labour contract with the agency employer. Between 1975 and 1980 the number of agency firms has increased from 891 to 1,670. The number of agency workers increased over the same period from 9,000 to 33,000. Because every agency worker is hired out many times there were some hundreds of thousands of hirings in 1980.[44] Agency workers can be employed according to requirements. They serve, as a rule, to eliminate bottlenecks, for which the employer does not need to engage workers himself. Of much greater importance than the officially registered agency work is illegal hiring, mainly of foreigners. Several investigations estimate that the proportion of legal to illegal agency work, i.e. 'lump labour', is one to seven.[45] In addition there is sub-contracting of firms which deal, for example, with maintainance, erection work, cleaning, and which also undertake regular production tasks. Altogether an increasing number of employees have no regular employment contract with the company in which they work.

These strategies of evasion affect the nature of the contract of employment, and equally affect the nature of management. Through privatisation of publicly owned enterprises, the protection afforded, for example, by collective agreements is removed. By the splitting-up of undertakings into a number of small establishments the right to co-determination of the works councils is eliminated.[46]

Summary and Conclusions

It has been shown that there is no uniform dismissal protection in West Germany. The legal dismissal protection gives a minimum of protection which only applies to a limited extent to small firms. These minimum conditions can be extended by the concluding of social plans, collective agreements and negotiated rationalisation protection agreements which, however, according to the initial economic conditions in the various firms and industries, and the trade union strength, vary a great deal. Dismissal protection varies greatly according to which company the employee is working in.

The weakest dismissal protection exists for employees in firms with fewer than 20 employees (about 25 per cent of the workforce) (see Table 6.7). These employees can be dismissed without a reason being given. There is no works council in existence which can object to the dismissal, or enforce a social plan in this situation. The rationalisation protection agreements and the dismissal arrangements taken from various collective agreements are not applicable. In addition, there is, as a rule, a lower level of trade union representation (Table 6.17). The development of dismissal protection has passed these firms by, and the employers are able, without much hindrance, to hire and fire.

The most comprehensive dismissal protection is experienced by the employees of large firms with a powerful trade union influence,

Table 6.17: Trade Union Density and Size of Establishment

	Employees					
	1–10	11–100	101–500	501–2000	above 2000	Total
Density in percentages of employees	7	26	38	46	56	31

Source: Infas Survey April 1977 up to June 1978.

as in the steel industry and mining where equal repesentation and co-determination operate (about 22 per cent of the workforce) (see Table 6.7). In these enterprises, dismissals are the 'last resort'. All improvements in the protection of employees in the case of dismissals operate in these establishments. Because of this situation, employee transfer and other measures have been gradually enforced during the past 20 years instead of dismissals. The change in personnel policy has only been made possible by using public funds. One of the alternatives to dismissal has shifted the problem of adaptation on to small firms.

The labour market policy of West Germany has up to now — possibly with the exception of short-time working — not been used as a preventive measure to hinder dismissals. The branches of the Department of Employment offer a number of services, but their funds are not directed into depressed regions or endangered firms. The distribution of money is therefore directed by the demands of firms. As a consequence, the labour market policy is taken advantage of primarily by the large firms who have formal and informal connections with the Department of Employment, and who are easily able, with their competent personnel departments, to satisfy all the bureaucratic requirements when applying for financial resources. The established unequal job security in large and small firms is thereby reinforced.[47]

The job security in the large firms is often held responsible for employment insecurity in the small- and medium-sized firms. Implied in such an assertion is the implicit demand that the trade unions in the large firms should be prepared to make concessions so that the 'misery' can be distributed equally. Such a point of view cannot be maintained if the developing situation is considered historically. In the first place, nearly all improvements in dismissal protection are based on collective agreements which were concluded in large firms. There, the trade unions were able, because of their strong position, to achieve social plans, improved protection for older workers in case of dismissal, protection against rationalisation measures, and were able to gather experience in handling such new arrangements. When such agreements were operating in important industries and enterprises, it became easier to establish such measures universally, either through legislation or through collective bargaining for the majority of employees.

Trade union policy, as applied in large undertakings, takes on the role of an advance guard and without it job security would not have been improved for all the employees working in firms with more than 50 employees (which constitute 75 per cent of all employees, see Table 6.7) in the last few years. The inequality in job insecurity between the large, medium and small firms presented an advantage, therefore, for everyone because it led to the development of improvements. Achieving equality by the reduction in social provision in the large enterprises would have resulted in a reverse development, and a worsening of conditions for everyone. At the present time all efforts to reduce trade union influence are aimed at weakening trade unions in the large enterprises, because the employers have realised that it is there that the significant obstacle for cutting down social expenditure exists.

Job protection in the large enterprises has positive macro-economic effects and in a period of economic crisis it is only those firms which are able to match the number of their employees with the reduction in demand after some delay. Through such a temporary stabilisation of employment the effect is to slow down the total reduction in demand. By involving the state in the employment policies of enterprises (through short-time payment to employees, early retirement, etc.) an increase in payment of social benefits has the effect of economic stimulation, which can be abrogated by legislation, but in any case will stabilise the situation temporarily.

The above empirical research results are nearly all drawn from the 1970s. And, because of the growing numbers of unemployed and the altered political situation in West Germany, the research results have certainly in part to be up-dated. The renaissance of the small firm, which has been forecast for the 1980s,[48] is possibly the employers' reaction to the difference in dismissal protection as well as making the workforce more flexible by sub-contracting. It is obvious as well that social plans are less all-embracing today then a few years ago. It is likely that this trend will be reinforced under present conditions. During the past few years a number of state benefits have been cut which provided fixed orientation points when negotiating about social plans at an enterprise level. This applies to unemployment benefits, which have in the meantime been reduced on several occasions, the reduced maintenance grants when re-training, and the increased pressure on the unemployed to accept work with less pay and requiring fewer qualifications. The monetarist economic policy reduces the framework within which negotiations on a company basis take place.

Since a main aim of the present Federal government is to lower wage costs, further direct intervention into the legal dismissal protection procedures can be expected.[49]

The trade unions are demanding a development of the law on dismissal protection.[50] Their most important demands are:

(1) in the case of court action against a dismissal the employee must, up to the judgement by the court, continue to be employed; and
(2) all protective legislation has also to apply to small firms.

The trade unions have in addition drafted a number of agreements, which envisage a preventative content on the effects of new technology.[51] But the main emphasis of trade union demands in industrial relations policies is at the present moment the shortening of working hours and work schemes, because only by these methods can the number of unemployed be decisively reduced.[52]

Notes

1. G. Schmidt, *Wenn wir uns nicht rühren, rührt sich überhaupt nichts. Der Kampf gegen die Schließung des Kesselbaus in MAN-Werk Hamburg*, West Berlin, 1981; and H. Bär, *Betriebsbesetzung, eine Kampfform zur Sicherung von Arbeitsplätzen*, Frankfurt, 1976.
2. M. Kittner, *Arbeits- und Sozialordnung. Ausgewählte und eingeleitete Gesetzestexte*, Köln, 1983, p. 700.
3. *Bundesarbeitsblatt*, 3/1981, p. 24.
4. E. Nickel, 'Der Schutz der Arbeitnehmer bei ordentlicher, insbesondere betriebsbedingter Kündigung und seine arbeitsmarktpolitische Einschätzung', in M. Kittner (ed.), *Arbeitsmarkt — ökonomische, soziale und rechtliche Grundlagen*, Heidelberg, 1982, pp. 231-58.
5. J. Falke, A. Höland, E. Rhode and G. Zimmermann, *Kündigungspraxis und Kündigungsschutz in der Bundesrepublik Deutschland. Eine empirische Untersuchung durchgeführt vom Max-Planck — Institut für ausländisches und internationales Privatrecht Hamburg*, vols. 1 and 2, edn. Bundesminister für Arbeit und Sozialordnung, Bonn, 1981. The authors of this research report published some more articles in the book: R. Ellermann-Witt, H. Rottleuthner and H. Russig (eds.), *Kündigungspraxis, Kündigungsschutz und Probleme der Arbeitsgerichtsbarkeit*, Opladen, 1983.
6. R. Dombois, P. Friedmann, and P. Gockell, 'Vom Heuern und Feuern zur stabilen Mindestbelegschaft — drie Jahrzehnte betriebliche Beschäftigungspolitik eines Schiffbauunternehmens', *Mehrwert. Beiträge zur Kritik der politischen Ökonomie*, vol. 23, Berlin, 1982, p. 19.
7. The proportion of the valid dismissals which were dealt with by the courts amounted to only 6 per cent where economic reasons applied: where behavioural reasons applied, however, the proportion was 57 per cent. Falke, Höland, Rhode

and Zimmermann, *Kündigungspraxis und Kündigungsschutz*, p. 19.

8. G. Bosch and R. Lichte, 'Zur Funtionsweise informeller Senioritätssysteme', in K. Dohse, U. Jürgens and H. Russig (eds.), *Statussicherung im Industriebetrieb*, Frankfurt, New York, 1983.

9. G. Bosch, 'Interessenvertretung in Mittel- und Kleinbetrieben', *Die Mitbestimmung*, vol. 7, 1983, p. 965.

10. Falke, Höland, Rhode and Zimmermann, *Kündigungspraxis und Kündigungsschutz*, p. 965.

11. Ibid., pp. 860-3.

12. Ibid., pp. 37-8.

13. M. Kittner, *Arbeits- und Sozialordnung*, p. 706.

14. Para. 8, Work Promotion Act of 1969; and paras. 17 to 22, Dismissal Protection Law with the amendments of 1969.

15. B. Pollmeyer, *'Zwischenbericht zur Studie "Massenentlassungausschüsse"'*, unpublished manuscript, Düsseldorf, 1983.

16. The old Works Constitution Act 1952 included a right of consultation for the works councils by which they could force the employers to conclude a social plan. However, excluded were alterations in processes which were 'obviously based on a change in the market position' (para. 72, 1, Works Constitution Act, 1952). The right of consultation had become worthless in practice through this exclusion.

17. A. Vogt, *Sozialpläne in der betrieblichen Praxis*, Köln, 1974; Autorengemeinschaft, *Sozialplanpolitik in der Eisen- und Stahlindustrie*, Köln, 1979.

18. With the reorganisation of mining in the Ruhr area by bringing all the pits in the Ruhrkohle AG in 1968, an all-embracing social plan was passed having the force of law. This plan contained minimum provisions for all social plans based on enterprises. See: 'Gesamtsozialplan über die öffentlichen und betrieblichen Leistungen und Vorsorgemaßnahmen für die von Stillegungen betroffenen Arbeitnehmer des Steinkohlenbergbaus vom 15. Mai 1968'; *Bundesanzeiger*, no. 94, 1968.

19. P. Ochs, *Analyse betrieblicher Sozialpläne*, Saarbrücken, 1976.

20. Ibid., p. 73.

21. G. Bosch, *Arbeitsplatzerlust. Die sozialen Folgen einer Betriebsstillegung*, Frankfurt, New York, 1978, pp. 236-9.

22. P. Ochs, *Analyse*, p. 108; and R. Lichte, *Betriebsalltag von Industriearbeitern*, Frankfurt, New York, 1978.

23. P. Ochs, *Analyse*, p. 121.

24. V. Gessner and K. Plett, *Der Sozialplan im Konkursunternehmen*, Bonn, 1982, p. 121.

25. Ibid., p. 35.

26. Ibid., p. 45.

27. R. Judith, *et al.*, *Die Krise der Stahlindustrie — Krise einer Region. Die Beispiel Saar*, Köln, 1980.

28. From 1983 up to the time of writing, rationalisation protection has been agreed only in the service industries, i.e. private and state banks, corporative banks and insurance companies.

29. Para. 3 'Tarifvereinbarung zur Absicherung von Arbeitsplätzen und Einkommen bei Rationalisierungsmaßnahmen für das private Bankgewerbe sowie die öffentlichen Banken', 14 April 1983.

30. Para. 3 'Tarifvereinbarung zur Absicherung von Arbeitsplätzen und Einkommen bei Rationalisierungsmaßnahmen für die Genossenschaftsbanken,' 16 April 1983.

31. H. Kohl, 'Probleme des Rationalisierungsschutzes', *WSI-Mitteilunger*, 4/1977; and H. Lühr, 'Tarifvertragliche Regelungen zum Schutz der Beschäftigten

bie Rationalisierungsmaßnahmen', *Kritische Justiz*, 1980, pp. 90-102.

32. 'Manteltarifvertrag für die gewerblichen Arbeitnehmer der Metallindustrie Nordwürttemberg/Nordbaden', 20 October 1973.

33. 'Manteltarifvertrag für die Arbeitnehmer der Zigarettenindustrie', 18 December 1975.

34. Falke, Höland, Rhode, Zimmermann, *Kündigungspraxis und Kündigungsschutz*, p. 946. In this book 98 rationalisation protection agreements, which were valid in 1979, are evaluated.

35. 'Rationalisierungsschutzabkommen für das Private Versicherungsgewerbe', 16 April 1983.

36. 'Tarifvertrag über die Einführung und Anwendung rechnergesteuerter Textsysteme in der Druckindustrie', 20 March 1978, and B. Robak, M. Schlecht, 'Tarifliche Gestaltung des Einsatzes neuer Technologien. Erfahrungen und Konsequenzen aus der Anwendung des RTS-Tarifvertrages in der Druckindustrie', *WSI-Mitteilungen*, 2/1983, pp. 133-41.

37. 'Manteltarifvertrag für die gewerblichen Arbeitnehmer der Druckindustrie', 2 August 1974.

38. R. Schultz-Wild, *Betriebliche Beschäftigungspolitik in der Krise*, Frankfurt, New York, 1978, p. 90.

39. H.G. Mendius and W. Sengenberger, 'Konjunkturschwankungen und betriebliche Politik. Zur Entstehung und Verfestigung von Arbeitsmarktsegmentation', in H.G. Mendius *et al.* (eds.), *Betrieb — Arbeitsmarkt — Qualifikation I*, Frankfurt, 1976, pp. 15-82.

40. R. Schultz-Wild, *Betriebliche Beschäftigungspolitik*, p. 168.

41. The results of the questionnaire have been analysed in G. Bosch, H. Seifert and B.-G. Spies, *Arbeitsmarktpolitik und gewerkschaftliche Interessenvertretung*, Köln, 1983.

42. I. Kurz-Scherf, 'Arbeitszeitflexibilisierung und gewerkschaftlicher Regelungsbedarf', in *WSI Arbeitsmaterialien Arbeitszeitverkürzung*, Düsseldorf, 1983; and *WSI-Tarifarchiv*, 'Tarifvertragliche Bestimmungen zur Teilzeitarbeit,' unpublished paper, Düsseldorf; in 1983 the trade unions succeeded in including part-time employees of the private banks in the rationalisation protection agreements.

43. WSI, *Informationspaket Flexible Arbeitszeiten*, Düsseldorf, 1983; and K. Löcher, 'Die Vergebeitung von Zeitarbeitsverträgen im öffentlichen Dienst', *Mitteilungen aus der Arbeitsmarkt- und Berufsforschung*, 1/1982, pp. 58-68.

44. J. Frerichs *et al.*, *Leiharbeit und betriebliche Interessenvertretung*, Köln, 1981; and *Arbeitsplatz und Arbeitsmarktsituation in Bremen*, vol. 3, Research report of der zentralen Wissenschaftlichen Einrichtung 'Arbeit und Betrieb', Universität Bremen, Bremen, 1982, pp. 29-99.

45. *Arbeitsplatz und Arbeitsmarktsituation in Bremen*, p. 37. The trade unions are demanding a general prohibition of agency work because through agency work the social rights of the employees are endangered. Since the beginning of 1982 agency work in the building trade has been prohibited. There the proportion of illegal agency workers, i.c. 'lump labour', had risen more than the average.

46. W. Krüer-Bucholz, 'Unternehmensaufspaltungen und ihre wirtschaftlichen Hintergründe am Beispiel der Bekleidungsindustrie', *WSI-Mitteilungen*, 1/1983, pp. 26-34.

47. G. Bosch and J. Priewe, 'Perspektiven und Handlungsspielräume der Arbeitsmarktpolitik', *WSI-Mitteilungen*, 2/1982.

48. D. Garlichs, H. Maier and K. Semlinger (eds.), *Regionalisierte Arbeitsmarkt- und Beschäftigungspolitik*, Frankfurt, New York, 1983.

49. A spokesman for the CDU/CSU parties has claimed, for example, that dismissal protection bears part of the responsibility for the high rate of

unemployment. It is claimed that the present dismissal protection restricts the willingness of the firms to engage new labour. Compare CDU/CSU-Arbeitsgruppe 'Arbeit und Soziales', *Eine Analyse der wichtigsten Ursachen der Arbeitslosigkeit und Vorschläge zur Eindämmung*, Frankfurter Rundschau, 30 July 1983 and 1 August 1983.

50. Deutscher Gewerkschaftsbund, *Grundsätze des Deutschen Gewerkschaftsbundes zur Weiterentwicklung des Betriebsverfassungsrechts*, Düsseldorf, 1983.

51. R. Bispinck, 'Tarifvertragliche Regelungen von Arbeitsbedingungen und Entlohnungsverfahren — zu den Forderungen der IG-Metall zu einem Lohnrahmentarifvertrag für Südwürttembert/Hohenzollern und Südbaden', *WSI-Mitteilungen*, 9/1982.

52. A good synopsis of the discussion dealing with the demand for reduction of working hours and work schemes in the Federal Republic is contained in the 'Memorandum 83' *Qualitatives Wachstum, Arbeitszeitverkürzung, Vergesellschaftung — Alternativen zu Unternehmerstaat und Krisenpolitik*. Köln, 1983.

NOTES ON CONTRIBUTORS

Douglas Anthony: Joint Lecturer, Centre of Japanese Studies, Division of Economic Studies, University of Sheffield, Sheffield S10 2TN, England.

Gerhard Bosch: Wirtschafts — und Sozialwissen — schaftliches Institut des DGB, Hans-Böckler — Str. 39, 4000 Düsseldorf 30, West Germany.

Michael Cross: Senior Research Fellow, The Technical Change Centre, 114 Cromwell Road, London SW7 4ES, England.

W.W. Daniel: Deputy Director, Policy Studies Institute, 1/2 Castle Lane, London SW1E 6DR, England.

Morris L. Sweet: Principal Planner, Department of City Planning, City of New York, 2 Lafayette Street, New York, New York 10007, USA.

Vic Taylor: Senior Lecturer in Management, Australian Graduate School of Management, University of New South Wales, PO Box 1, Kensington, New South Wales, Australia 2033.

Di Yerbury: Professor of Management, Australian Graduate School of Management, University of New South Wales, PO Box 1, Kensington, New South Wales, Australia 2033.

INDEX